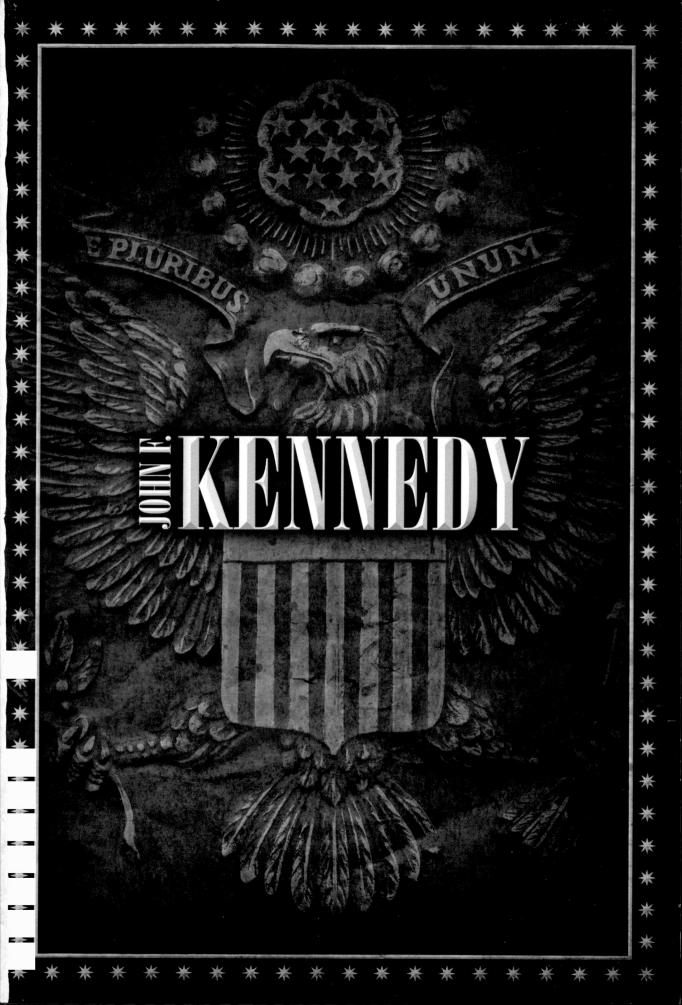

JOHN F. KENNEDY

THE LIFE AND DEATH
OF A US PRESIDENT

CHARLOTTE
MONTAGUE

CHARTWELL
BOOKS

And so, my fellow Americans, ask not what your country can do for you—ask what you can do for your country.

John F. Kennedy (1917 – 63)

CONTENTS

INTRODUCTION

John Fitzgerald Kennedy was a new kind of politician, one who recognized the value of not just programs and policy but also of image and presentation. With his glamorous wife Jacqueline, he formed the prototype for the politician of the future, and created an excitement among the American people that had rarely, if ever, been seen for a president.

Since his death, he has been mythologized and lionized but even during his presidency he was a magnetic figure. In fact, so much did people want to be associated with the urbane young man from Massachusetts that in a mid-1963 survey, 59 percent of Americans claimed they had voted for him in 1960 when, in fact, only 49.7 percent had actually done so. Following his assassination, the number of Americans who claimed to have cast their vote for him rose to 65 percent. Moreover, in opinion polls, he consistently scores the highest approval rating of any president since Franklin D. Roosevelt.

These numbers are all the more astonishing when one considers that he was president for only three years and those three years were not exactly covered in glory. Just a few months after his inauguration, his administration became embroiled in the fiasco of the Bay of Pigs invasion when Cuban exiles, trained by the CIA, landed at the Bay of Pigs with the objective of unseating Cuban leader, Fidel Castro. Kennedy was badly advised but made the fateful decision to keep America out of the whole escapade, refusing to authorize air support for the invasion force.

The venture dismayed the people of the United States and the world but from it he seems to have learned valuable lessons that he applied to the other major crisis of his brief time in the Oval Office—the Cuban Missile Crisis. In that case, he did not listen to the Joint Chiefs of Staff and other agencies and advisors. He succeeded in saving the world from a nuclear holocaust as well as in creating

President John F. Kennedy, First Lady Jacqueline Kennedy, and their children, John Jr. and Caroline, in Hyannis Port, Massachusetts, 1962.

President John F. Kennedy proposing a program to land men on the Moon to Congress in May 1961.

an image of a statesman who could stand tough against the threat of Communism.

Like a number of presidents, Kennedy was restricted in what he could do by Congress, especially by congressmen from the American South who were concerned about civil rights legislation being passed. Thus, they blocked other legislation that Kennedy was trying to pass in order to persuade him to back off. Much of what Kennedy wanted became law after his death, including the important 1964 Civil Rights Bill that outlawed segregation. Perhaps it was more as a tribute or memorial to a fallen leader than anything else.

Kennedy the man was notoriously flawed and since his death many stories of his philandering have emerged. But they somehow do not tarnish his reputation as a great American president. It would seem that people want to hang on to the vision of Camelot—as his administration was called—that the idealism and hope of the 1960s and Kennedy's notion of a "New Frontier" somehow represented a better time when anything was possible.

Of course, he lived a privileged life, born into a wealthy family with all the benefits, both

personal and professional, that are associated with such an upbringing. But Kennedy had his personal struggles, too. Firstly, he had to emerge from the shadow of an older brother who was being groomed for greatness until his death in the Second World War. Secondly, he had to position himself carefully regarding his powerful father, a man who had made the wrong decisions as war approached and destroyed his own political ambitions. Kennedy became his own man and in mid-1963 was starting to create a successful presidency. Whether he would have won a second term or withdrawn the United States from Vietnam are matters of conjecture which will be debated long into the future.

One matter that will also be long debated is the manner of President Kennedy's tragic death that fateful November day in Dallas. Thousands of books have been written about it and countless theories have been concocted. We may never know exactly what happened, but it says much about the extraordinary life of John Fitzgerald Kennedy that we are still trying to solve the mystery of his tragic death.

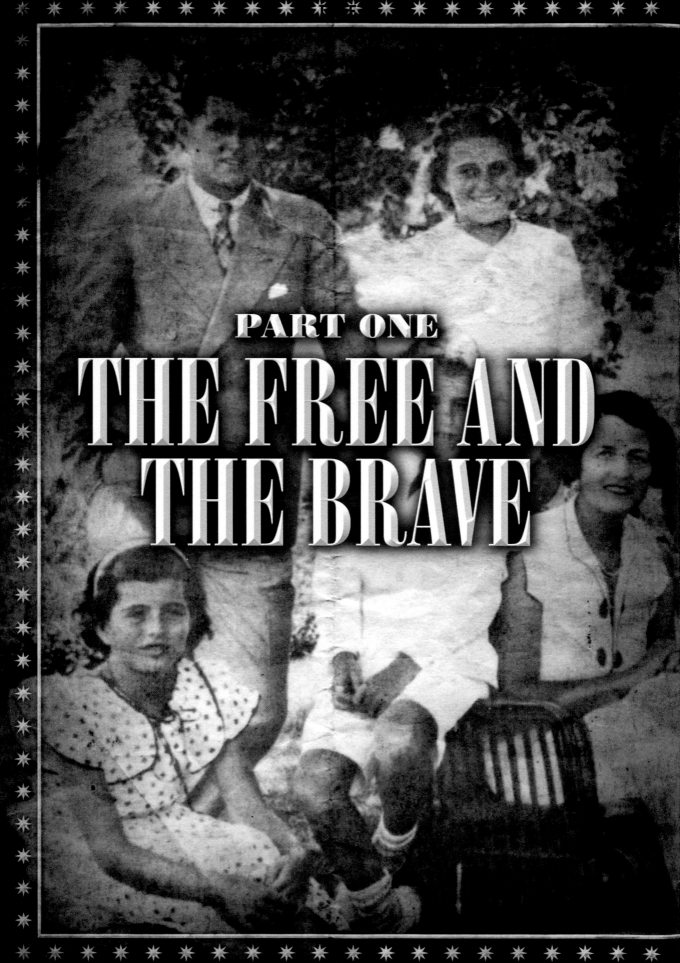

PART ONE

THE FREE AND THE BRAVE

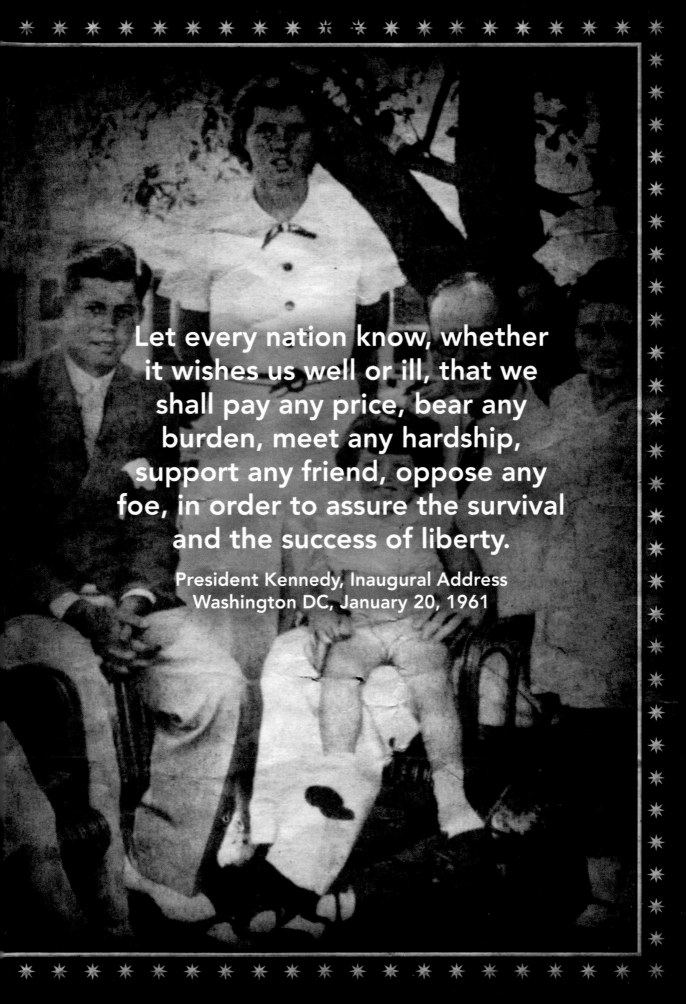

Let every nation know, whether it wishes us well or ill, that we shall pay any price, bear any burden, meet any hardship, support any friend, oppose any foe, in order to assure the survival and the success of liberty.

President Kennedy, Inaugural Address
Washington DC, January 20, 1961

CHAPTER 1

AN ANCESTRY OF IRISH IMMIGRANTS

THE KENNEDYS

Both sides of President John F. Kennedy's family originated in Ireland. His great-grandfather Patrick Kennedy (c. 1823 – 58) was the son of James Kennedy (c. 1770 – c. 1840) and his wife Maria (maiden name and birth dates unknown). Patrick Kennedy was forced, like many Irish people, to flee Ireland in the face of the dreadful potato famines of the late 1840s that killed thousands. He made his way to East Boston, where he married Bridget Murphy (c. 1824 – 88), and found work as a cooper. But in 1858, at age just 35, Patrick Kennedy died of cholera, leaving a wife, three daughters, and a son, Patrick Joseph "P.J." Kennedy—John Kennedy's paternal grandfather.

THE FITZGERALDS

Thomas Fitzgerald (1823 – 85), a farmer born in Bruff, County Limerick, Ireland, was John Kennedy's great-grandfather on his mother's side. In 1854, the potato famine also forced Thomas Fitzgerald to immigrate to America, ending up in the overcrowded wood-built slums of Boston's North End Irish ghetto.

He married Rose Anna Cox and the couple had twelve children, nine of whom survived to adulthood. Thomas Fitzgerald worked as a peddler of household goods and then took over a grocery store that became a tavern at night, managing to earn enough to buy tenements that he rented to Irish laborers. When he died in 1885, Rose having passed away six years earlier, he left his large family well provided for. The fourth of the twelve Fitzgerald children was John Francis Fitzgerald (1863 – 1950),

John F. Kennedy's maternal grandfather.

It was John F. Kennedy's two grandfathers who really set his family on the road to success. Both men were very prosperous and became well-known local celebrities. They were great political rivals who created comfortable lives for all their children.

MOVING UP IN SOCIETY

John Francis Fitzgerald married his second cousin, Mary Josephine Hannon (1865 – 1964), whom he met when he was fifteen and she was thirteen. It was love at first sight, he claimed and they would be married for sixty-two years. They had three sons and three daughters. The oldest was Rose Elizabeth Fitzgerald (1890 – 1995) who would lead a privileged life. Fitzgerald saw her as his entrée into polite society.

The Fitzgeralds moved from Acton, where the family had originally settled after arriving from Ireland, to Dorchester. Fitzgerald made a great deal of money from acquiring *The Republic* newspaper. It had been failing when he had purchased it, but he turned it into a thriving success.

In Dorchester, Rose was brought up far from the rough and tumble of Fitzgerald's political life in Boston and she led a sheltered existence. She was well-known in the city, though, having attended, at age 17, a number of social and political events. She went to a Catholic school, the Convent of the Sacred Heart where young ladies learned deportment and feminine virtues, with the intention of turning them into model wives and mothers.

In 1907, Fitzgerald took his wife and

two oldest daughters on a European tour, ostensibly to enhance the girls' education, but in reality he was taking them away from press coverage claiming that during his two-year term as mayor of Boston, he had lined his own pockets. The trip was also to separate Rose from P.J. Kennedy's son, Joseph Patrick "Joe" Kennedy, of whom Rose had become enamored.

* * * * * *

LOOKING DOWN ON THE KENNEDYS

The Fitzgeralds considered the Kennedy family to be of inferior social standing. To maintain the distance, John Fitzgerald decided to enroll Rose and her sister Agnes (1892 – 1936) in the Sacred Heart Convent school in Holland for the 1908 – 09 term. It was an establishment attended by the daughters of French and German aristocrats and affluent European families.

In 1909, Rose enrolled for another year at the Sacred Heart Convent in Manhattanville, New York, before returning to Boston to work for her father who had won a second term

as mayor. She effectively became Fitzgerald's First Lady as his wife was happy to stay home and look after the other children. Rose traveled with him to other US cities, went to Europe with him and met President William Howard Taft (1857 – 1930) at the White House. She appeared regularly in Boston's newspapers and was glowingly described by one biographer:

Fitzgerald delighted in the good looks of his daughter, in her intelligence, her presence of mind and superb social skills … She proved to be her father's equal in conversation, curiosity, dancing, athletic ability and powers of endurance and even in the capacity of fascinating reporters.

At Rose Fitzgerald's coming-out party in 1911, there were 450 guests including the Massachusetts elite. The next step should have been marriage and there were a number of eligible young men who vied for her hand. All of them were Catholic as at the time Protestants and Catholics in Boston gave each other a wide berth. But among the young men was the one she was looking for—Joe Kennedy.

The Fitzgerald family *c.* 1915. Center, John F. Fitzgerald and wife Mary Josephine Hannon. Surrounded by daughters Mary Agnes Fitzgerald, Eunice Fitzgerald, and Rose Elizabeth Fitzgerald; and sons Thomas Acton Fitzgerald, John Francis Fitzgerald Jr., and Frederick Hannon Fitzgerald.

"P.J." KENNEDY

Patrick Joseph "P.J." Kennedy (1858 – 1929) was the father of Joseph Patrick "Joe" Kennedy Sr. and the paternal grandfather of President John F. Kennedy. Born in East Boston, the son of Irish immigrants, he ended his schooling at age 14 to work in the Boston docks. By the 1880s he had saved enough money to buy a saloon in Boston's Haymarket Square. Soon, he owned three bars and a whiskey-importing business.

By the time he was 30, P.J. Kennedy was a well-known figure in East Boston. He was popular, described as "likable, always ready to help less fortunate fellow Irishmen with a little cash and some sensible advice." He converted this popularity into votes in 1884, when he was elected to serve in the Massachusetts House of Representatives. He then served in the Massachusetts Senate, becoming one of the most high-profile of Boston's Democrats.

In 1887, P.J. married Mary Augustus Hickey (1857 – 1923), daughter of a well-off Boston Irish family from the affluent suburb of Brockton. Her father James was a successful businessman, signifying P.J. Kennedy's move into Boston's newly emergent Irish middle class. Such families as his would become known as First Irish Families, or FIFs.

Leaving the Senate in 1895, he became involved as the behind-the-scenes boss in the complex world of Boston politics. He and the other three members of the Boston Democratic Party's Board of Strategy chose candidates for local and state positions and distributed favors as necessary.

By the time of his death in 1929, P.J. had an interest in a coal company and shares in a bank, the Columbia Trust Company. On his death, his son Joseph Patrick Kennedy Sr. and his two daughters inherited a beautiful home on the upscale Jeffries Point in East Boston.

"HONEY FITZ" FITZGERALD

John Francis "Honey Fitz" Fitzgerald (1863 – 1950) was Rose Fitzgerald's father and President John F. Kennedy's maternal grandfather. Born in Boston, the son of an Irish businessman, after attending Boston Latin School and Boston College, Fitzgerald enrolled at Harvard Medical School. But following his father's death in 1885, he left to take a job in Boston Customs House to enable him to feed his six younger brothers. Around this time, he became involved with the local branch of the Democratic Party.

In 1891, Fitzgerald was elected to Boston's Common Council where he succeeded in having $350,000 spent on a public park to benefit the poor inhabitants of Boston's North End. A year later, he was elected to the Massachusetts Senate and in 1894 was elected to the United States Congress. Five years later, he was elected Mayor of Boston, the first American-born Irish Catholic to hold that office.

Popularly known as Honey Fitz, his theatrical style of campaigning, and warmth of personality endeared him to voters. But underneath his "Fitzblarney," he was, above all, a master of politics.

During his years in Congress, Fitzgerald supported measures that served local and state needs, championed laws for progressive income taxes rather than high, protective tariffs, and always supported the continuation of unrestricted immigration.

His later years were devoted to his business interests and on aiding the political ambitions of his grandsons. When John F. Kennedy decided to run for Congress in 1946, Honey Fitz, by this time 83, helped him plan his campaign strategy.

When he died, at age 87, his funeral was one of the biggest Boston had ever seen. A crowd of many thousands lined the route taken by his coffin.

JOSEPH P. KENNEDY SR.

Joseph Patrick "Joe" Kennedy Sr. (1888 – 1969) was the son of P.J. Kennedy, and the father of President John F. Kennedy. He was born at a time of great entrepreneurship when prominent men accumulated vast personal wealth through steel manufacture, energy creation, railroad construction, and finance.

At age 15, Joe Kennedy launched a neighborhood baseball team named the Assumptions. He was the team's business manager, coach, and also played. He rented the ballpark, purchased uniforms, and collected the money from spectators ensuring he made a profit.

His mother believed in her son's potential so much that she moved him from the Catholic Xaverian School to Boston Latin, the preferred educational establishment of the Boston elite. Although as an Irish boy, Joe was in a distinct minority at the school, he was not inhibited. He was appointed colonel of an award-winning drill team and captained the school's baseball team.

From Boston Latin, he moved on to Harvard where old attitudes still prevailed and snobbery was endemic. Joe was surrounded by the sons of millionaires. But he lived with the less well-off students in less salubrious dormitories. Nonetheless, he served on the student council, as a class leader, and gained membership of some of the university's most important clubs.

He was also successful in business dealings at Harvard. He and a friend purchased a business that was going under and gained a licence from Mayor John Fitzgerald. The business took off and with an initial investment of $600, Joe and his friend made $10,000 profit over the next two years.

He graduated in 1912 and started work in his father's bank, Columbia Trust. He gained the requisite qualifications to be put on the list of potential state bank examiners. Through his Irish American connections he was fast tracked by Mayor Fitzgerald and the governor to the position and did the job for eighteen months.

A Boston bank made an approach to buy the Columbia Trust in 1913, but Joe wanted it to remain independent. He got a loan from another bank and bought Columbia Trust himself, becoming president at age 25. The press provided countless pages of publicity for the young bank president and deposits at the bank doubled.

THE IRISH POTATO FAMINE

The Potato Famine—also known as the Great Famine—was a dreadful time for Ireland, a period of four years between 1845 and 1849 when the country suffered mass starvation and disease leading to mass migration.

The potato had become a staple food in Ireland because it was nutritious, hardy, and provided a lot of calories. It was also easy to grow for Ireland's farmers. Thus, by the early 1840s, around 50 percent of the Irish population depended on the potato for food. There was also a reliance on a couple of high-yielding varieties, increasing the chances of the crop being completely wiped out.

In 1845, a deadly potato fungus, *Phytophthora infestans*, arrived from North America and conspired with unusually cool, moist weather to decimate much of the potato crop. The British government failed to provide sufficient help, and when the Whigs under Lord John Russell came to power in 1846, the government adopted a policy of relying on Irish resources and the free market to resolve the crisis. This led to catastrophe.

Irish and British absentee landowners were given the responsibility of providing aid but as the tenant farmers fell behind with payments to their landlords, the owners also fell into financial difficulties. Hundreds of thousands of tenant farmers were evicted and many had no option but to enter the workhouse.

The British government opened soup kitchens and employment was provided on road building and public works. Astonishingly, as millions starved, Ireland continued to export grain, meat, and other foodstuffs to Britain. The situation did little to assuage the deep resentment about British rule in Ireland.

At the beginning of the famine, the Irish population was 8.4 million. By the end, it was 6.6 million. A million died of starvation or famine-related diseases such as typhus, while almost a million more Irish migrated to the United States. They were the first wave of poor refugees to land in America. Almost 37,000 impoverished Irish immigrants disembarked in Boston in 1847. They took any unskilled jobs available, and settled in tough areas near the Boston waterfront, in the North End, and in East Boston. Since then, almost 4.7 million Irish have arrived in America. A 2002 census showed that, out of the total United States population, more than 34 million people claimed Irish ancestry, making Irish Americans the second-largest ethnic group in the USA.

Starving Irish families at the gate of the work-house.

CHAPTER 2

A FAMILY UNLIKE ANY OTHER

★ ★ ★ ★ ★ ★ 🦅 ★ ★ ★ ★ ★ ★

Joe Kennedy and Rose Fitzgerald had been in love since he was 18 and she was 16 but, Rose's family believed the Kennedys to be a bit beneath them. Rose's father, Honey Fitz, had tried to bring their relationship to an end, prohibiting Rose from attending a Boston Latin School dance and the Harvard Junior Prom. Between 1906 when they first met and 1914 he would not even allow Joe Kennedy to set foot inside his house. It was pointless, however, as the couple were hopelessly in love.

★ ★ ★ ★ ★ ★

HONEY FITZ AND "TOODLES"

They got round Rose's father's wishes by meeting secretly at the houses of friends, although never alone. Eventually, Honey Fitz was forced to give in, especially when

it emerged that he himself had been having an affair with a beautiful cigarette girl by the name of "Toodles" Ryan.

Suddenly, as Honey Fitz was forced by his philandering with "Toodles" to abandon another tilt at the mayorship, the young banker Joe Kennedy did not seem an altogether bad prospect. The couple were engaged in June 1914 and married the following October. Joe was 26 and Rose was 24.

They began married life in a seven-roomed house in Beals Street in Boston's middle class Brookline area. Joe Kennedy incurred the substantial debt for the time of $6,500 to buy the house, but he was confident that the future was rosy. He also borrowed in order to purchase a new Model T Ford. A maid costing seven dollars a week was hired to cook and keep the house clean and tidy.

Joseph P. Kennedy Sr. and bride Rose Elizabeth Fitzgerald on their wedding day in Boston, Massachusetts, 1914.

TWO SONS AND A WORLD AT WAR

Joe and Rose's first child, a boy, was born the following summer at the house they were renting next to his in-laws at Nantasket Beach, Hull, Massachusetts. Honey Fitz was disappointed to learn that instead of being named after him, the boy was to be named Joseph Patrick "Joe" Kennedy Jr. (1915 – 44) after his father. Nonetheless, he was full of pride at the birth of his grandchild, excitedly telling a journalist:

> *He is going to be President of the United States. His mother and father have already decided that he is going to Harvard, where he will play on the football and baseball teams and incidentally take all the scholastic honors. Then he's going to be a captain of industry until it's time for him to be President for two or three terms. Further than that has not been decided. He may act as Mayor of Boston and governor of Massachusetts for a while on his way to the presidential chair.*

It was said in jest, of course, but such was the ambition of the Fitzgerald and Kennedy families that it was not entirely a joke.

A second child followed less than two years later. This time they made Honey Fitz even more proud by naming him John Fitzgerald Kennedy (1917 – 63). Born on May 29, 1917, at the house in Beals Street, less was said about this child. The United States had, after all, just entered the First World War and many young Americans were risking their lives overseas.

* * * * * *

MAKING JUDGMENTS

That day marked not only the birth of their second son, however, it was also the day that Joe Kennedy Sr. was elected to the board of the Massachusetts Electric Company. He was still only 28. He was cynical about the war effort that had become something of a crusade in America.

He saw little point in sacrificing his own or other American lives in a European war which he considered senseless slaughter. A number of his friends from Harvard disagreed and volunteered, but Joe remained at home.

It was symptomatic of his foreign-affairs thinking. Always insightful on domestic matters, he consistently made bad decisions on overseas matters. Making judgments based on how his business ventures or his family would be affected by events outside America, rendered him a lifelong advocate of isolationist policies.

* * * * * *

STEEL FOR AMERICA

In September 1917, Joe left the bank and took a job as general manager of Bethlehem Steel's Fore River shipbuilding plant in Quincy, Massachusetts, at a salary of $15,000 a year. He managed to salve his conscience somewhat about not volunteering to fight with the thought that the steel being produced was vital to the United States' war effort.

It was a wonderful opportunity to demonstrate that he could manage a multi-million dollar business and Joe was able to make some useful contacts. He also worked very hard, remaining there for eighteen months, often sleeping for no more than two hours a night in the office. He left in the summer of 1919 with a bonus and a letter thanking him "for services rendered at a time when no one else could have done what you did."

* * * * * *

MAKING A MILLION

Joe became a stockbroker with the well-respected Boston firm, Hayden, Stone and Company. Although he earned just $10,000 a year, he was able to use what he learned on a daily basis to accumulate a $2 million fortune in the next six years. He had once said that he would be a millionaire by the time he was 35 but he had managed this early.

In 1923, he launched his own stockbroking business, adding many more millions to his fortune. He also made money from the purchase of Massachusetts' first cinemas. He sold all his movie business in 1930 but made still more money from the drinks industry when Prohibition was repealed in 1933.

By this time, he and Rose had added to their growing family—Rose Marie, known as "Rosemary" (1918 – 2005), Kathleen Agnes (1920 – 48), Eunice Mary (1921 – 2009), Patricia Helen (1924 – 2006), Robert Francis (1925 – 68), Jean Ann (b. 1928) and Edward Moore (1932 – 2009).

* * * * *

RELATIONSHIP ISSUES

They had nine children over a seventeen-year period but loved having a large family. In 1921 they moved into a bigger house to accommodate everyone. Again it was in Brookline, but it had twelve rooms. They employed a full-time, live-in nursemaid so that Rose Kennedy could have some time off from caring for her brood.

Despite the wealth, the children and the large house, all was not well, however. Joe and Rose had issues in their relationship. Rose's devotion to her faith got in the way of her enjoyment of her comfortable situation. Meanwhile, Joe always suffered from an inferiority complex as a result of the social slights he had endured at Harvard and in the world of banking.

To some extent, however, they were made for each other. Rose was very conservative while Joe, although still conservative, was more adventurous, never happier than when he was breaking the rules. He was imaginative in his thinking and it paid off in his work life. It was a characteristic that several of his children inherited.

* * * * *

GLORIA SWANSON

Joe Kennedy was also something of a womanizer, although it has been suggested that he turned to other women simply because of Rose's dislike of intimacy. She believed that sex was purely for the procreation of children. Indeed, it is reported that after the birth of their last child, Edward in 1932, Rose announced to Joe, "No more sex" and from then on, it is said, she slept in a separate bedroom.

Nonetheless, it seems unlikely, given the type of man that Joe was, that he would have been satisfied with just one woman. A journalist who knew him well, said that women "were another thing that a rich man had—like caviar. It wasn't sex, it was part of the image … his idea of manliness."

The Kennedy family at Hyannis Port, 1931. Left to right: Robert Kennedy, John F. Kennedy, Eunice Kennedy, Jean Kennedy (on lap of) Joseph P. Kennedy Sr., Rose Fitzgerald Kennedy, Patricia Kennedy, Kathleen Kennedy, Joseph P. Kennedy Jr. (behind), Rosemary Kennedy. The dog in the foreground is "Buddy."

Incredibly, he even brought several of the women he was seeing into his own home, telling the curious that they were merely friends of his daughters. His affair with the glamorous Hollywood star Gloria Swanson, was an open secret and one that came close to ending his marriage. Rose's father even threatened to tell her about the affair if he did not end it. Although Honey Fitz was a man of experience in such matters, Joe refused to give up seeing Gloria. The affair eventually came to an end, but it resonated throughout the lives of the Kennedy family from then on.

* * * * * *

FACING INFIDELITIES

Rose Kennedy meanwhile, was forced to reluctantly stay at home and be a mother to the children. This contrasted greatly with the type of life she had led with her father before she married. In fact, during the first eighteen years of the marriage she was pregnant for nearly 40 percent of the time, and even though she did, of course, have a large retinue of servants to help her, she still felt the pressure of having to care for so many children.

She had to persevere, in the face of her husband's infidelities and his many absences. They came to an arrangement whereby she could travel both in the United States and abroad. She traveled to Europe no fewer than seventeen times in the mid-1930s. During both their absences, they had an agreement not to share any bad news about the family. So they made it work, appearing to the outside world to be a normal happy family.

* * * * * *

YOUNG JACK KENNEDY

John Fitzgerald Kennedy (known as "Jack") attended the local public school, Edward Devotion from 1922 to 1923. The following year he and his elder brother, Joe Jr., at age seven and nine respectively were enrolled at a local private school, Dexter. Their absence from the house allowed Rose Kennedy to devote more attention to her daughter Rosemary who had been born with learning difficulties.

Dexter was another opportunity for Joe Sr. to improve his social status. His sons were mixing with the children of Boston's elite families.

Leisure time was often spent with Grandpa Honey Fitz, attending Boston Red Sox baseball games, or even accompanying him on the campaign trail during his failed attempt to win the Massachusetts governorship. Jack Kennedy was a willing reader, enjoying Walter Scott's tales of chivalry and adventure as well as histories and biographies.

Summers were spent away at Cohasset on the South Shore, where in 1922 the family received a cool welcome from the Protestant families who gathered there. They felt more at home in the Cape Cod villages of Craigville Beach where they summered in 1924, and Hyannis Port which they first visited in 1926. They rented an estate that overlooked the harbor at Hyannis Port, and it was there that the young Jack Kennedy learned to swim.

* * * * * *

CHILDHOOD RIVALRY

Joe Jr. was a great rival to Jack during his childhood. The two often fought and Joe would push his younger brother around. One woman who was a friend of Jack when he was young said:

> *He talked about him all the time—"Joe plays football better, Joe dances better, Joe is getting better grades." Joe just kind of overshadowed him in everything.*

Joe Sr. had created a hugely competitive, goal-oriented family and these two siblings took it to the limit. Joe Jr. bullied Jack, but Jack always refused to be intimidated by him. At the same time, Jack also worshipped him, missing him terribly if he went away for the summer.

* * * * * *

BRONXVILLE AND BOARDING SCHOOL

When Jack Kennedy was ten, the family moved from Brookline to Riverdale, New York. By this time, engaged in the film industry, Joe Sr. was spending most of his time flying between

New York and Los Angeles, and the move made sense. He also felt, however, that New York was a better place for an Irish Catholic family, remembering the social stigma of being Irish Catholic when he was growing up. They still spent summers at Hyannis Port and Joe Sr. purchased the large estate they rented to ensure they could summer there in perpetuity.

The new house, owned previously by former US Secretary of State Charles Evans Hughes, had thirteen rooms and was situated in a wooded area that overlooked the Hudson River. But Rose Kennedy found it hard to adjust and soon they were on the move again, this time to a six-acre estate in Bronxville. It was home to some of the nation's wealthiest families and Rose was much happier there.

Jack went to Riverdale Country Day School where he did well. Joe Jr., meanwhile, was sent to boarding school in Connecticut. After Joe Jr. was sent away, his younger brother's work began to suffer and it was decided to send him away to boarding school, too.

He was enrolled in the Canterbury School in New Milford, Connecticut, a different establishment to the one his brother was attending. He was homesick much of the time and generally unimpressed by the strict regime. He did well in English, math, and history, but was let down by his performance in science, and Latin.

* * * * * *

THE DEPRESSION

Meanwhile, Jack Kennedy developed an abiding interest in world affairs, asking his father in the fall of 1930 to send him the *Literary Digest* because, he wrote "I did not know about the Market Slump until a long time after …" But the Depression did not seem to affect the Kennedy fortune as Jack Kennedy later said:

I have no first-hand knowledge of the depression. My family had one of the great fortunes of the world and it was worth more than ever then. We had bigger houses, more servants, we traveled more. About the only thing I saw directly was when my father hired some extra gardeners just to give them a job so they could eat. I really did not learn about the depression until I read about it at Harvard.

In fact, during the Crash, Joe Sr. greatly enhanced his fortune by investing a huge amount of it in real estate. In 1929, his fortune was estimated at $4 million and by 1935 he was said to have $180 million which would be equivalent to around $3.11 billion in today's terms.

* * * * * *

A FAMILY UNLIKE ANY OTHER

There is little doubt that the money and the social standing separated the Kennedys from everyone else. Charles Spalding, a childhood friend, provides us with an idea of what it was like to be around the Kennedys at that time:

You watched these people go through their lives and just had a feeling that they existed outside the usual laws of nature; that there was no other group so handsome, so engaged. There was endless action …endless talk … endless competition, people drawing each other out and pushing each other to greater lengths. It was as simple as this: the Kennedys had a feeling of being heightened and it rubbed off on the people who came into contact with them. They were a unit. I remember thinking to myself that there couldn't be another group quite like this one.

From the outside they appeared arrogant and there were many who disliked the Kennedys. Even more disliked Joe Sr., who did not suffer fools gladly. It may have been a result of the humiliations of his youth but he could be disturbingly abrupt with people. He gained a reputation for being opinionated and difficult to work for. The Kennedys were often slow in paying bills too, which did not go down well with local tradesmen. Like royalty they did not carry cash which led to awkward situations at places such as gas stations.

CHAPTER 3

IN SICKNESS AND IN HEALTH

In 1931, Jack Kennedy passed the entrance exams for Choate boarding school in Wallingford, Connecticut, which his brother had attended. The school had educated generations of upper-class New England children, and was delighted to have another boy from this wealthy and prominent family. But during the next four years Jack suffered a series of baffling health problems.

He had endured a dangerous bout of scarlet fever at age 3, and his father had to use all his influence to get a hospital bed for his son in the middle of an epidemic. In the fall of 1930, he was laid low by a mysterious illness, losing a considerable amount of weight, and feeling tired all the time. In April 1931, he was struck by abdominal pains that led to an appendectomy.

At his new school his health problems persisted, and he was often in the school infirmary. His weight was of concern and he suffered from colds and coughs. His second year was no different. His knees began to hurt, the doctor diagnosing growing pains.

In the summer of 1933 he turned 16, but was still not putting on any weight leading his classmates to nickname him "Rat Face" because of the thinness of his face. The following January, his health deteriorated to such an extent he was rushed to hospital. Doctors feared that he had leukaemia but later his symptoms disappeared.

Members of the Muckers Club at Choate, c.1934. Left to right: Ralph Horton, Lem Billings, Butch Schriber, and John F. Kennedy.

THE WEAKER BROTHER

All the time, he was in the shadow of his high-achieving brother. Joe Jr. proved successful in his studies and was a star on the sports field, winning the school's prestigious Harvard Trophy when he graduated in 1933.

Jack Kennedy would never achieve the degree of parental approval lavished on his brother, but that did not mean they did not expect him to be a high achiever. All the Kennedy children were expected to excel in whatever they did. Thus, Joe Sr. was irritated by his son's many health problems but they were also a continual embarrassment to his son, as a friend pointed out:

> *Jack's very frame as a light, thin person, his proneness to injury of all kinds, his back, his sickness, which he wouldn't ever talk about … he was heartily ashamed of them, they were a mark of effeminacy, of weakness which he wouldn't acknowledge.*

* * * * * *

MOST LIKELY TO SUCCEED

But his parents were also worried about Jack's academic weakness. He was forced to attend the summer session of 1932 to try to improve his performance in Latin and French. His mother feared he did less well in subjects that did not interest him. In fact, he was more interested in current affairs than in his schoolwork. He was a *New York Times* subscriber and around this time his lifelong interest in Winston Churchill (1874 – 1965) began.

Although deemed "most likely to succeed" by his classmates, Jack was disorganized and untidy. His father wrote to the school's assistant head, worried that his son may perhaps have been over-indulged. But what Jack had going for him was his great charm and the assistant head recognized this trait:

> *In any school he would have got away with some things, just on his smile … a very likeable person, very loveable.*

Jack's small rebellions at Choate—such as forming a club called "The Muckers" dedicated

to bucking the system—can be viewed, however, as little more than an expression of the traits that his father had worked so hard to instill in his boys—independence and irreverence.

When Joe Jr. graduated from Choate, his father dispatched him to England to study with the socialist academic, economist and author, Harold Laski (1893 – 1950). Joe Jr. even traveled to the Soviet Union with Professor Laski, returning full of the virtues of socialism.

* * * * * *

KENNEDY'S HEALTH PROBLEMS

In June 1934, the 17-year-old Jack Kennedy was ill again. He was sent to the famous Mayo brothers' clinic in Rochester, Minnesota, where he had a miserable time. He spent two weeks at the clinic before being transferred to St. Mary's Hospital in Rochester, all the while writing about his experiences to his schoolfriend Lem Billings (1916 – 81) who later recalled:

> *We used to joke about the fact that if I ever wrote a biography, I would call it "John F. Kennedy: A Medical History."*

The doctors thought initially he might be suffering from a peptic ulcer but it was later recorded that he had "spastic colitis." He lost weight and complained that no one really knew what was wrong with him. He was put on special diets and subjected to an array of invasive and embarrassing tests. His family were secretive about the seriousness of his condition.

* * * * * *

TREATMENT AND DIAGNOSIS

His colitis and digestive problems made it hard for him to put on weight and the condition could become very serious if his colon became ulcerated or bled. A later diagnosis—in July 1944—by a gastroenterologist at the Lahey Clinic in Boston said that he had "diffuse duodentitis and severe spastic colitis," both of

HAROLD LASKI

Educated at Manchester Grammar School and New College, Oxford, Harold Laski was a professor at the London School of Economics from 1926 until his death in 1950. He taught modern history at McGill University and also lectured at Harvard.

After 1930, he took a Marxist viewpoint, advocating the need for a violent workers' revolution if necessary. This was in contradiction to the beliefs of the leaders of the Labour Party. They wanted to achieve the same goals but via non-violent democratic means.

Laski became Chairman of the Labour Party in 1945, and was criticized by Winston Churchill, leader of the Conservative Party who lost that year's British general election. While campaigning in Nottinghamshire on behalf of a Labour candidate, Laski said that if Labour did not obtain what it needed by general consent, "we shall have to use violence even if it means revolution." There was uproar in the media and Laski was, as a result, not given a role in the government of new prime minister Clement Attlee (1883 – 1967).

Laski continued to work on behalf of the Labour Party until his death but his influence was greatly diminished. He died of influenza in March 1950, at the age of 56.

which could be very dangerous. At the time it was believed that emotional stress was a big factor in the creation of ulcers and colitis; therefore, it was essential that stress should be kept to a minimum. He also had to be put on a diet that would relieve his condition.

He returned to Choate for his senior year and the school infirmary kept a close watch on him, their results being passed on to the doctors at the Mayo clinic. It is probable, however, that the changes in his blood count were as a result of the drugs he was being administered. In fact, he was comparatively healthy during that year. Although he was briefly hospitalized, he recovered quickly enough in time to enroll for university.

We're puttin' on our top hat,
Tyin' up our white tie,
Brushin' off our tails,
In order to
Wish you
A Merry Christmas

Rip.   Leem.   Ken.

A Christmas card featuring (left to right) Ralph Horton, Lem Billings, and John F. Kennedy, Princeton, 1935.

GOING TO PRINCETON

Even though his grades were not what might have been hoped for—he was 65th out of a class of 110—there was little doubt that Jack Kennedy would gain admission to Harvard. His father was a prominent alumnus and his brother was already a good student there.

He elected, however, to go to Princeton, a decision that his father was happy to accept, given that it could be seen as an expression of the independence he had encouraged in his children. He also asked if, like his brother, he could go to England to study under Harold Laski. So, in 1935, at age 18, he traveled to Europe for the first time.

It was an interesting but tense time for the continent. There was concern over the Rhineland, occupied by the Allies since the end of the First World War, but which German leader Hitler was threatening to reoccupy in the first overtly aggressive act of Nazi Germany. In October 1935, Mussolini's Italian troops invaded Ethiopia. But Jack was only interested in these events in as much as they offered him reasons to return home and even while he was in Europe, he was more interested in his social life than what Professor Laski had to say.

He fell ill in October and returned to the United States where he was enrolled to begin his studies at Princeton in November. Illness interrupted his studies, however, and by December he was in hospital again in Boston. He recuperated in Palm Beach, Florida and then in April, at his father's suggestion, he went to Arizona for two months. With time to think, he decided that Princeton was not for him and in July 1936 re-applied for Harvard.

* * * * * *

AT HARVARD

In terms of Jack's application to his studies in his first two years at Harvard, little had changed from his time at Choate. His grades were unimpressive and he made no effort to improve them, apart from taking on the odd tutor or using a "cram school."

He was, according to the memories of his teachers and fellow students, as charming and good-humored as ever, but it is interesting to note his lack of enthusiasm for the progressive politics of the day. He also seemed uninterested in the activities of those who were responding to the rise of fascism, communism, Nazism or the New Deal.

He worked hard on his social life and on his sporting activities. In his first year, he played football and golf, swam, and was a member of the Smoker and Annual Show committees. His second year was occupied with junior varsity football, varsity swimming, and the Spee and Yacht Clubs.

He also served on the business board of *The Harvard Crimson*, the Harvard newspaper. Given Jack's skinny stature—six feet and only 150 pounds—and his poor health, his sporting achievements were completely eclipsed by his brother's.

* * * * * *

POLITICS AND GIRLS

Joe Jr. was completely immersed in campus politics. The Kennedy family had decided that he was the one to have a political career, and his ambition was to be president.

He was elected to the Winthrop House Committee. Winthrop House being one of the twelve undergraduate residential houses at Harvard. He was a class representative to the student council and acted as business manager for the class album. His politics, he admitted, reflected those of his father. He was against any US intervention in Europe where tensions were rising.

Jack, too, began to develop an interest in politics and he studied economics, history, and government. But, in his first two years at Harvard, he was extremely popular and began to display an interest in girls. And girls liked him, too. He described his numerous conquests in letters to his friend, Lem Billings:

> I can now get my tail, as often and as free as I want which is a step in the right direction.

TENDENCY TO PROWL

In fact, Jack enjoyed the favors of so many women that he often could not remember their names. Of course, he had not been set a very good example by both his father and his maternal grandfather. He was well aware what his father got up to when he was away in New York, Hollywood or Europe, and Honey Fitz also played the field. Jack told the story of how his father had tried to climb into the bed of one of his sisters' friends. He often warned women visitors:

> Be sure to lock your bedroom door. The Ambassador has a tendency to prowl late at night.

* * * * * *

EUROPEAN GRAND TOUR

Jack paid for Lem Billings to accompany him on a grand tour of Europe in 1937. It was customary for privileged young American men at the best universities to undertake such a tour, visiting all the historical sites of the great European cities. It served to broaden their understanding and interest in foreign affairs.

They started in France, touring in a convertible Jack had had shipped across the Atlantic, visiting all the major towns and sights, including the First World War battlefields. They quizzed the French about their views on America, and about recent developments in Europe. He wrote in his travel diary:

> The general impression also seems to be that there will not be a war in the near future, and that France is much too well prepared for Germany. The permanence of the alliance between Germany and Italy is also questionable.

In Spain they were told stories of the atrocities committed during the Spanish Civil War. But Italy made a huge impression on the two young men. It seemed cleaner and more prosperous than they had expected. Jack wrote, "Fascism seems to treat them well."

In Germany they found that Americans were not well liked, as Lem Billings later remembered:

We had a terrible feeling about Germany, and all the Heil Hitler stuff ... They were extremely arrogant—the whole race was arrogant— the whole feeling of Germany was one of arrogance; the feeling that they were superior to us and wanting to show it.

* * * * * *

UNDERSTANDING THE CONSEQUENCES

The European trip was hugely important to Jack Kennedy. He began to understand that it was necessary to investigate a situation and understand it, rather than just have personal opinions with nothing to back them up. This was, of course, a view that contrasted greatly with his father's and was, perhaps, the first step in his separation, politically at any rate, from his father and his older brother.

Jack was arriving at his own independent viewpoint and beginning to understand that despite the distance between the two continents, what happened in Europe impacted upon the United States. This was an opinion in direct contradiction to his father's isolationist view.

* * * * * *

UNITED KINGDOM AMBASSADOR

Joe Kennedy Sr. had been serving as chairman of the newly created US Maritime Commission and had been featured in a cover article for *Fortune* magazine. Then in December 1937, President Franklin D. Roosevelt (1882 – 1945) appointed him as United States Ambassador to the United Kingdom.

This was a huge honor, as the British ambassadorship was the most prestigious of all American diplomatic posts. It gave a massive boost to the Kennedys' social standing. Joe Sr. had, in fact, lobbied Roosevelt hard for the post. He had been offered the position of Secretary of Commerce but, as a man of Irish origins, London was where he really wanted to be. Now he would have access to London society, as he told an aide who was traveling with him:

Don't go buying a lot of luggage. We're only going to get the family on the Social Register. When that's done, we come on back.

* * * * * *

ON THE BRINK

So, Jack Kennedy found himself, for a short time anyway, mixing with the higher echelons of English society. He spent the summer of 1938 working in the US embassy in London as well as attending tea parties, balls, regattas and horse racing. Then in August 1938, the Kennedys decamped to a villa in Cannes, south of France, and vacationed with some members of the British royal family.

Jack returned to Harvard in the fall of 1938. Meantime, in Europe tensions were developing rapidly. Britain was trying to broker an agreement over the Sudetenland question. Hitler was supporting the claims for self-determination of the Germans in the Sudetenland which was part of Czechoslovakia. Nazi Germany was gearing up for an invasion and Europe was on the brink of war.

John F. Kennedy (right) and his brother Joseph Kennedy Jr. (left) with their father, on the deck of the French liner *Normandie*, 1938.

LEM BILLINGS

Kirk LeMoyne "Lem" Billings was born in Pittsburgh, Pennsylvania, in 1916, son of a prominent physician and a mother who was descended from one of the families that had sailed on the *Mayflower*. He first encountered John F. Kennedy at Choate in the fall of 1933 and spent that Christmas with the Kennedys at Palm Beach.

For the remainder of his life he was very much a member of the Kennedy family circle, spending holidays with them and participating in family events. Kennedy and Billings were drawn together by a shared dislike for the strict regime at Choate. Billings even repeated his senior year there so that he and Kennedy could graduate at the same time.

Billings attended Princeton, majoring in art and architecture, while Kennedy left that university for Harvard after a bout of ill health. But they would spend weekends together in New York City and embarked on a European tour together in 1937. He failed the medical tests required to enlist in the army when the United States entered the Second World War in 1941.

Billings solicited help from Joe Kennedy Sr.—who described him as "my second son"—to be accepted by the American Ambulance Field Service. He served in North Africa, and the South Pacific. On leaving the military, he worked on Jack Kennedy's successful Congressional election campaign in 1946 before touring South America with Robert Kennedy.

He gained an MBA from Harvard and worked in several jobs before taking leave to help on Jack Kennedy's 1960 presidential campaign. During Kennedy's presidency, Billings was a fixture in the White House inner circle, visiting most weekends. When the president was away, he kept the First Lady company.

Many have questioned his relationship to President Kennedy, speculating on his homosexuality. Some historians suggested that he expressed his sexual interest to Kennedy in 1934 but was rebuffed by him. After Kennedy's assassination, he was described by one historian as "Probably the saddest of the Kennedy widows."

Billings continued to be a presence in Kennedy family circles long after the death of his friend and he served for many years with Sargent Shriver (1915 – 2011)—husband of Eunice Kennedy—as a trustee of the Kennedy family trusts. He died on May 28, 1981.

President John F. Kennedy with Lem Billings (right) in the Oval Office, 1962.

CHAPTER 4

WHY ENGLAND SLEPT

★ ★ ★ ★ ★ ★ ★ ★ ★ ★ ★ ★ ★

Jack Kennedy was determined to return to Europe. Therefore, he obtained permission from Harvard to take a term's leave of absence. In the spring of 1939, he planned to travel to Europe to work on his honors thesis about the developing political situation. During the previous fall term, his grades had improved considerably, and he excelled in his government classes. One of his teachers wondered if he might become a journalist.

At the end of February 1939, he flew down to New Orleans for Mardi Gras before flying back to New York to board an ocean liner for Europe.

★ ★ ★ ★ ★

MOVING IN DIPLOMATIC CIRCLES

Around this time, Joe Kennedy Sr. was making waves by publicly supporting the British policy of appeasement toward Nazi Germany. But as soon as Jack Kennedy arrived in London he threw himself into the social life of a diplomat and he described it to Lem Billings:

> … having a great time … [met the king] at a Court Levee. It takes place in the morning and you wear tails. The King stands & you go up and bow. Met Queen Mary and was at tea with the Princess Elizabeth with whom I made a great deal of time … Friday I leave for Rome as J.P. has been appointed to represent Roosevelt at the Pope's coronation.

He next spent a month in Paris, went skiing in Switzerland and was able to write to Billings that he was "seeing life." Meanwhile, he did actually research material for his senior thesis. They were heady times and he was fascinated by the political situation in Europe that made war seem almost inevitable to many observers.

His letters to his father and Billings were full of the political machinations of the time.

He was right in the middle of it, traveling to Danzig and Warsaw in May to have meetings with Nazi and Polish officials. He then went on to Leningrad, Moscow, Kiev, Bucharest, Turkey, Jerusalem, Beirut, Damascus, and Athens. Everywhere he went he had discussions with US senior diplomats at the various embassies where he stayed.

August was spent in England, France, Germany, and Italy. In Munich he and another Harvard student and future Congressman, Torbert MacDonald (1917 – 76), were subjected to abuse when some Nazi storm troopers spied the British number plate on their car. His father arranged for him to visit Czechoslovakia which annoyed members of the embassy staff who had to spend time looking after him and arranging his tour.

The family returned to the south of France in August 1939 and Jack joined them there, socializing and flirting with the German actress Marlene Dietrich (1901 – 92).

★ ★ ★ ★ ★

THE END OF THE WORLD

Everything changed on September 1, 1939, when Hitler invaded Poland, and Britain and France declared war. Joe Kennedy Sr. was devastated, complaining on the phone to President Roosevelt: "It's the end of the world … the end of everything."

Jack Kennedy also got to do some real work when his father sent him to Glasgow. He was instructed to look after the interests of two hundred Americans who had been rescued following the sinking by a German submarine of the liner carrying them. Of the hundred passengers who had lost their lives, twenty-eight were Americans.

The American survivors were reluctant to board another ship without a naval escort but Jack tried to explain to them that the Germans

PEACE IN OUR TIME

Appeasement is the term most often used to describe the policy of the British government to avoid war with Nazi Germany. The policy came to the fore following the failure of the League of Nations to prevent aggression that might lead to another war.

In 1936, Adolf Hitler sent his forces into the Rhineland which, under the 1925 Locarno Treaties, was supposed to be a demilitarized zone. Britain and the League of Nations took no action. The policy of appeasement was implemented still further when Stanley Baldwin (1867 – 1947) resigned as prime minister and was replaced by Neville Chamberlain (1869 – 1940) in May 1937.

When the Anschluss happened—German troops entering and annexing Austria, something strictly prohibited by the Allies at the end of the First World War—no action was taken and America more or less concurred.

In 1938, when Germany threatened to invade the Sudetenland—part of Czechoslovakia—Neville Chamberlain flew to Berchtesgaden to negotiate with Adolf Hitler.

Hitler threatened the British PM with war if the Sudetenland was not allowed to be absorbed into Germany. At a second meeting of the two leaders, Chamberlain agreed to the cession of the Sudetenland to Germany.

On September 29, 1938, Chamberlain, Hitler, French prime minister Édouard Daladier (1884 – 1970), and Italian leader Benito Mussolini (1883 – 1945), all attended a conference. Neither Czechoslovakia nor the Soviet Union was invited. The four agreed to allow Germany to hold onto the Sudetenland and created an international commission to decide the future of other disputed areas. Czechoslovakia was told that if it did not accept the agreement, it would stand alone.

Hitler and Chamberlain signed a peace agreement allowing the British prime minister to famously announce "Peace in Our Time," when he returned to Britain. Soon, however, German troops took control of all of Czechoslovakia ignoring the agreement. When war eventually broke out those who had advocated appeasement were vilified.

Adolf Hitler (right) greets British Prime Minister Neville Chamberlain (left) at Munich, Germany, 1938.

were unlikely to attack a US vessel. Jack was supportive of their view and tried to persuade his father to accede to their wishes, but Joe Sr. refused and they returned to America on board an unaccompanied freighter.

* * * * * *

THE HARVARD CRIMSON

As he said in an article he wrote for *The Harvard Crimson*, Jack was convinced that the warring European powers were keen for a settlement, although it would probably mean the sacrifice of Poland to obtain such an agreement. He advocated Germany being given a "free economic hand" in Eastern Europe and some overseas colonies in return for which Hitler must agree to disarm.

The emergence of this new political sensibility seems to have happened with his brother out of the way—Joe Jr. had gone to law school. At this time Jack's new-found confidence in his abilities led him to make an attempt to become a member of *The Crimson* editorial board. There was no place open for him, however, and he ended up on the business board.

His first-hand experience of European politics led him to focus on contemporary international politics in his government classes. He took a class on elements of international law, as well as courses on Modern Imperialism, Principles of Politics and Comparative Politics: Bureaucracy, Constitutional Government and Dictatorship.

* * * * *

APPEASEMENT AT MUNICH

Jack's honors thesis was on the origins of Britain's policy of appeasement. His social status undoubtedly helped him to meet the right people and make the right contacts for this work. He had three months to write the paper and devoted all his time and energy to doing so. His friends made fun of his sudden dedication, teasing him about his "book" as they called it.

The result was a 148-page document, "Appeasement at Munich: The Inevitable Result of the Slowness of Conversion of the British Democracy to Change from a Disarmament policy to a Rearmament Policy." In it, Jack told Americans that the British experience should provide a warning. He did not blame the advocates of appeasement, and was adamant that if Britain had gone to war with Germany earlier, it would have ended in catastrophe.

Joe Kennedy Sr., always anxious to enhance his sons' achievements, pushed to get it published as a book, even though Harold Laski warned against it:

> While it is the book of a lad with brains, it is very immature, it has no structure, and dwells almost wholly on the surface of things. In a good university, half a hundred seniors do books like this as part of their normal work in their final year … I don't honestly think any publisher would have looked at that book of Jack's if he had not been your son, and if you had not been ambassador.

* * * * *

WHY ENGLAND SLEPT

Nonetheless, Joe Sr. secured the help of Henry R. Luce (1898 – 1967), publisher of magazines such as *Time*, *Life*, *Fortune*, and *Sports Illustrated*, to provide a foreword, and former bureau chief of the *New York Times*, Arthur Krock (1886 – 1974), helped re-draft the work. He also put Jack in touch with an agent who eventually found a publisher in Wilfred Funk, after Harper & Brothers and Harcourt Brace had each turned down the chance to publish it.

It was given the title *Why England Slept*—a play on Winston Churchill's 1938 book, *While England Slept*—and published in 1940. Reviews were very good and the book sold 80,000 copies in Britain and the United States, earning Jack $40,000 royalties. The British royalties were generously donated to the town of Plymouth, on the southern coast of England, recently the target of heavy Nazi bombing raids. The American royalties were used to buy a Buick convertible.

Jack spent the summer promoting the book, doing interviews for the press and radio, signing copies, making sure bookshops were stocking it and answering letters. His father was very pleased, seeing it, as ever, as another step in helping his family climb the social ladder. He wrote to his son:

> *The book will do you an amazing amount of good … You would be surprised how a book that really makes the grade with high-class people stands you in good stead for years to come.*

✶ ✶ ✶ ✶ ✶
WHAT NEXT?

The plan had been to go to Yale Law School after Harvard but Jack's poor health meant he had to abandon that idea for the moment. Of course, it was a difficult time to be thinking about the future. America was on the verge of going to war and planning for the future seemed to the graduates of 1940 pretty pointless.

This feeling was exacerbated by the passing of the Selective Training and Service Act of September that year, introducing the first peacetime conscription in US history. It required that men between the ages of 21 and 35 registered with local draft boards. Men were then selected by a lottery system and if drafted, served for twelve months.

Jack decided to go to Stanford University in California for a term, taking business studies as his subject. But he remained fixated by current affairs. He attended an Institute of World Affairs conference in December.

✶ ✶ ✶ ✶ ✶
SUPPORTING APPEASEMENT

Meanwhile, Joe Sr. continued to support Neville Chamberlain's appeasement policy. Throughout 1938 he had even tried to stage a meeting with Adolf Hitler. In 1940, not long before the Nazis began their bombing campaign of British cities, he once again tried to arrange a meeting with the German leader purportedly "to bring about a better understanding between the United States and Germany."

These efforts were without the approval of the US Department of State. It has been suggested that Joe Sr. feared war partly because he was concerned that his sons would enlist. But he also argued against giving aid to Britain. He insisted that the war was not a matter of saving democracy from National Socialism or Fascism. As he told *The Boston Globe* and the *St. Louis Post-Dispatch*:

> *It's all a question of what we do with the next six months. The whole reason for aiding England is to give us time … As long as she is in there, we have time to prepare. It isn't that [Britain is] fighting for democracy. That's the bunk. She's fighting for self-preservation, just as we will if it comes to us … I know more about the European situation than anybody else, and it's up to me to see that the country gets it.*

His isolationist stance did not go down at all well with British politicians. One Member of Parliament, Josiah Wedgwood, 1st Baron Wedgwood, saw Joe Kennedy's utterings as self-serving and ignorant:

> *We have a rich man, untrained in diplomacy, unlearned in history and politics, who is a*

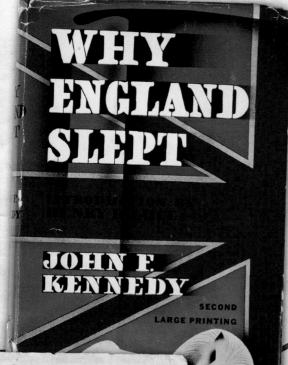

The front cover of *Why England Slept*.

great publicity seeker and who apparently is ambitious to be the first Catholic president of the US.

* * * * * *

AMBASSADOR KENNEDY RESIGNS

Joe Sr. was viewed as defeatist by the British and did not make himself any more popular by leaving London for the countryside during the Blitz. It was noted the British royal family, the government and other ambassadors remained in London during the bombing. One member of Britain's Foreign Office famously quipped: "I thought my daffodils were yellow until I met Joe Kennedy."

The American administration and the American public were horrified by his comments and in the face of growing public outrage and pressure from the Department of State, he was forced, in November 1940, to tender his resignation. He effectively sat out the remainder of the war and any ambitions he may have had to be president were gone.

At the end of his time at Stanford, in early 1941, Jack Kennedy returned east where he tried to find a ghostwriter for his father's memoirs. His mother and sister Eunice were planning a trip to Latin America in the spring and he decided that he would accompany them. The three took in Argentina, Brazil, Chile, Uruguay, Peru, Ecuador, Colombia, and Panama. He returned still unsure about what direction his life should take.

* * * * * *

THE DRAFT

Following the introduction of the Selective Training and Service Act, Jack Kennedy was among the first young Americans to be drafted but, of course, his various health problems made it unlikely that he would be passed fit to join the army. His call-up was delayed as he was enrolled at Stanford and he was given until the end of the academic year. He really wanted to serve, however. "They will never take me into the army," he wrote to Billings, "and yet if I don't, it will look quite bad."

He realized that rejection by the military would finally make it common knowledge that there was something wrong with him and that could inhibit his future career, wherever that lay. His father's vehement opposition to US involvement in the war would also make it look suspicious. For his part, he thought it would be exciting to join the war effort, certainly more attractive to a young man than a law career.

As expected, he was rejected by the army and then failed the physical examination to become a naval officer. Finally Joe Kennedy Sr. pulled strings for him via Captain Alan Kirk (1888 – 1963) who had been his naval attaché in London and was now head of the Office of Naval Intelligence. Kirk had organized for Joe Jr. to join the navy and train as a pilot in spring 1941. Now, in the summer of that year he also got Jack Kennedy into the military.

* * * * * *

OFFICE OF NAVAL INTELLIGENCE

A month later, Jack Kennedy, a man who had spent so much of his life sick, who had been in and out of hospitals and clinics for years, and who had a catalog of ailments, was given a clean bill of health by the board of medical examiners.

"Usual childhood diseases" was noted on his record and mention was also made of his diet of no fried food or roughage. Incredibly, they pronounced that he did not have any ulcers. He was going into the Office of Naval Intelligence (ONI) in Washington DC, which should at least have cut down on any exposure to physical danger or strenuous activity, except that of the brain.

In October 1941, Ensign John F. Kennedy entered the navy, working in the Foreign Intelligence branch of the ONI. It was a desk job, 9 to 5, six days a week and pretty stultifying for a young man in search of adventure. But on December 7, 1941, when Japan launched a surprise attack on Pearl Harbor in Hawaii, it suddenly got very busy in Jack's office. He was working seven nights a week, from 10 p.m. until 7 a.m. the following morning. It was, needless to say, exhausting.

CHAPTER 5

THE HERO OF PT-109

At the same time as he was working round the clock in Washington, however, Jack Kennedy somehow fitted in a rich social life, mainly because his sister Kathleen was now working as a journalist for the *Washington Times-Herald*. Around this time, he met a "perfect example of Nordic beauty," Inga Arvad (1913 – 73), who wrote a column for the *Times-Herald*. She was four years older than him and married twice.

* * * * * *

DATING A SPY

"Inga-Binga" as Jack called her, even wrote a column about him, describing him as "a boy with a future." They began a fleeting affair with her later describing him as a man who "knows what he wants," which she found refreshing. "He's got a lot to learn," she said, "and I'll be happy to teach him."

Of course, Joe Sr. found out about their affair, despite their efforts to keep it secret. Although he let it pass without comment, it can hardly have been in his and Rose's plans for their son to marry a divorcée who, to make matters worse, was not a Catholic. She was even suspected of being a spy, having worked in Germany for a while with access to Hitler and other high-level Nazis. She was under surveillance by the FBI but nothing came of it.

* * * * * *

FBI WIRETAP

There was the possibility that his affair with Inga might lead to Jack being forced out of the service, especially after their relationship was made public by the nationally syndicated columnist, Walter Winchell (1897 – 1972). Instead of that, however, he was transferred to another desk job in South Carolina but he persevered with their affair even after his transfer.

They wrote to each other, spoke on the phone, and spent weekends together when they could. Soon, however, the relationship began to founder, as testified to by stormy exchanges on wiretaps that the FBI continued to plant wherever they were together. He seemed to her to be irresponsible and unable to commit when she said she would have her marriage annulled. She became despondent.

Perhaps one reason Jack was being hesitant was that his father had warned him in no uncertain terms that he would be risking everything by marrying her, especially whatever career he chose after the war. He also emphasized to him the effect it would have on his family.

Some speculated that Joe Sr. might well have paid off Inga to leave his son alone. It would not have been the first time he had paid for a woman's silence. Inga withdrew gracefully.

Legendary broadcaster, Walter Winchell.

INGA ARVAD

Inga Arvad was born Inga Marie Arvad Petersen in Denmark, in 1913. She changed her name to her middle name Arvad in 1931 when she won a beauty contest in the Danish newspaper *Berlingske Tidende*.

She became a journalist and, in 1935, she traveled to Germany to interview Adolf Hitler, one of the few Scandinavian journalists to do so. In fact she interviewed him several times more. She said: "You immediately like him. He seems lonely. The eyes, showing a kind heart, stare right at you. They sparkle with force."

As a freelance, she was the first journalist to announce that Hitler's deputy, Hermann Göring (1893 – 1946), was going to marry the German actress Emmy Sonnemann (1893 – 1973). Inga was invited to the wedding where she met all the Nazi leaders. At the summer Olympics of 1936, she was a guest of Hitler which made the FBI suspicious of her when she worked for the *Times-Herald* and dated Jack Kennedy.

FBI chief, J. Edgar Hoover (1895 – 1972), authorized the use of listening devices while Kennedy and Arvad were together but the couple were well aware of the interest in them, sometimes speaking to "whoever is listening." But nothing was ever proved against her and her journalism was really no more than society gossip.

Arvad's second husband was the Hungarian film director Paul Fejos (1897 – 1963). She appeared in two Danish films and was still married to Fejos when she began her affair with Jack Kennedy, divorcing the film director in 1942.

For a while she was engaged to the colorful British Member of Parliament, Robert Boothby (1900 – 86) in 1945, but the British press had a field day with her Hitler connections. Boothby was facing an election and had to call the engagement off. She eventually married American actor, Tim McCoy (1891 – 1978) in 1946, and became an American citizen. Inga Arvad died in Nogales, Arizona, in 1973, at age 60.

SERVICE AT SEA

The work in the Office of Naval Intelligence (ONI) was deadening for Jack and the break-up with Inga probably made him want a change. In July 1942, therefore, he requested a transfer into something that would provide a chance for service at sea. His request granted, he was sent to midshipman's school at Northwestern University in Chicago.

He undertook the sixty-day course that churned out junior naval officers ready to be thrown into combat situations. He wanted to be given command of a motor torpedo boat. These were popularly nicknamed PT boats.

Short for Patrol Torpedo, PT boats were built to be fast and were highly maneuverable. They were ideal vessels for use in night operations where they would make little noise and create no wake. The aim was for them to gain sufficient proximity to a target to unleash their torpedoes. They were not heavily protected with armor and relied, therefore, on surprise and their good handling at high speeds to get in and out of a hostile situation without being targeted by large vessels.

* * * * * *

GLAMOR OF COMMAND

The biggest champion of the PT boat was Lieutenant Commander John Bulkeley (1911 – 96). He had been awarded a Congressional Medal of Honor for transporting General Douglas MacArthur, his family and staff in a PT through 500 miles of enemy waters from Corregidor in the Philippines to Australia.

Bulkeley probably exaggerated the success of the PT boats in an effort to attract young officers to command them. Jack Kennedy was keen on the glamor they represented, and they provided him with the opportunity to have his own command. He would also be free of the boredom of his desk-bound job and would no longer be restricted by tiresome naval bureaucracy.

But the competition for places was keen and Jack's back pain issues did not help. Once again his father stepped up and had a word with Bulkeley. Jack also gave a very good account of himself in the interview and Bulkeley knew that the presence of the ambassador's son would only be good publicity for the PTs.

For his part, Jack was worried that he would not make it through the tough physical training. He suffered badly and shipmates recall him sleeping on a plywood board because of his back pain. Nonetheless, he loved it, bringing to good use the experience of all his summers of sailing off Cape Cod.

* * * * * *

DESPERATE MEASURES

Jack Kennedy spent seventeen months in the Pacific on active duty and was exposed to combat on his first day in March 1943. His transport ship was approaching Guadalcanal when Japanese planes attacked his vessel, killing the captain. A Japanese pilot was brought down and started firing a revolver at the bridge. Next to Jack was an old soldier who fired his weapon, blowing off the pilot's head. He realized that with this kind of desperate attitude, the enemy would take some stopping.

He was distinctly unimpressed by the commanding officers he saw, and, like many others, he was concerned about the quality of the young officers emerging from the colleges. He also questioned the high estimation of the contribution made by PTs to the war effort. He knew the truth about the endless night patrols, sailing slowly through rough seas, sleeping for a couple of hours and then going on watch again.

He complained about the inadequate equipment, radios that didn't work, guns that malfunctioned. They were also poorly protected and if they had the misfortune to be hit, they went up in flames very quickly. He further bemoaned the quality and enthusiasm for fighting of the American serviceman, claiming to have seen "too much bellyaching and laying off."

COMMANDING *PT-109*

In the spring and summer of 1943, Jack Kennedy saw some action. The PTs were sent to take part in the re-capture of the New Georgia Islands from the Japanese. They were up against what was nicknamed the "Tokyo Express," the fleet of Japanese destroyers that had the job of escorting vessels carrying troops and equipment to New Georgia. They had to sail through what was known as "the Slot," a passage through New Georgia Sound.

In June, Jack's boat—*PT-109*—was sent to the Russell Islands which were situated southeast of New Georgia. In July, it was Lumbari Island which lay in the middle of the combat zone to the west of New Georgia. At the beginning of August, *PT-109* joined fourteen other PTs sent to Blackett Strait, southwest of Kolombangara, to attack a Japanese convoy.

The ensuing action was described in the navy's official history as "the most confused and least effective action the PTs had been in." It was later described as "a personal and professional disaster" for the PT commander Thomas G. Warfield, who, in turn, firmly placed the blame on the PTs' lack of discipline.

It was a total failure. Only just over half the available torpedoes were fired and nothing was hit. Jack's vessel was cut in half by a Japanese destroyer and two crewmen were killed while the others were thrown into the water. The fact that PTs should easily have been able to outmaneuver a destroyer, led to questions about Jack's performance.

* * * * *

IMPOSSIBLE DARKNESS

Warfield did not consider Jack to be a particularly good PT boat commander, and others were critical of his tactics on the day. He had positioned his vessel in the middle of Blackett Strait and only ran one engine, so there was less water being churned up, making it hard for his boat to be seen by Japanese planes. However, it made it more difficult for *PT-109* to evade an approaching vessel.

But it was more complex than that. Only the four lead boats had radar and it was impossible on the dark night for the others to follow them or even to know the locations of the enemy craft. The lead boats with the radar, having exhausted their supply of torpedoes, returned to base leaving the others floundering in the darkness. Thus, Jack had no idea he was so close to a Japanese ship until it was on top of him.

Lieutenant John F. Kennedy, USNR (extreme right), with the crew of *PT-109*.

Jack and five members of the crew succeeded in making it to the upturned hull of their distressed vessel and clung to it. Then he and a couple of others swam out to five other survivors and led them back to the safety of the hull.

* * * * *

SLOWLY SINKING

Pat "Pappy" McMahon, *PT-109's* engineer, had been badly burned and it was only with difficulty that Jack managed to get him back to the upturned hull against a strong current. With Pappy safe, Jack jumped back into the water and led two others back. The two men who had been lost left Jack devastated. One had been with him from the beginning and the other had arrived very recently and was just 19 years old.

The hull was slowly sinking and they were in a dangerous situation. For nine hours they clung on until fearing it was about to sink, Jack told the men their only hope was to swim to a tiny island, just seventy yards wide—its name was either Bird Island or Plum Pudding Island. Jack towed wounded crewmen and Pappy McMahon and they struggled through choppy seas for five hours.

DISTRESS SIGNALS

On reaching the island, Jack swam out into the Blackett Strait, hoping to flag down a passing PT as this was a passage they normally used. He had now been awake for around 36 hours and was swimming against very strong currents. He swam for an hour with a lantern to signal to passing vessels, but there were no PTs in the passage that night. No one was searching for them as commanders were convinced there were no survivors. As Jack exhaustedly swam back to his shipmates, he lost consciousness several times, arriving back with them at midday.

It was now August 3, and they had set off on August 1. Another crew member swam out into the strait to have another go at finding a passing PT, but he returned on August 4, having found none. They made the short crossing to another island, Olasana Island, hoping to find drinking water but there was none. A storm provided them with a little refreshment that they caught in their mouths.

* * * * *

RESCUE MISSION

On August 5, Jack and another officer named Ross swam to Cross Island where they discovered a canoe—only big enough for one man. They also discovered a fifty-gallon drum filled with fresh water and some crackers and sweets. It would be a welcome relief from the coconuts on which they had been surviving so far. There were also inhabitants on the island.

They loaded the water and the crackers and candy onto the canoe and Jack paddled it back to Olasana Island. Returning to Cross Island, he used a knife to scratch a message on a coconut, saying:

> NATIVE KNOWS POSIT HE CAN PILOT 11 ALIVE NEED SMALL BOAT KENNEDY

He gave it to some of the local people who had agreed to take it to the PT base at Rendova. They returned with a letter from an infantry lieutenant in the New Zealand army who was working with the US troops on New Georgia. He advised Jack to return to New Georgia with the native people, leaving his crewmen behind. He promised to let Rendova know the situation and they would organize for the others to be rescued. Seven days after the destroyer had crashed into them, Jack arrived at the New Zealand camp. The rest of the crew were rescued the following day.

* * * * * *

REMEMBER THE REAL HEROES

It was a great story because it said to the American people that it was not just ordinary working-class young men that were risking their lives, but wealthy, privileged scions of great American families like the Kennedys were also putting their lives on the line for American values. *PT-109's* escapade became front-page news:

> ### Kennedy's Son is Hero in Pacific as Destroyer Splits his Boat
>
> *New York Times*

> ### Kennedy's Son Saves 10 in Pacific
>
> *Boston Globe*

Jack was amazed by the coverage he received but was sanguine about the experience. He later wrote:

> *The real heroes are not the men who return, but those who stay out there, like plenty of them do, two of my men included.*

* * * * * *

PAYBACK TIME

Throughout the incident and its aftermath, Jack never once admitted his back or health problems. His back issue was known as he wore a "corset-type thing" and, as has been noted, slept with a board under his mattress. But his other issues were kept hidden. Joe Kennedy Sr. was worried about him and wanted to bring him home, writing to Joe Jr. he said, "I imagine he's pretty well shot to pieces by now."

But Jack was unwilling to give up, desperate to make redress for what had happened to his

boat and his crewmates. So, on August 16, after ten days' rest and recuperation, he returned to duty. His commanding officer recalled:

> *He wanted to pay the Japanese back. I think he wanted to recover his own self-esteem—he wanted to get over this feeling of guilt …*

* * * * * *

FIT TO FIGHT

With the reputation of the PTs in tatters, it was decided to transform them into gunships with much more weaponry. Jack helped with the re-design of his vessel and it was the first of this new style boat to enter service.

By this time, it was early October and Jack made up for lost time by engaging in a lot of action over the next six weeks, succeeding in causing the enemy losses. He was beginning to lose heart, however. He wrote to Inga Arvad that the places being fought over were no more than "just God damned hot stinking corners of small islands in a part of the ocean we all hope never to see again."

His back continued to trouble him, and he was still plagued by interminable stomach pains. However, he refused to share his real condition with the medics at the base. He even passed a medical exam to get promotion, writing to Lem Billings:

> *Everyone is in such lousy shape here that the only way they can tell if he is fit to fight is to see if he can breathe. That's about the only grounds on which I can pass these days.*

* * * * * *

FROM BAD TO WORSE

His stomach pains became so bad, however, that he was forced to pay a visit to a hospital at Tulagi in the Solomons on November 23. They x-rayed him and found an early duodenal ulcer. It was the end of his time with the PT squadron. He was ordered back to the PT training center at Melville, Rhode Island, arriving in January and taking the thirty days' leave to which he was entitled. He visited Inga Arvad in Los Angeles and then went to the Mayo Clinic.

This time the clinic suggested surgery to stop the pain in his lower back, but he decided against it, visiting his brothers and sisters then going off to Palm Beach and New York for some fun. Before returning for duty there was another hospital visit.

At the New England Baptist Hospital in Boston, back surgery was once again prescribed but he decided he would wait until after the war. It was complex, of course, because if the true nature of his ailments became known to the authorities, he could possibly be given a dishonorable discharge for not telling the truth.

* * * * *

BLAMING POST TRAUMATIC STRESS

The work at a PT base in Miami was dull. He was now also suffering from malaria and seriously in need of medical help. So, he agreed in May to put himself under the knife and the navy authorized it. They operated at Chelsea Naval Hospital, having diagnosed a ruptured disc. What they actually found was unusually soft cartilage that they removed.

After the operation, he experienced severe pain when walking or standing and was told he would not be returning to active duty for at least six months. His duodenal ulcer had been cured by x-ray but he was now suffering from an irritable colon. Soon he was consuming a constant supply of codeine for the abdominal pain from which he was suffering.

His condition was known but he managed to convince the doctors that, although he had suffered this pain before the war, he had lately felt fine. They conveniently ignored visits to the Mayo Clinic and other institutions and believed him when he told them that his current problems had begun after the *PT-109* incident on the Solomon Islands.

* * * * *

IN THE LINE OF DUTY

Eventually, as his back pain subsided and his abdominal agony got worse, he was declared "unfit for service." The doctors diagnosed chronic colitis. It was concluded that he would never be fit again to return to service which was "the result of an incident of the service … suffered in [the] line of duty." They retired him on March 1, 1945.

He tried to get himself fit again through the first part of 1945, traveling to Castle Hot Springs, Arizona in an effort to recover his health. He had not confided in his father how bad he was, but one physician who saw him in Phoenix, Arizona, Dr. Lahey, wrote to Joe Sr. that he was not doing well. He looked jaundiced and was frighteningly thin. Not much had changed by mid-April when he returned to Rochester but there was nothing more that could be done for him.

* * * * *

LIFE-THREATENING CONDITION

In May 1945, as the war drew to a close, Jack took a job with Hearst newspapers. He was to cover the United Nations Conference in San Francisco as well as the important elections in Britain and the Potsdam Conference in Germany. Winston Churchill was attending the conference on behalf of the United Kingdom, Joseph Stalin (1878 – 1953) for the Soviet Union, and the new US president, Harry S. Truman (1884 – 1972) who had succeeded to the position following the death of Franklin D. Roosevelt, was attending on behalf the American people. Jack was ill throughout each of these major events.

In 1947, when he became ill in London, a prominent physician, Sir Daniel Davis, diagnosed Addison's disease. The symptoms of the disease were all evident—nausea, vomiting, fever, fatigue, the failure to put on weight and a brownish, yellow skin color. It may have been caused by the hormonal supplements Jack had been taking for a number of years. His sister Eunice also suffered from Addison's, therefore, inheritance of the disease cannot be ruled out. Although it could be treated back then, Addison's was considered a dangerous condition, even life threatening.

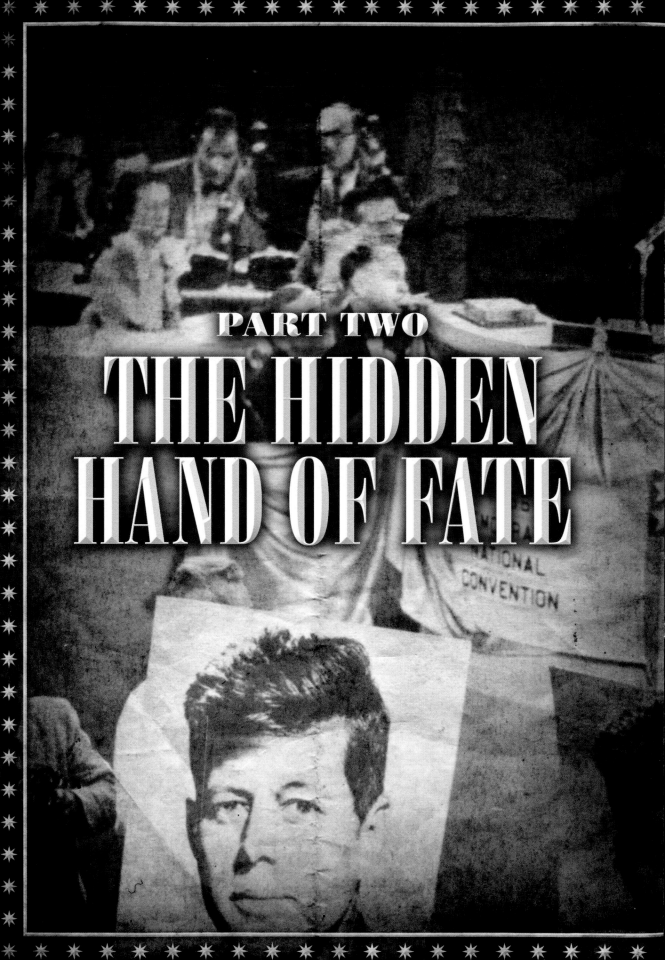

PART TWO

THE HIDDEN
HAND OF FATE

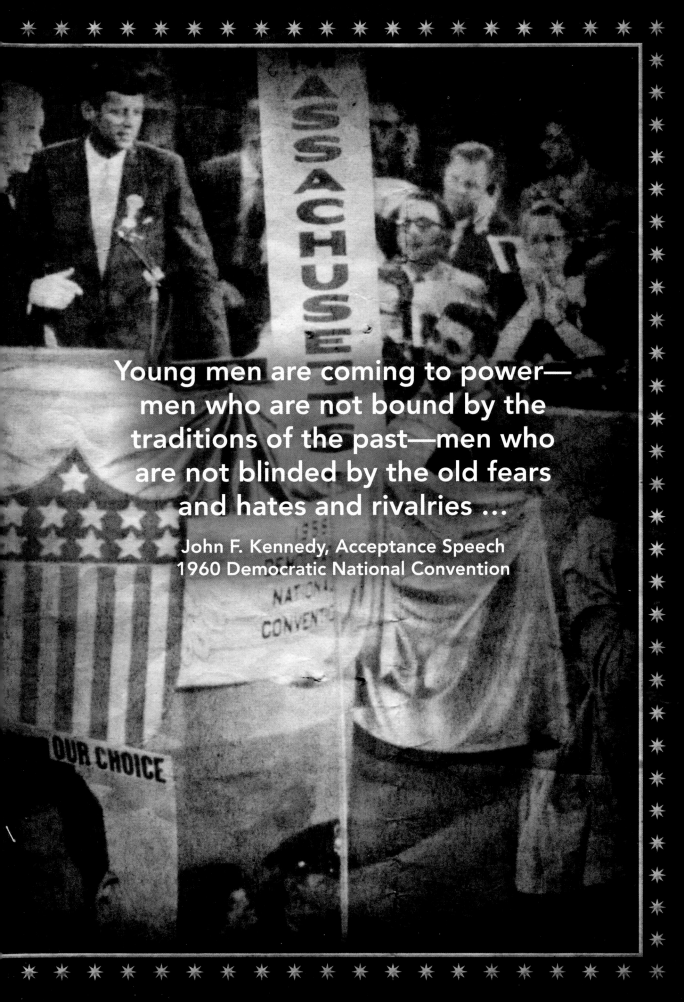

Young men are coming to power—
men who are not bound by the
traditions of the past—men who
are not blinded by the old fears
and hates and rivalries ...

John F. Kennedy, Acceptance Speech
1960 Democratic National Convention

CHAPTER 6

GHOSTS AND DEMONS

ROSEMARY KENNEDY

Rose Marie "Rosemary" Kennedy (1918 – 2005) was the oldest daughter of Joe and Rose Kennedy. It was obvious that all was not right with the little girl by the time she was five. She couldn't feed herself and had learning difficulties with limited vocabulary.

To their credit, Rosemary's parents opted to care for her at home. She had a governess and a tutor, and her mother devoted a great deal of time to looking after her and playing with her. Something she rarely did with her other children. At home they ensured Rosemary was treated the same as their other children who all behaved impeccably toward their sister.

Calm and gentle as a child and teenager, Rosemary became rebellious, and subject to violent mood swings as she grew older. The

family had problems with her wild temper and unpredictable behavior. They expected the children to conform. Her father thought his daughter's state of mind would embarrass the family or may even be detrimental to his career.

VIOLENT MOOD SWINGS

Around the age of 21, Rosemary became increasingly violent, raging at those who were tasked with looking after her and throwing terrible tantrums. Finally, it all became too much and in 1941, without telling his wife, Joe Kennedy arranged for Rosemary to have a prefrontal lobotomy—a new neurosurgical procedure that would help calm her violence and mood swings. Sadly, it had disastrous results and left her incapacitated permanently. She had the mentality of a two-year-old child, unable to walk or talk intelligibly.

From the age of 23, Rosemary spent the remainder of her life in Jefferson, Wisconsin, in the grounds of the St. Coletta School for Exceptional Children, an institution run by nuns for people with disabilities. Her father built a private house for her about a mile outside St. Coletta's, which the nuns called "the Kennedy cottage." She had minimal contact from her family. Rose Kennedy did not visit her for twenty years and they explained away her sudden absence by saying she was reclusive.

Rosemary Kennedy died in January 2005, at age 86. Her sisters Jean, Eunice, and Patricia, and brother Edward were by her bedside. She was buried beside her parents in Holyhood Cemetery in Brookline, Massachusetts. Ironically, she was the first child of Joe and Rose Kennedy to die from natural causes.

Rosemary Kennedy, at age 21.

BEING A KENNEDY

Perhaps one of the reasons that Joe and Rose Kennedy cared for Rosemary at home for so long was to keep her condition secret from the outside world. The attitude toward mental health problems was very different back then and they were seen often as something of an embarrassment to a family, something not to be discussed.

For the Kennedys and their image as an achieving, highly active family of intellect and status, it was a bitter blow and they feared it would open them to ridicule. Health weaknesses were not permitted. They were thought to be an impediment to progression whether in political spheres or otherwise. If a Kennedy child fell and hurt themselves they were told to get up at once and behave as they should.

The Kennedy family did not publicly explain Rosmary's absence until 1961. Even then they scaled back the reason, saying she was "mentally retarded," rather than revealing she had been committed to a psychiatric hospital due to a failed lobotomy arranged by her father.

* * * * *

KATHLEEN "KICK" KENNEDY

Kathleen Agnes Kennedy (1920 – 48), the younger sister of John F. Kennedy, was known as "Kick" by the family, which suited her vivacious and quick-witted personality perfectly.

Born in Brookline, Massachusetts, she had settled into London life well and made many friends when her father was United States Ambassador to the United Kingdom from 1938 to 1940. She had been dubbed "debutante of the year" in 1938 by the English press, and wanted to remain in England when the Kennedys left. She signed up for work in an English center for servicemen that had been set up by the Red Cross.

She was becoming more independent of both her family and the Catholic Church. Her mother was horrified when she became

romantically linked with the politician William "Billy" Cavendish, Lord Hartington (1917 – 44), heir apparent to the Dukedom of Devonshire. Rose Kennedy was against the relationship from the start because marriage would mean that Kathleen's children would be brought up in the Church of England rather than the Catholic Church.

Nonetheless, despite Rose's best efforts, Kathleen married Cavendish on May 6, 1944, and became Lady Hartington. Her eldest brother, Joe Jr., was the only Kennedy present at the ceremony. But tragically, she and her new husband had a mere five weeks together. Cavendish was killed in Belgium during the war by a bullet from a German sniper's gun.

* * * * *

QUIETLY WRITTEN OUT

Kathleen then became romantically involved with Peter Wentworth-Fitzwilliam, the 8th Earl Fitzwilliam (1910 – 48). Rose Kennedy was again decidedly unhappy with Kathleen's choice of partner, especially as he

Kathleen "Kick" Kennedy, at age 23.

was in the process of divorcing his wife. Rose threatened to disown her, and said all financial support would be withdrawn if she married Fitzwilliam. Joe Sr. was in Paris for a business meeting and Kathleen decided to meet him to plead her case.

On May 13, 1948, having talked to her father, Kathleen and the Earl left Paris for the French Riviera. An hour into the flight, the airplane hit a storm and crashed in the Cevennes Mountains, killing everyone on board instantly.

Her father was the only family member to attend Kathleen's funeral and Rose refused to attend her daughter's memorial service. It was a scandal that resulted in Kathleen "Kick" Kennedy being quietly written out of the Kennedy family history and barely spoken of again.

Ensign Joseph P. Kennedy Jr., USN, 1942.

JOSEPH "JOE" KENNEDY JR.

In September 1943, Joseph Patrick "Joe" Kennedy Jr. (1915 – 44), John Kennedy's older brother, was serving as a lieutenant in the US Navy as a bomber pilot. Posted to Britain, in 1944 he became a member of Bomber Squadron 110, Special Air Unit 1. During two tours of duty, he patrolled the English Channel on missions to locate German submarines. After twenty-five combat flights Joe Jr. was eligible to return to the United States. However, he insisted on remaining on flying duty at least until June 6, the D-Day allied invasion of northern France, when he would provide protection against German U-Boats for the craft carrying the invasion forces.

But even after he had flown through D-Day, he still refused to go home. It may have been the Kennedy family's competitive spirit that pushed him to outdo his younger brother who had received the Navy and Marine Corps Medal for his action in the South Seas. Possibly Joe Jr. was slightly jealous of the fighting action his brother had seen, and he volunteered for the perilous Operation Aphrodite.

* * * * * *

OPERATION APHRODITE

Operation Aphrodite used unmanned robot bombers laden with explosives that were deliberately crashed into their targets under remote control. These aircraft could not take off safely on their own, so needed pilots to take off and fly to an altitude of 2,000 feet before setting the detonators, and parachuting out.

On August 12, 1944, Joe Jr. was one of the pilots on the US Navy's first Aphrodite mission. It was a dangerous operation during which he would fly a BQ8 Liberator bomber carrying 22,000 pounds of explosive, the highest amount ever carried during the entire war up to that point. The destination was the U-boat pens at Heligoland in the North Sea.

Approaching the target, the two pilots were to parachute out of their craft which would then continue under remote control. Before the flight, he told a friend that if he didn't come back he should "tell my dad … I love him very much."

Near the North Sea coast, Joe Jr. and his co-pilot, Wilford John Willy, removed the safety pin, arming the flying bomb. Joe Jr. radioed the agreed code "Spade Flush," his last known words. Two minutes later, well before the planned crew bailout, the explosives detonated prematurely, destroying the Liberator and killing Joe Jr. and Willy instantly.

A report into the explosion concluded that it could have been caused by a number of possibilities from static to a faulty fuse. Lieutenant Joseph Patrick Kennedy Jr. was reported as killed in action and was posthumously awarded the Navy Cross.

* * * * * *

AS WE REMEMBER JOE

The loss of Joe Jr. was devastating for all the Kennedy family, especially his father who had high expectations for him to become President. He told an acquaintance: "You know how much I had tied my whole life up to his and what great things I saw in the future for him." His resolve only grew that America should isolate itself from involvements on foreign soil.

Jack Kennedy was also overwhelmed by the loss of his older brother. He compiled a book of memories of Joe Jr. from family and friends, entitled *As We Remember Joe*. He was left with conflicting emotions. He had no big brother now with whom he could compete and, as he wrote to Lem Billings:

[Joe would now be]… forever in his father's heart. I am shadowboxing in a match the shadow is always going to win.

* * * * * *

OUR OBLIGATIONS AS CITIZENS

In May 1945, Jack Kennedy turned 28. His father had always pushed his children in the direction of a useful life. He had rejected the notion of a business career for the boys. After all, he had earned for his family sufficient millions for them never to have to worry about making a living.

Politics seemed like the ideal career, following in the footsteps of their illustrious forebears, Honey Fitz and P.J. Kennedy. Joe Kennedy Sr. was of the belief, since the economic crash of 1929, that people in government and not businessmen were the most important people in the United States.

Jack Kennedy had never stopped thinking about politics during his time in the US Navy and in 1941 had begun researching a book on the subject of isolationism versus internationalism in the United States. He was deeply concerned and even pessimistic about the way the war was being conducted:

It will take death in large quantities to wake us up … I don't think anyone really realizes that nothing stands between us and the defeat of our Christian crusade against Paganism except a lot of Chinks who never heard of God and a lot of Russians who have heard about him but don't want Him.

He became more optimistic in the Solomons, but his interests in the politics of the war remained. He constantly discussed politics with his colleagues, one recalling how Jack spoke to them just before he returned to the United States:

He made us all very conscious of the fact that we'd better … be concerned about why the hell we're out here, or else what's the purpose of having the conflict, if you're going to come out here and fight and let the people that got us here get us back into it again … He made us all very aware of our obligations as citizens of the United States to do something, to be involved in the process.

* * * * *

AN EXPERIMENT FOR PEACE

As he recuperated from back surgery in Phoenix in the winter of 1944 – 45, Jack Kennedy wrote an article, "Let's Try an Experiment for Peace," that he hoped would feed into the efforts to regain stability in the world after the war. The article cautioned against an arms race after the end of hostilities, because, in his opinion, that could lead only to another war.

He feared that if the USA tried to match the Soviet Union in weaponry, smaller states might ally against America. Furthermore, if all efforts were directed at matching the Russians, resources would be withdrawn from other more worthwhile domestic projects. What he forgot, however, was that the domestic economy prospers from an arms race. He feared for democracy in the middle of an arms race.

A number of the major magazines rejected the article—*Life*, *Reader's Digest*, and the *Atlantic* among them. In fact all Jack was doing was reflecting thoughts that were fairly common at the time—limitation of arms production, disarmament and some kind of world government. The editor of the *Atlantic* described the piece as:

… an oversimplification of a very complicated subject. Some profounder thinking is needed here and conclusions not based on clichés.

* * * * * *

THE UNITED NATIONS CONFERENCE

Perhaps Jack Kennedy saw himself as a journalist in the years to come. If so, the commission by the *Chicago Herald-American* to cover the United Nations Conference in San Francisco was a wonderful opportunity. Or perhaps a journalistic career would give him a springboard into politics. But for the moment it seemed, neither his father nor Jack himself foresaw him running for office any time soon.

The *Herald-American* was getting a good deal. It was paying only $250 for the work but they were getting a writer with whom the public were familiar, who was exceedingly well connected and who was seen as something of an expert in international affairs. He was also a war hero and that would do the newspaper no harm.

As ever, Jack had fun in San Francisco, but he also filed seventeen 300-word articles from April 28 until May 28, 1945, often focusing on the behavior of the Russian delegation and the tensions created by them. He made special mention of the overbearing nature of Soviet Foreign Minister, Vyacheslav Molotov (1890 – 1986). Looking on at the politicking, however, dampened Jack's spirit and he saw war between the United States and its Western allies and the Soviet Union as extremely possible. The United Nations, he believed, would be ineffective in preventing such a conflict.

* * * * * *

BRITAIN AND GERMANY

Next, it was the British General Election of 1945. Jack spent a month following Winston Churchill's campaign for re-election. It was fairly inevitable that he was going to lose to a groundswell of support for the Labour Party of Clement Attlee (1883 – 1967). But Jack admired the great war leader to such an extent that he predicted a Conservative victory although he added that it would be only a matter of time before Labour would be in government. Not only did Labour win, but it was a landslide victory.

He was invited to Germany by US Navy Secretary James Forrestal, a friend of his father who was eager to recruit Jack for his Navy Department. Forrestal invited him to attend the Potsdam Conference, and then visit parts of Germany to assess what challenges would be faced in the rehabilitation of a country whose cities had been devastated by years of relentless bombing.

Jack Kennedy met and was in the company of some of the most important men of the day—President Truman, General—and future President—Dwight D. Eisenhower (1890 – 1969), British Prime Minister Clement Attlee and his Foreign Minister, Ernest Bevin (1881 – 1951), Molotov, and Soviet ambassador to the United Nations, Andrey Gromyko (1909 – 89).

* * * * * *

ONE POLITICIAN IS ENOUGH

It had always been thought that Joe Jr. would be the family politician and Jack had never really seriously considered it:

I never thought at school or college that I would ever run for office myself. One politician was enough in the family, and my brother Joe was obviously going to be that politician. I hadn't considered myself a political type, and he filled all the requirements for political success … I think his political success would have been assured … I didn't even start to think about a political profession for more than a year later.

He was possibly being a little disingenuous because it seems that his father had already raised the idea of a political career. As Joe Sr. later told a reporter:

I got Jack into politics. I was the one. I told him Joe was dead and that therefore it was his responsibility to run for Congress.

Jack Kennedy himself said subsequently:

My father wanted his eldest son in politics. "Wanted" isn't the right word. He demanded it. You know my father.

* * * * * *

TIME TO WAIT AND SEE

In December 1944, Jack's health was still giving cause for concern and, anyway, he was still in the navy at that time. He remained reluctant to commit to a political career throughout 1945 and when Lem Billings asked him in a January 1946 letter if he had a political career in mind, he replied that he was returning to Harvard Law School in the fall and "if something good turns up while I am there I will run for it."

He saw politics as a far more exciting option than any others that he had to choose from. It seemed much more interesting to be writing "legislation on foreign policy or on the relationship between labor and management" than the normal work of a law firm. He later wrote:

How can you compare an interest in [fighting an anti-trust suit] with a life in Congress where you are able to participate to some degree in determining which direction the nation will go?

Journalism also lacked, for him, the power to change things. "A reporter is *reporting* what happened. He is not making it happen," he

later said. Some have suggested that, like other veterans of the Second World War, he went into politics to prevent others having to go through what they experienced.

* * * * * *

FILLING DEAD MAN'S SHOES

Joe Sr. meanwhile, was doing his best behind the scenes. It had to be thus because his reputation as an isolationist would do nothing but damage to any political campaign. Many said, however, that he had been out of touch with Massachusetts politics for so long that he had little influence any more.

But what is certain is that Joe Sr. threw himself into the fray, announcing a half-million dollar investment in the state and accepting the role of chairman of a body to plan Massachusetts' economic future. He took on a more prominent role in the state.

Joe Sr. eventually persuaded Congressman James Michael Curley that he should make another run at being Mayor of Boston thus vacating his 11th Congressional District seat. Still unsure, with the shadow of Joe Jr. constantly hanging over him, Jack told his friends, "I'm just filling Joe's shoes. If he were alive, I'd never be in this."

* * * * * *

UNDER PRESSURE

Jack's continuing poor health also gave him cause for doubt. He was taking steroids but his stomach still ached as did his back.

Campaigning for Congress put considerable strain on his ailing body. As for shaking hands and slapping backs, it was not really his style. Jack said, "I think I'd rather go somewhere with my familiars, or sit alone somewhere and read a book."

It was noticeable that he found glad-handing and mingling with the crowds at his rallies difficult and he often made a quick escape. He was not even terribly good with the volunteers that were working for him. One said, "… I don't know if he was shy or a snob."

CONGRESS SEAT FOR SALE

Neither was Jack Kennedy at this time a good public speaker. His voice was "scratchy and tensely high-pitched," according to one observer, and there was never a trace of humor in what he said. His family realized he needed help, and made suggestions about how to improve his performance.

The main things that were against him were his youth, his inexperience, his wealth and, critically, his lack of knowledge of the district he was fighting to represent. As one of his competitors for the seat said:

He comes from New York. His father is a resident of Florida and because of his money is favored by the newspapers of Boston ... insofar as certain responsibilities are concerned, this candidate does not live in the district ... and knows nothing about the problems of its people.

John F. Kennedy for Congress, Boston, Massachusetts, 1946.

The *East Boston Leader* went further with a parody advertisement:

Congress seat for sale—No experience necessary—Applicant must live in New York or Florida—Only millionaires need apply.

* * * * *

CHARM OFFENSIVE

But Jack was more than capable of withstanding such personal attacks and, in fact, he enjoyed them. He threw himself into a fight which was really to win the blue-collar vote, to gain the confidence of the mainly Irish and Italian working class of the district. The challenge was to get more voters to turn-out than the customary 20 or 25 percent.

Jack knew that his family connection to Honey Fitz and P.J. Kennedy would help, and he was also very different to the usual politicians of Irish ethnicity in Boston. "He never even went to a wake unless he knew the deceased personally," one of his backers said. He dropped into bars and barbershops, pool halls and restaurants, meeting the ordinary people and eventually his natural charm began to have an impact.

He worked hard, rising around 6:15 in the morning, standing at factory gates or at the docks, knocking on doors, and meeting workers as they left for home. In the evenings he would attend parties that his sisters Eunice and Pat organized. He would talk on these occasions to anything from fifteen to seventy-five young women. A few days later they would be invited to become volunteers for the Kennedy campaign.

* * * * *

HEROES ON THE HOMEFRONT

Jack employed war heroes on his campaign, and of course, the fact that he was a veteran himself added to his appeal. Although he was reluctant to exploit it, he knew the value of his military experience. He agreed to chair a national Veterans of Foreign Wars convention and became a member of the American Legion.

One of the regular speeches that he delivered featured the story of *PT-109* but focusing on the heroism of his shipmates rather than his own. Joe Sr. paid for 100,000 copies of an article by John Hersey (1914 – 93) in the *New Yorker* about *PT-109* to be distributed across the district.

Importantly, however, Jack also dealt with the basic issues—the economy, housing, and jobs. He promised that if he were to win he would ensure that there was housing for the homecoming troops and assured them of jobs that paid better than when they went away to fight.

On one occasion, he listed the most important issues facing the country—housing, military strength in order to maintain national security, the expansion of Social Security benefits, an increase in the minimum wage to 65 cents an hour, and the modernization of the US Congress.

* * * * * *

THAT'S OUR MAN

It takes cash for a politician to get his message across. Although the true figure is unknown, it has been estimated that Joe Sr. spent as much as $300,000 on his son's campaign—a huge amount for a congressional race at the time.

The money was used to hire a public relations firm, for billboards, subways, radio, and newspapers. The advertisements featured the headline "Kennedy for Congress," beneath which was a picture of Kennedy and a war veteran's father pointing at him and saying to his veteran son "That's our man, son." The money was also spent on polling which told them, for instance, that focusing on Jack's war record would reap dividends.

It paid off. In the primary, Jack polled 40.5 percent of the votes cast, but with a paltry 30 percent turnout, it meant he had won his seat in Congress with just 12 percent of the district's Democrats. There was no huge victory celebration. It was not viewed as a great result. Jack was disappointed in the turnout, given the recent sacrifices, a feeling he had already expressed in a talk he gave at Choate in September:

> *In Brookline, a very well-to-do community, only twenty percent of the people voted in the primary. We must recognize that if we do not take an interest in our political life we can easily lose at home what so many young men so bloodily won abroad.*

* * * * * *

FIGHTING THE ELECTION

Jack tried to establish his credentials as a Democrat, stating in a major speech entitled "Why I am a Democrat" that he was a member of the party because it had for years—especially under the leadership of Franklin D. Roosevelt—taken care of the national interest both at home and overseas. He began to use the national need and not just party need to guide his political principles. As he said in a speech on a Boston radio station that he repeated during his campaign:

> *The time has come when we must speak plainly on the great issue facing the world today. The issue is Soviet Russia.*

He described Russia as "a slave of the worst sort," that had "embarked upon a program of world aggression." He added that if the nations of the free world did nothing to stop the Soviet Union, they would be wiped out.

But, in the election, the Republicans performed well nationally, scoring impressive gains in Congress and recapturing both the House and Senate for the first time since the 1930s. Their task was made easier because of the many strikes that were staged in 1946. The Truman administration also made a number of mistakes in 1945 and 1946 and the Republicans jumped on these, using slogans such as "To Err is Truman" and "Had Enough?"

The Republicans won the election with a landslide. Nonetheless, in Massachusetts, Jack polled 69,093 votes against the 26,007 votes of Lester Bowen, his Republican rival, winning 72 percent of the vote in a resounding victory. Congressman John F. Kennedy entered the US House of Representatives as Member for Massachusetts's 11th District on January 3, 1947. He was 29 years old.

MAKE SURE THAT
_ AND YOUR FRIENDS
ARE REGISTERED
ST DAY IS MAY 29

The NEW Generation Offers A Leader
JOHN F.
KENNEDY
FOR
CONGRESS
11th DISTRICT
PRIMARIES: TUESDAY, JUNE 18th

John F. Kennedy at one of his campaign headquarters during his run to represent Massachusetts in Congress, 1946.

CHAPTER 7

KENNEDY IN CONGRESS

✶ ✶ ✶ ✶ ✶ ✶ 🦅 ✶ ✶ ✶ ✶ ✶ ✶

Strikes, growing inflation, the communist threat, and a failing Democratic Party all greeted Congressman John F. Kennedy when he arrived in Washington to take his seat in the House of Representatives. The Republicans had been returned as the government with a 58-seat majority in the House, while in the Senate they enjoyed a 4-seat majority. Most of the blame for the failure of the Democrats fell on the shoulders of President Truman.

There were constant fears of a Third World War, exacerbated by the inroads the Soviet Union was making in Eastern Europe, Turkey, Iran, and Greece. Of course, the United States possessed a far greater atomic weapon capacity, but the idea of using the weapons was opposed by most American people.

Elsewhere in the world, there were grounds for concern. China was engaged in a brutal civil war being fought between the communists of Mao Zedong (1893 – 1976) and the nationalists led by Chiang Kai-shek (1887 – 1975). Meanwhile, there were fears of infiltration into the United States government by sympathizers or even members of the Communist Party.

✶ ✶ ✶ ✶ ✶

STEPPING-STONES

For Kennedy every job was little more than a stepping-stone to the next position. Junior congressmen had little hope of passing legislation or achieving much more than dealing with issues that related to their own constituencies. As Arthur Krock said:

I think from the time he was elected to Congress, he had no thought but to go to the Senate as fast as he could. He wanted scope, which a freshman in the House cannot have, and very few of the seniors; so I think the House was just a way-station.

But, it would have been a great mistake to make a play for the next role too soon. He still had a lot to learn. Nevertheless Lem Billings remembered Kennedy's frustrations:

[He] found most of his fellow congressmen boring, preoccupied as they all seemed to be with their narrow political concerns. And he also had terrible problems with all the arcane rules and customs which prevented you from moving legislation quickly and forced you to jump a thousand hurdles before you could accomplish anything. All his life he had troubles with rules externally imposed and now here he was, back once again in an institutional setting.

✶ ✶ ✶ ✶ ✶ ✶

BUILDING A PROFILE

While Kennedy was at the House, his father began to use his money and connections to build his son's profile, both in Massachusetts and nationally. The objective was to link him, wherever possible, with major national issues. At the same time, staff were paid to run offices in Boston and Washington that would help Kennedy deal effectively with constituency matters. Thus, he was seen to be working hard on behalf of his constituents as well as in the national interest.

Kennedy's office at 322 in the Old House Office Building was headed by Ted Reardon. A talented young man, Reardon had no real ambition and was happy to be Kennedy's assistant. One colleague recalled:

[He] had a brain but unfortunately he didn't use it that much. I used to get annoyed with him. He just wouldn't apply himself. Much of the time, he wasn't in the office.

MORRISSEY AND ROSETTI

Also in the Boston office was Frank Morrissey, a lawyer and a very close confidant of Joe Kennedy Sr. But as Morrissey was absent much of the time, practicing law on behalf of Joe Sr., the day-to-day running was left to Joe Rosetti, a war veteran. Rosetti was going to night school at Northeastern University to learn hotel management. Politics was not a business he enjoyed. He later said:

No matter how many good things you did for Jack's constituents, the only thing they remembered is what you couldn't do for them. That irritated me a great deal.

* * * * * *

BEHIND THE SCENES

In January 1947, John F. Kennedy was named number one of the ten outstanding young men of 1946 by the US Junior Chamber of Commerce. Of course, it had not come without his father's maneuvering. Joe Kennedy Sr. used a New York publicist to secure the selection and a succession of orchestrated favorable newspaper and magazine articles followed in the ensuing months. Joe Kennedy Sr. also ensured his son was appointed to the House Education and Labor Committee, where he could have a say on some important matters.

But there came a point when Kennedy had to separate himself from his father's influence and stand on his own two feet. He said to Lem Billings:

I guess Dad has decided that he's going to be the ventriloquist, so I guess that leaves me the role of dummy.

* * * * * *

ENDLESS GIRLS

Meanwhile, Kennedy was seeing a divorcée named Florence Pritchard, fashion editor of the *New York Journal-American*, who lived in New York. Some weekends were spent with her, others in Palm Beach with his friend, the congressman from Florida, George Smathers (1913 – 2007). There seemed to be an endless supply of girls around them. As one journalist later described the two men:

Together or singly, they were wolves on the prowl, always able to find or attract gorgeous prey …

* * * * * *

CREATING LABOR TENSIONS

As a freshman or junior congressman, Kennedy had little power to stop Republican efforts to dismantle New Deal welfare programs. He supported failed efforts to build more low-cost housing—something he had promised his constituents when running for election. He also cast his vote against the Taft-Hartley Act that was designed to limit the growing power of trade unions.

John F. Kennedy having dinner with his family, friends, and campaign workers, 1946. Seated left to right: Frank Morrissey, Mary Josephine Fitzgerald, Eunice Kennedy (center), John F. Kennedy, Honey Fitz, and Joseph F. Timilty. Lem Billings is standing behind on the left.

One outcome of this legislation was the outlawing of the closed shop. Labor leaders described it as the "slave-labor bill," while President Truman called it a "dangerous intrusion on free speech" that would "conflict with important principles of our democratic society." The law was passed despite a presidential veto. Kennedy's reason for voting against the bill was complicated, however. He feared that its passing into law would create tensions with labor leaders and would play into the hands of the left.

* * * * * *

CLEMENCY FOR CURLEY

Kennedy supported federal aid for education, leading opponents to claim he was in the pocket of the Catholic Church. But he supported the idea of the money being allocated to the individual child rather than to the school. This allowed him to escape the assertion that aid to parochial schools was in fact blurring the line between Church and state. His proposal failed to win the day, but questions about his closeness to the policies of the Church would return later.

He did not always see eye to eye with his heavily Catholic constituents and the Catholic political establishment. He refused to put his name to a petition seeking clemency for the four-time Mayor of Boston, James Curley (1874 – 1958) who faced charges relating to his corrupt activities during the war.

It was Curley's seat that Kennedy had won and his refusal to sign was seen as an act of treachery by some. Respected Boston politicians such as Representative John McCormack were disappointed by Kennedy's decision. Although the president eventually commuted Curley's sentence, the seething anger in Boston may have been a reason for a delay in Kennedy's candidacy for higher office.

* * * * * *

MORE HEALTH SCARES

Kennedy's bid for higher office might also have been hindered by his continuing bad health. By September 1947, the Addison's disease from which he was suffering was now so bad that while returning from England on board the liner *Queen Mary*, he was given the last rites.

But after nine months of recovery, he was dealt another blow when his sister Kathleen "Kick" Kennedy was killed in an airplane crash in France in 1948. Kennedy was devastated and very depressed at the loss of another sibling. In fact, he confided to journalist Joseph Alsop (1910 – 89) that he did not expect to live beyond the age of 45 himself, and was, therefore, determined to make the most of what little time he had left.

CRASHES

FRENCH WRECK KILLS KENNEDY GIRL, 4 OTHERS

31 Mis

Newspaper headline reporting Kathleen Kennedy's death, 1948.

THE KENNEDY INNER CIRCLE

TED REARDON

Timothy "Ted" Reardon (1915 – 93) was a roommate of Joe Kennedy Jr. at Harvard and had been promised a role in the oldest Kennedy son's Washington staff, should he ever win national office. Reardon had served in the Army Air Corps during the war. After he left the army, he married and accepted a job offer in Ohio.

At the start of his 1946 campaign, John Kennedy asked him to help run a storefront campaign office in his hometown of Somerville. When Kennedy won, Reardon told him that he was leaving to take a public relations job. But Kennedy asked him to come with him to Washington. Reardon worked as Kennedy's administrative assistant and from 1961 was Special Assistant to the President for Cabinet Affairs.

BILLY SUTTON

In 1946, Sergeant William "Billy" Sutton (1914 – 98) had just completed two years overseas and, having been discharged from Fort Devens, took a train to see his mother in Boston. As he was walking up School Street, he ran into Joe Kane, a cousin of the Kennedys and a highly respected and knowledgeable Boston politician.

Billy Sutton had already worked on a couple of campaigns in the 11th District and was very well connected in the area. Kane knew that Sutton could prove invaluable to Kennedy's campaign and persuaded him that night to go to the Bellevue Hotel because there was someone he had to meet.

When Sutton met Kennedy there was an instant bond between the two men. By the time Sutton walked out through the doors of the Bellevue he was a fully signed up member of Kennedy's staff. The following morning he began to assemble the organization that would bring Kennedy victory in 1946, hiring Dave Powers (1912 – 98), a friend and a fellow veteran.

Billy Sutton was with Kennedy during his early years in Washington, living on the third floor of a house Kennedy was renting on 31st Street in Georgetown. Then, when Kennedy was considering a Senate run, Sutton was the first to tell him that the seat was winnable. He returned to Boston and organized Kennedy's victorious campaign. He never went back to Washington, having missed his family and friends but he helped in all the other Kennedy family campaigns. He died in 1998, at age 84.

MARY DAVIS

In the early days, Mary Davis (1918 – 2004) was Kennedy's secretary and remained in that role until 1952. A year younger than the congressman, she was vital to the Washington office, joining his staff after eight years working for other congressmen.

Billy Sutton could not praise her highly enough:

> Mary Davis was unbelievable. She could answer the phone, type a letter, eat a chocolate bar all at once. She was the complete political machine, knew everybody, how to get anything done … When Mary came in, you could have let twelve people go.

She herself said:

> Everything that came into the office was handed to me. I took care of everything. If I had any questions, I'd take them into him at a specific time and say, "Here, what do you want me to say about that?" Nothing would land on his desk. I'd pin him down on the spot, get his decision, then do it.

Unfortunately, Davis was never happy about her $60 weekly wage and complained about it to Kennedy, remembering that his family had many millions in the bank. He told her he'd get round to it one day. But he never did and she eventually left him for a higher-paid position. She worked in the US Congress for 45 years.

GRACE BURKE

Born in Boston's West End, 50-year-old Grace Burke started out working for Kennedy's campaign, hired by Joe Kane. Formerly secretary for Judge John P. Higgins, she became Kennedy's secretary in the Boston office and remained there throughout his three terms as a congressman. One member of Kennedy's team has described her as "the most dedicated person to Jack Kennedy of anybody I ever knew."

DAVE POWERS

The son of Irish immigrants, Dave Powers was born in Boston in 1912. His father died when he was two and he found work at ten as a newsboy, getting to know almost everyone in the area. A succession of jobs followed his graduation from high school and he also attended night school. He served three years in the US Air Force during the Second World War, ending up as a master sergeant.

Powers first met Kennedy when the congressional hopeful knocked on his door, canvassing. The two bonded instantly and Kennedy realized that Powers' local knowledge was an invaluable asset. While Kennedy was in Washington, Powers remained in Boston, working for the city housing authority and the state housing board but he was involved in all Kennedy's campaigns.

When Kennedy became president, Powers was appointed his special assistant in the White House, which meant meeting and greeting visitors. Powers reportedly told the Shah of Iran, "I want you to know you're my kind of Shah." Known as the First Friend, his loyalty, sense of humor, and contacts throughout Boston's Irish community made him a close aide to Kennedy. He was a man who made the president laugh and they often watched ball games together.

After Kennedy's death, Powers went on to assemble and catalog thousands of items of memorabilia for the Kennedy Library and to raise money for it. Dave Powers died at the age of 85 in 1998.

President John F. Kennedy throws out the ceremonial first pitch at a baseball game, 1962. Dave Powers (in the hat) stands to the president's right with Vice President Lyndon B. Johnson.

CHAPTER 8

A SEAT IN THE SENATE

✶ ✶ ✶ ✶ ✶ ✶ 🦅 ✶ ✶ ✶ ✶ ✶ ✶

Kennedy's contemporaries, Richard Nixon (1913 – 94) and George Smathers, both made the move to the Senate in 1950, their progress facilitated by their zealous work in sniffing out communist sympathizers. Kennedy began to prepare the ground for his own move by focusing on America's relationship with the Soviet Union. America now saw the world outside by means of the communist threat.

Winston Churchill, Kennedy's political hero, had described the situation in his customarily eloquent manner in a famous speech in Westminster College in Fulton, Missouri:

> From Stettin in the Baltic to Trieste in the Adriatic, an iron curtain has descended across the Continent.

It was because of this fear of the communists taking over Europe that President Truman managed to defeat the isolationists and gain approval for the Marshall Plan, a means of providing aid to the beleaguered countries of Europe. He also won support in 1949 for the formation of North Atlantic Treaty Organization (NATO), a military alliance between the nations of the West. Kennedy supported these initiatives fully but worried that the Truman government should be doing more.

✶ ✶ ✶ ✶ ✶ ✶

PUSHING FOR A SENATE SEAT

An imminent move to the Senate was now firmly in Kennedy's plans. Like many others he had been dismayed that China had fallen to the Communists, saying that what "our young men had saved [in World War II], our diplomats and our president have frittered away."

In 1950, the Korean War had also begun badly for a poorly prepared America

and Kennedy railed against the Truman administration and had little time for Secretary of State Dean Acheson's foreign policy. He also showed his colors as a politician who was willing to go against the party line, displaying support for communist-chasing Republican Richard Nixon against the Democrat and former actress Helen Douglas (1900 – 80) in the California senatorial election of 1950.

Kennedy reportedly said that he could not endorse Nixon, but that he would not be heartbroken if Douglas had to return to her acting career. Furthermore, Kennedy gave Nixon a donation of $1,000 on behalf of his father who considered Douglas to be a communist.

✶ ✶ ✶ ✶ ✶ ✶

CHANGING ELECTORATE

America was changing in the years following the end of the Second World War. Migration westward and southward, coupled with the growth of the suburbs and the move from an industrial economy to a service economy rendered the old party structures and approaches fairly redundant.

The senior party officials remained all-powerful, but perhaps their grasp on power was weakening and their ability to deliver votes was not what it once was. They remained important to any young politician running for national office but he or she could now run their own campaign, putting together their own electoral organization. There was also a new way to connect with voters—television.

The voters that Kennedy had to chase in his senatorial campaign were mainly Catholic trade union members . But their politics had shifted with the changes in society and living conditions. Away from the urban centers with their slums and overcrowding, these voters had different aspirations and values.

THE RED SCARE

By the 1930s, Communism had begun to gain a foothold in America and by 1939 the Communist Party of the United States of America (CPUSA) boasted 50,000 members. After America's entry into the Second World War in 1941, the Smith Act or Alien Registration Act restrained anyone trying to overthrow the US government, and was used principally against communists. The CPUSA eventually became pro-war.

Many disparate events provided the background to the growing fear of communism in the United States. The trial and executions of Ethel (1915 – 53) and Julius Rosenberg (1918 – 53) for spying for the Soviet Union caused a sensation; the Soviet Union's first nuclear weapon test surprised and alarmed Americans in 1949; a spy-ring was uncovered in Canada; and Chinese Communists won the Chinese Civil War, founding the People's Republic of China.

In March 1947, President Truman signed Executive Order 9835 that established review boards to determine the "Americanism" of federal government employees. Meanwhile, the House Committee on Un-American Activities (HUAC) headed by the Republican Senator for Wisconsin, Joseph McCarthy (1908 – 57) carried out investigations on suspected communists. This process provided a launchpad for future-president Richard Nixon's political career as well as that of John F. Kennedy's brother, Robert Kennedy.

McCarthy, a good friend to the Kennedy family and godfather to Robert Kennedy's daughter Kathleen, appointed Robert as assistant counsel of the US Senate Permanent Subcommittee on Investigations.

McCarthy exploited the American fear of communism and the process became known as "McCarthyism." The clampdown on communists has often been seen as anti-intellectual and often targeted filmmakers, writers, and artists. It undoubtedly, changed America.

Ethel and Julius Rosenberg, separated by a heavy wire screen, as they leave court after being found guilty by the jury.

Their political thinking had moved from the Left to the Center. They were happy with the new President Dwight D. Eisenhower's "Modern Republicanism" that seemed to hold onto important elements of Roosevelt's New Deal, maintaining Social Security and allowing a limited role for organized labor. They did want limits placed on things such as federal aid for education and public housing, however. What was certain, though, was that anticommunism was an absolute necessity for any candidate seeking public office at that time.

* * * * * *

AMERICAN INFLUENCE FADING

Kennedy did his research, traveling to Europe for five weeks in early 1951. He reported on his return that there was little need to fear that the Russians would launch an attack in Europe while the nations of the West were concentrating on the war in Korea. Military preparedness was still necessary, however, and it should be shared equally by the members of NATO.

In the fall of the same year, he traveled to Israel, Iran, Pakistan, India, Singapore, Thailand, French Indochina, Korea, and Japan. He concluded that American influence was weakening in these regions, recognizing that their nationalist aspirations would inevitably mean that the United States would merely become an imperialist replacement for the colonial powers that had previously ruled them.

* * * * *

CHAMPION OF THE WORLD

The deciding factor in whether Kennedy ran for the Senate lay in the hands of the Democratic Governor of Massachusetts. Paul Dever (1903 – 58) had been elected in 1948 and was re-elected in 1950. If he decided to stand for the Senate in 1952, the party machinery would no doubt be put at his disposal, closing out Kennedy's chances.

Nonetheless, Kennedy threw himself into a punishing schedule of speaking engagements across the state, made even more difficult by his debilitating back pain. Outwardly, all appeared well. Dave Powers remembers the young congressman running up onto the podium "looking as fit and healthy as the light-heavyweight champion of the world." But when they returned to the privacy of their hotel, they had to supply him with crutches to get up the stairs. His customary long, hot bath would be the prelude to sleep.

* * * * * *

A NATION SEEKING CHANGE

In the early 1950s, the Republicans were making a comeback, despite Truman's 1948 victory. The Red Scare had played into Republican hands and with Eisenhower saying he would bring the Korean War to an end, Henry Cabot Lodge was favorite to regain his Massachusetts seat in the Senate. This created complacency in the Lodge camp and they also seriously underestimated Kennedy's capabilities. He had been working hard, criss-crossing the state and as he did so he had assembled a powerful team of young, enthusiastic volunteers led by his dynamic younger brother Robert Kennedy.

Once again, Joe Kennedy Sr. was the force behind the scenes, spending money on a huge advertising campaign that took in newspapers, television, radio, and billboards. The celebrated Kennedy charm was evident at "teas" across the state that hosted some 70,000 women.

It began to look bad for Lodge when the *Boston Post* came out for Kennedy a few weeks prior to election day. Of course, it was Joe Sr. pulling the strings. Apparently, he gave the owner of the paper a loan of $500,000 on generous terms to help his precarious financial situation.

Against all the odds, with the country veering to the Republicans, Eisenhower defeating Adlai Stevenson (1900 – 65) and Dever losing the governorship, Kennedy defeated Lodge by 51.4 percent to 48.4 percent, the number of votes separating the two only 70,737. The same as the number of women that attended Kennedy's "tea parties" and the joke circulated that Lodge had "drowned in tea."

The electoral vote had changed. There was an increased turnout in ethnic districts and Catholic and Jewish voters had swung to Kennedy. It was as if the minorities were saying that not only had they arrived but they were also going to put into a position of power another from outside the elite. John F. Kennedy was elected Senator for Massachusetts on January 3, 1953. He was 35 years old.

SENATOR KENNEDY

Kennedy had forty proposals aimed at getting New England back on its feet again, and the first job Ted Sorensen was given was to craft three speeches explaining them. To reassure the voters that he meant business, 30,000 copies of the three speeches were distributed. He also took a stand against the Eisenhower approach to foreign policy, especially with regard to Russia.

Eisenhower had introduced a policy named "New Look" that focused on strategic nuclear weapons as a deterrent to threats from the Eastern Bloc, something of a shift in focus from conventional military capability to "air-atomic" capability. This entailed a reduced military establishment with fewer land and naval forces. It became embedded in the doctrine of "Massive Retaliation" using nuclear weapons, but Kennedy was against it, insisting that it represented nothing but danger for America.

INFAMY SO BLACK

Concern about the communist threat continued, even though Eisenhower made good on his promise to bring the Korean War to an end. The president had a huge issue with the right wing of his party that explains to some extent why he allowed the McCarthy hearings to go on—he was appeasing that part of the Republican Party.

Eisenhower refused to cooperate or endorse in any way what McCarthy was doing. He remained quiet about his opposition to it, even when McCarthy accused General George Marshall (1880 – 1959)—the man for whom the Marshall Plan was named—of being involved in "a conspiracy so immense and an infamy so black as to dwarf any previous such venture in the history of man."

DODGING THE McCARTHY VOTE

Eisenhower was proved right to keep his distance when, in December 1954, the Senate voted to censure Senator McCarthy. The only Democrat in the entire Senate who did not vote to censure McCarthy was John F. Kennedy. Why did he do it? Probably not because of the family ties.

By 1954, McCarthy and the young senator were not on the best of terms, largely due to Kennedy blocking appointments of some associates of the Wisconsin senator. It is more likely that Kennedy had one eye on McCarthy's popularity, especially with the Catholic voters of Massachusetts.

Instead of going with the flow, and possibly upsetting his constituents, Kennedy avoided voting by going into hospital for back surgery. It would be a decision that haunted him for years. He said:

> *I went into hospital, and I heard nothing about it and cared less and I didn't have any contact with anyone at my office and maybe Ted [Sorensen] should have paired me, but at the time I didn't care about the thing. I couldn't care less. I was in bad shape and had other things on my mind.*

For the next six years Kennedy had to explain away that vote, or lack of it. He understood he had made a bad call and wished he had demonstrated more courage.

THE INNER CIRCLE
EVELYN LINCOLN

Evelyn Norton was born in 1909 in Polk County, Nebraska, her father was a member of the House of Representatives. After graduating from George Washington University, she married Harold Lincoln, a federal worker, in 1930. She was John F. Kennedy's personal secretary from the day he entered the Senate until his death and her relationship to the president has often been described as being like a marriage.

A 43-year-old congressional aid at the time, Lincoln started to work for Kennedy in 1953. She was soon indispensible to the young senator, in his private as well as his professional life. When Kennedy won the presidential election, Lincoln became a public figure, occupying the office next to the Oval Office.

It is said that when Lyndon Johnson arrived in the White House as president the day after Kennedy's assassination, he gave her until 11:30 to clear her desk so that his "girls" could move in. She never forgave the former vice president. In her 1968 book, *Kennedy and Johnson*, she recalled that Kennedy told her he was thinking about Governor Terry Sanford of North Carolina as a vice-presidential running mate rather than Lyndon Johnson.

After Kennedy's death, it transpired she had saved virtually every scrap of paper that had crossed the president's desk. She donated it all to the John Fitzgerald Presidential Library and Museum in Boston. Her devotion to Kennedy was clear and every year until her death in 1995, age 85, she left three red roses at his grave.

THE INNER CIRCLE
TED SORENSEN

Theodore "Ted" Sorensen (1928 – 2010) was born in Nebraska, the son of Christian A. Sorensen who was Nebraska attorney general. He joined John F. Kennedy's staff in January 1953 as his chief legislative aide.

Sorensen served as Kennedy's special counsel, advisor and main speechwriter, and it is for the latter role that he is best remembered. Kennedy's inaugural address, famous for the words "Ask not what your country can do for you; ask what you can do for your country," was written by him although he always maintained that Kennedy wrote those words. In his 2008 memoir, *Counselor: A Life at the Edge of History*, Sorensen claimed, "The truth is that I simply don't remember where the line came from."

Sorensen helped draft Kennedy's correspondence with Nikita Khrushchev (1894 – 1971) during the Cuban Missile Crisis and contributed to Kennedy's first address to the American people on the crisis. Kennedy referred to Sorensen as his "intellectual blood bank."

Consumed by grief following Kennedy's assassination, Sorensen tendered his resignation immediately although he was persuaded to stay on for the transition. He was responsible for President Lyndon Johnson's first speech to Congress, and the 1964 State of the Union Address, but after

that, he left the White House. Sorensen's biography, *Kennedy*, was published during 1965 and became an international bestseller.

Sorensen remained close to the Kennedys and was an advisor to Robert Kennedy during his 1968 presidential campaign. For the next forty years he practiced as an international lawyer, advising governments and businesses around the world.

On October 31, 2010, Sorensen died in New York City of complications after a stroke. He was 82 years old.

Jacqueline Bouvier, June 1953.

JACQUELINE BOUVIER

In 1951, 22-year-old socialite, Jacqueline Bouvier (1929 – 1994) entered Kennedy's life. Her parents were stockbroker John Vernou "Black Jack" Bouvier III (1891 – 1957) and socialite, Janet Norton Lee (1907 – 1989). She was extremely close to her father who described her as "the most beautiful daughter a man ever had." Her mother and father divorced in 1936, the marriage having been put under strain by her father's drinking and financial troubles caused by the Wall Street Crash of 1929. The divorce greatly affected the young Jacqueline. Her mother re-married Standard Oil heir, Hugh Dudley Auchincloss Jr. (1897 – 1976) in 1942.

In the fall of 1947, Jacqueline enrolled at Vassar College and became an accomplished student. But she was also a familiar figure at New York social functions and was dubbed "debutante of the year" by one newspaper columnist. From 1949 to 1950, she spent a year at the University of Grenoble and the Sorbonne in Paris and on her return to the United States, attended George Washington University in Washington DC from which she graduated with a degree in French literature in 1951.

While at George Washington, she won a 12-month junior editorship at *Vogue* magazine, but after spending the summer of 1951 traveling in Europe with her sister, Lee (born 1933) she decided against the *Vogue* position, resigning after just one day in the job. Given that she was 22, she was apparently concerned about her marriage prospects and wanted to get on with the job of finding a suitable husband. She found a part-time position with the *Washington Times-Herald* and was briefly engaged to a young stockbroker, John G.W. Husted Jr. (1926 – 99).

* * * * * *

KINDRED SPIRITS

Jacqueline Bouvier and John Kennedy moved in the same social circles and met for the first time at a dinner party in May 1952, introduced by mutual friend, the journalist Charles L.

Bartlett (1921 – 2017). The two were instantly attracted to one another and had much in common. They were both Roman Catholic and both were writers. They also had a mutual love of reading and had both lived abroad. As a couple Jacqueline added to Kennedy's allure which was no bad thing for his political career.

They had other things in common. Jacqueline had been scarred by her parents' divorce, having also endured the tensions of a difficult family life when her parents had been together. She had issues with her mother, and her father's drinking and womanizing had created unbearable tensions at home.

Jacqueline had become wary of trusting people too much and became withdrawn and reserved. Kennedy, too, had had to endure tensions at home with his devout, unaffectionate mother and a father who was also frequently absent and who enjoyed many liaisons outside marriage. Lem Billings, a close friend of the Kennedy family, confirmed this:

> *He saw her as a kindred spirit. I think he understood that the two of them were alike. They had both taken circumstances that weren't the best in the world when they were younger and learned to make themselves up as they went along … They were so much alike. Even the names—Jack and Jackie: two halves of a single whole. They were both actors and I think they appreciated each other's performances. It was unbelievable to watch them work a party …*

It was not plain sailing, however. At the start of their relationship Jacqueline was away in Europe and on her return Kennedy was preoccupied with winning his Senate seat. He was understandably spending a great deal of time in Massachusetts and was still seeing other women. But some suggest that Jacqueline enjoyed her future husband's philandering, saying she was attracted to dangerous men.

* * * * * *

TRUE RAPTURE

The wedding at the Newport, Rhode Island estate of Jacqueline's stepfather, Hugh Auchincloss, on September 12, 1953 was described by the media as the social event of the year. There were more than 700 guests at the ceremony at St. Mary's Church in Newport and 1,200 at the Hammersmith Farm reception. They honeymooned in Acapulco from where Kennedy wired his parents:

> *At last I know the meaning of true rapture. Jackie is enshrined forever in my heart. Thanks Mom and Dad for making me worthy of her.*

Soon, however, tensions began to appear. Kennedy was obsessed with work and Jacqueline often felt ignored, even when he was home. She said:

> *I was alone almost every weekend. It was all wrong. Politics was sort of my enemy and we had no home life whatsoever.*

* * * * * *

A PRICE TO PAY

For his part, Kennedy felt that Jacqueline spent too much money and was irritated by her constant re-decoration of their homes. She was also annoyed by his deep-rooted independence—habitually disappearing with male friends—and, there was a constant argument over other women.

What had seemed an attractive trait before, now disturbed her. She was often embarrassed at parties when Kennedy vanished with a pretty young girl. One friend of the couple said that after the first year of marriage, "Jackie was wandering around like the survivor of an airplane crash."

By the summer of 1956, Jacqueline was pregnant with their first child. Kennedy took off to a yacht in the Mediterranean with fellow philanderer George Smathers, picking up girls in every port. Even when Kennedy was informed of Jacqueline's miscarriage, he was not inclined to return home immediately. But Smathers reminded him of the consequences. Being divorced was unlikely to endear him to the voters if one day he were to fulfil his ambition of the presidency. Kennedy packed his bags and flew home.

THE DEMOCRATIC CANDIDATES

John F. Kennedy was, in reality, sculpting a presidential candidate of himself. Most of his moves were calculated with that goal in mind. But there were other candidates in the Democratic Party at that time who might pose a threat to his chances of reaching the White House in 1960.

ADLAI STEVENSON

The Governor of Illinois had won the Democratic nomination for president in both 1952 and 1956. He was a liberal, a witty and smart man, but was seen as something of an "egghead." Although liked by intellectuals, he never proved popular with the people who found him just a little too cerebral. He lost both presidential elections to Dwight D. Eisenhower.

LYNDON B. JOHNSON

The youngest ever majority leader in the Senate, the senator from Texas was making a name for himself in the legislature, but his problem was his national profile. Well-known in his own state and in the South, he was still a relative unknown to the rest of the United States.

ESTES KEFAUVER

After fronting a highly publicized investigation into organized crime in the early 1950s, Tennessee Senator Estes Kefauver went for the 1952 nomination, campaigning in a coonskin cap and often on a dog-sleigh. His defeat of the incumbent president, Harry Truman in the New Hampshire primary forced Truman to withdraw from the race. But even though he was ahead of Adlai Stevenson in the polls, Democratic Party bosses chose Stevenson as the 1952 presidential nominee. In 1956, Kefauver was Stevenson's choice as vice president but they went on to lose again to Eisenhower.

STUART SYMINGTON

The senator from Missouri was highly critical of President Eisenhower's defense policy and in so doing was creating a name for himself. He had been the first Secretary of the Air Force before being elected to the Senate in 1952. He was a poor public speaker, leading some to describe him as the best presidential candidate right up to the moment he opened his mouth.

HUBERT HUMPHREY

The Minnesotan senator was a favorite of liberals following his fight at the 1948 Democratic Party Convention for a strong civil rights policy and for his support for organized labor. His civil rights stance was, however, unlikely to attract southerners.

CHAPTER 9

PROFILES IN COURAGE

Kennedy's health was still a battle. Addison's disease had been diagnosed in 1947 but for the next six years he was plagued by other health issues. He suffered headaches, respiratory infections, stomach pains, and urinary tract problems and spent every minute of the day with back pains. His life was an endless intake of drugs and implants, and he consulted specialists and consultants in an effort to find relief from his miseries. He had been so ill from his stomach problems during a 1951 trip to Japan that doctors feared he was going to die. This episode made him much more circumspect about taking his various medications.

In 1953, Kennedy's back became excruciatingly painful. It was discovered that the corticosteroids he had been taking for Addison's had resulted in the collapse of his fifth lumbar vertebrae. By May, he was using crutches and becoming increasingly short-tempered. It was so bad that his secretary Evelyn Lincoln almost quit. He consulted with a team from Lahey Hospital in Massachusetts who told him of a complex new surgical procedure that might help relieve his pain. Without it, they warned, there was a chance he might end up confined to a wheelchair.

SURGICAL COMPLICATIONS

His father tried to dissuade him from having the surgery, bringing up the fact that Roosevelt used a wheelchair, although he was rarely seen using it in public. But Kennedy was determined to go ahead with the surgery which took place in October 1953. During a three-hour operation at New York's Hospital for Special Surgery, surgeons inserted a metal plate to stabilize his spine.

All went well, until following the operation, a urinary tract infection sent him into a coma. It was feared once more that he was not going to make it, and as his father wept, a priest was brought in to deliver the last rites. But, Kennedy pulled through and began his recuperation in Palm Beach. Unfortunately, the plate became infected and another operation was needed in January 1954 to remove it.

He had been away from his desk for quite a time and it could no longer be a secret that he had problems. His surgery and back problems were made public by the Kennedy family but instead of being a problem, he seemed to gain some benefit from it. People were impressed that he was so committed to doing his public service duty despite suffering such debilitating problems. They saw him as courageous.

ONLY A HEARTBEAT AWAY

Kennedy's health had been an issue for him through much of the 1950s, but now the health of others began to have an impact on his political advancement. Firstly, Lyndon Johnson, a sixty-a-day smoker suffered a near-fatal heart attack in July 1955. He had been a contender for the presidency after his brilliant performances in the Senate, but his health took him out of the running.

Later in that same year, President Eisenhower also suffered a heart attack. Although his doctors advised him that he would be fit enough to run for a second term, the spotlight fell on his running mate. The vice president, after all, would be only a heartbeat from the presidency. Many were distressed to think that Richard Nixon, who had relentlessly pursued Alger Hiss (1904 – 96), could become president if Eisenhower were to fall ill again.

The Democrats, faced with the popularity of Eisenhower, even though they had gained control of Congress, focused on the possibility

PROFILES IN COURAGE

Kennedy began to think about writing a book on the subject of courage. It was tied in partly to the lack of courage he had shown in not taking part in the McCarthy censure vote but he was also returning to a philosophical conundrum that had always been in his mind. At what point should a politician put aside the needs of the people who voted for him or her and, instead, go with whatever is best for the national good? He sent Ted Sorensen off to find examples where senators went against the wishes of their constituents. Sorensen came up with the list of eight senators who showed bravery and integrity in their political careers, defying their party or constituents to do what they felt was right.

Profiles in Courage told the stories of: John Quincy Adams (1767 – 1848); Daniel Webster (1782 – 1852); Thomas Hart Benton (1782 – 1858); Sam Houston (1793 – 1863); Edmund G. Ross (1826 – 1907); Lucius Lamar (1825 – 1893); George W. Norris (1861 – 1944); and Robert Taft (1889 – 1953). The book became an instant bestseller and won the Pulitzer Prize for Biography in 1957.

But behind the scenes, it was rumored that Joe Kennedy Sr. had persuaded members of the prize board to vote for it, and there was also controversy over who had really written the book. The reality was that Ted Sorensen had worked with Professor Jules Davids (1920 – 96) of Georgetown University to draft chapters which Kennedy edited. He also dictated chapters to be typed, tapes of which can be found in the John F. Kennedy Library.

Kennedy undoubtedly played a large part in the creation of the book but did not write all of it. There were questions in the media, and at one point Joe Sr. wanted to sue journalist Drew Pearson (1897 – 1969) who implied that Ted Sorensen was the sole author. A retraction and apology were made by the ABC TV network, but many believed the story to be true. In his 2008 autobiography *Counselor: A Life at the Edge of History*, Sorensen said he wrote "a first draft of most of the chapters" and "helped choose the words of many of its sentences."

Nevertheless, the whole point of *Profiles in Courage* was for Kennedy to associate himself with courageous politicians, and that certainly worked. The book caused quite a stir and Kennedy also raised his intellectual standing, outshining his rivals in the Senate.

Profiles
IN
Courage

DECISIVE MOMENTS IN
THE LIVES OF CELEBRATED AMERICANS

Senator John F. Kennedy

Foreword by ALLAN NEVINS

The front cover of *Profiles in Courage*.

LYNDON B. JOHNSON

Popularly known as LBJ, Lyndon Baines Johnson was born in 1908 in Stonewall, Texas, to a farming family. After graduating from high school, in 1926 he enrolled in Southwest Texas State Teachers College—now Texas University. Graduating in 1930, he became a teacher.

Around this time he entered politics, campaigning for a Texas senator who recommended Johnson to Congressman Richard M. Kleberg (1887 – 1955) who made him his legislative secretary. In 1937, he won election to the House of Representatives, representing Texas's 10th Congressional District, serving in the House until 1949 when he won election to the Senate.

In 1960, Johnson ran for the Democratic presidential nomination but at the party's convention he was defeated by John F. Kennedy who offered him the vice presidency. In November 1963, Lyndon Johnson became the 36th president of the United States following Kennedy's assassination. In 1964, he stood for election, defeating Republican Senator Barry Goldwater in a landslide.

During his presidency, he introduced the "Great Society" legislation that supported civil rights, broadcasting, Medicare, Medicaid, help for education, the arts, urban and rural development, public services and launched his "War on Poverty." Millions of Americans were moved out of poverty during his time in office.

However, he was responsible for the escalation of American involvement in Vietnam. The Gulf of Tonkin Resolution placed in the hands of the president the power to use military force in Southeast Asia without asking Congress. A huge anti-war movement both at home and abroad disrupted public confidence in the conduct of the war and in their president.

In 1968, as his popularity declined, he ended his bid for a second presidential term following a poor showing in the New Hampshire primary. He returned to his ranch in Texas where he died in January 1973, at the age of 65.

that Eisenhower might not make it all the way through a second term. They suggested, therefore, that a vote for "Ike," as he was known, was in reality a vote for Richard Nixon. Thus, the vice presidential role was given greater emphasis than normal.

* * * * * *

HOPING FOR A GLAMOR TRANSFER

For Kennedy, there was a fear that his Catholicism would prove a big hurdle to his dream of becoming president. Ted Sorensen provided Kennedy with statistics that showed if the Catholics in the key election states who had voted for "Ike" in 1952, voted for Stevenson because Kennedy was on the ticket they could provide the deciding margin of victory.

Stevenson needed someone like Kennedy because his 1949 divorce did not sit well with Catholic voters. But he favored a vice-presidential candidate from the South. Nonetheless, he asked Kennedy to narrate a film that was to open the Democratic National Convention which in 1956 was being held in Chicago. It was mutually beneficial. Kennedy would derive terrific exposure among the party faithful and the outside world while Stevenson and the Democrats hoped that some of Kennedy's glamorous image might rub off on them.

Kennedy was further honored by being asked to give the nomination address. However good this might have sounded, all it said to Kennedy and his supporters was that this time round he was not going to be the vice-presidential choice.

Stevenson surprised everyone by announcing, however, that he was going to hand over the choice of vice president to the delegates, emphasizing the democratic nature of the party. Kennedy was made for

television and had already enjoyed a high profile at the convention. He hoped that this might conceivably pay off for him in the vice-presidential vote.

* * * * * *

LESS PROFILE MORE COURAGE

It had already been arranged behind the scenes that Estes Kefauver would be Stevenson's running mate and the more cynical surmised that Stevenson, by using Kennedy as he had, was merely trying to gain favor with the big city Democratic bosses, many of whom were Irish Catholics. Now he was faced with possibly being forced to make Kennedy his running mate.

When it came to the vote, Kennedy did very well, proving popular among delegates from both the North and the South. In fact, he did exceptionally well with delegates from the Deep South who were concerned about Kefauver's openness to civil rights. But Northern Liberals were not so supportive, guided as they were by the powerful personality of Eleanor Roosevelt (1884 – 1962) who did not like Kennedy. When *Profiles in Courage* was published, she said she wished that he had a little less profile and a little more courage.

Incredibly, some prominent Catholic Democratic figures also withheld support because they were afraid that if Kennedy and Stevenson lost, the party would turn on the Catholics and blame them. Furthermore, Kennedy's lack of support for farm subsidies recently turned agricultural states against his candidature. Soon, it became apparent that Kefauver was going to win and Kennedy delivered a gracious withdrawal speech in which he asked the party to unite behind Kefauver.

NEW ENGLAND PRESENTS

ELECT U. S. SENATOR JOHN F. KENNEDY VICE PRESIDENT

(Above) Kennedy campaign badge.

ELEANOR ROOSEVELT

Eleanor Roosevelt (1884 – 1962) was the longest-serving First Lady of the United States in American history, her husband having been president from March 1933 until his death in April 1945.

Born in 1884, Anna Eleanor Roosevelt's parents were socialites Elliott Bulloch Roosevelt (1860 – 94) and Anna Rebecca Hall (1863 – 92) and she was the niece of President Theodore Roosevelt (1858 – 1919). She tragically lost her parents early and was raised by her maternal grandmother, a member of the important Livingston family in Tivoli, New York. She was privately tutored before being sent to a private finishing school in London. At age 17, she returned home and was presented at a debutante ball at the Waldorf-Astoria Hotel in Manhattan.

In 1902, she met her father's fifth cousin, Franklin Delano Roosevelt on a train and the two started a secret romance, becoming engaged in November 1903. They married against the wishes of his mother in 1905. They went on to have six children although she confessed to a dislike of sex. In 1918, she learned that her husband had been having an affair with her social secretary but the marriage remained intact.

When her husband was attacked by polio in 1921, Eleanor stepped in to help him and in 1933 when he became president, she dramatically changed the role of First Lady, playing an active part in politics. She supported human rights, children's causes and women's issues. She spoke out against racial discrimination and visited troops during the war.

Following her husband's death in 1945, she was appointed as a delegate to the United Nations General Assembly and became chair of the UN's Human Rights Commission. She helped to write the Universal Declaration of Human Rights.

A controversial figure throughout her life, Eleanor Roosevelt died in 1962, at the age of 78.

WINNING HEARTS AND MINDS

Kennedy had lost, and defeat was not something his family were used to or were comfortable with. But it represented a defining moment for him. Kennedy had enjoyed the limelight throughout the convention, had sparkled on television a number of times, and had almost won the vice-presidential nomination without really trying. He realized that with a bit of work, he could do much better in 1960. The experience had taught him valuable lessons.

Rivals such as Johnson believed it was their performance in Congress and their influence in the party that would win the nomination. Kennedy knew it was about a lot more than that. It was about charisma and the ability to reach out through the new medium of television and win the hearts and minds of the American people. Importantly, he also learned that a moderate approach to civil rights would guarantee the support of the Southern states, who did not want liberals like Hubert Humphrey.

What could he do about the liberal wing of the party? His name was still attached in those circles to the way his father had behaved as an ambassador. His dodging of the McCarthy vote, too, was a burden. Losing may initially have been disappointing but it turned out to be beneficial because ultimately he was not on a losing ticket. And it was a devastating loss, Stevenson winning only six Southern states and Missouri. He even lost in his home state, Illinois.

Kennedy campaigned faithfully for them, speaking in twenty-four states, again raising his national profile. Robert Kennedy, part of the campaign team, was dismayed by Stevenson's lackluster operation, describing it as an example of how a presidential campaign should not be run. He, too, learned a great deal that year, lessons that he would apply to his brother's campaign in 1960 and that would eventually carry John F. Kennedy all the way to the White House.

Television host Jack Paar and John F. Kennedy, on *The Tonight Show* in 1959.

THE CIVIL RIGHTS BILL

In 1954, the US Supreme Court made a landmark decision in the Brown v. Board of Education of Topeka case. This effectively made state laws that supported segregation in public schools unconstitutional. Racial segregation was ruled to be a violation of the Equal Protection Clause of the Fourteenth Amendment of the United States Constitution. It opened the door to integration and represented a huge victory for the growing civil rights movement.

For politicians like Lyndon Johnson and Estes Kefauver, the huge opposition to the ruling was of deep concern. Unlike most other Southern congressmen, Johnson had already withheld his signature from the Southern Manifesto that opposed the desegregation of schools. But politicians who showed signs of moderation in racial matters were being voted out of office across the South. He was in a difficult position.

In 1956, during the Montgomery bus boycott, when a young African American woman Rosa Parks (1913 – 2005) refused to give up her seat in the "colored" section to a white passenger, a young black Baptist preacher, Martin Luther King Jr. came to prominence.

Years of peaceful protest followed, including Freedom Rides, lunch-counter sit-ins, huge marches and demonstrations. In 1963, President Kennedy delivered a historic televised speech calling on Congress to pass new civil rights legislation and urging the nation to embrace civil rights as "a moral issue … in our daily lives."

Southern senators consistently blocked Kennedy's legislation, but the Civil Rights Bill finally passed into law in 1964. It outlawed state and local laws supporting segregation and discrimination.

Soldiers from the 101st Airborne Division escort African American students into the all-white Central High School in Little Rock, Arkansas, 1957.

MARTIN LUTHER KING JR.

Martin Luther King Jr. (1929 – 68) was born in Atlanta, Georgia, the son of the Reverend Martin Luther King Sr. (1899 – 1984) and his wife Alberta (1904 – 74). At age 18, while attending the respected black Morehouse College in Atlanta, King chose to go into the ministry, believing the church offered him the best way to satisfy what he described as his "inner urge to serve humanity."

Early in his career, he became involved with civil rights and led the 1955 Montgomery bus boycott, a political and social campaign against the racial segregation that operated on the public transport system in Montgomery, Alabama. In 1956, the United States Supreme Court declared the segregation policy to be unconstitutional. In 1957, he founded and was first president of the Southern Christian Leadership Conference (SCLC) that went on to play an important role in the civil rights movement. The SCLC fought segregation in Albany, Georgia, in 1962 and organized non-violent protests in Birmingham, Alabama, in 1963.

In 1963, during the 300,000-strong "March on Washington," King delivered the "I Have a Dream" speech which is now one of the most famous speeches in American history. In 1964, he was awarded the Nobel Peace Prize for his work to defeat racial segregation using non-violence, and a year later organized the marches from Selma to Montgomery. Between 1964 and 1968, King concentrated his efforts on poverty and the Vietnam War. His controversial 1967 speech, "Beyond Vietnam," angered many, even the liberal elements with whom he had worked.

Martin Luther King Jr. was assassinated on April 14, 1968 at the Lorraine Motel in Memphis, Tennessee, by James Earl Ray. His assassination led to a wave of rioting across America.

PLAYING BOTH SIDES

Race became a big issue in the 1960 presidential election, further complicated by the Russians using America's treatment of its African Americans to exemplify the iniquities of the West. Meanwhile, those who favored the maintenance of the status quo, the segregationists, labelled civil rights activists communists. Campaigners responded by accusing the segregationists of causing problems for America in the Cold War. Kennedy and Lyndon Johnson were effectively caught in the middle, trying to gain the vote of both sides.

For his part, Johnson worked hard to get the 1957 Civil Rights Act through Congress but other Southern senators usually ensured the death of any civil rights legislation at the committee stage. The Judiciary Committee, chaired by inveterate segregationist, James Eastland, Senator for Mississippi, looked like it might prove the end of the road for the bill.

There was a procedural method of bypassing the committee stage and placing bills or resolutions directly on the Senate calendar—Rule XIV. The liberals in the Senate tried to invoke this rule on this occasion. Kennedy played to both sides with this bill.

IN AFRICAN AMERICAN EYES

Firstly, he tried to ingratiate himself with Southern senators by opposing the use of Rule XIV, believing that there were already enough votes without his that would enable the bill to progress. A few days later, to please the Northern liberals he spoke in favor of a part of the bill that would allow the attorney general powers to intervene in the South. It was unlikely to pass, anyway.

Johnson, meanwhile, knew that liberals very much doubted that a Southern white jury would return a guilty verdict on any registrar who hampered efforts to enable African Americans to register to vote. Therefore, he supported an amendment that affirmed the rights of all Americans to serve on juries. However, civil contempt cases would be heard by a judge alone, with no jury involvement.

Kennedy responded by backing the amendment on interracial juries, to please the liberals, but supported Southern senators in opposition to the denial of jury trials in civil contempt cases. White Southerners were pleased, but Kennedy lost credibility in African American eyes.

A civil rights picket line protesting against F.W. Woolworth's segregation policies, New York City, 1960.

PART THREE

THE EDGE OF A NEW FRONTIER

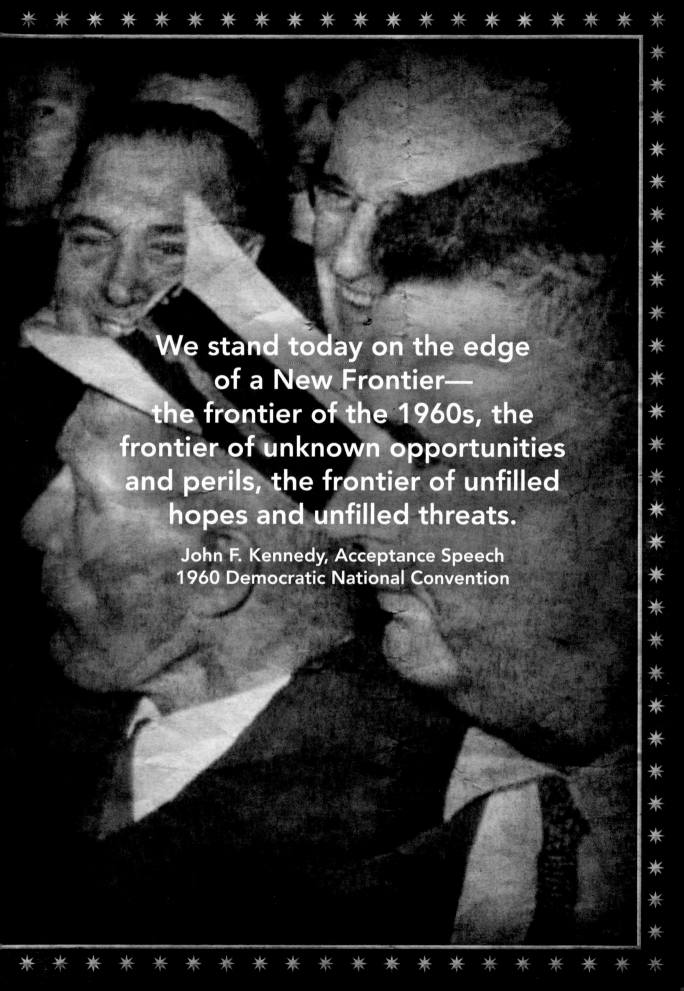

We stand today on the edge
of a New Frontier—
the frontier of the 1960s, the
frontier of unknown opportunities
and perils, the frontier of unfilled
hopes and unfilled threats.

John F. Kennedy, Acceptance Speech
1960 Democratic National Convention

CHAPTER 10

THE RACE FOR THE NOMINATION

John F. Kennedy sat on the Senate Foreign Affairs Committee, a position that gave him a platform to expound his foreign policy views. He was not overly critical, as some were, of the Eisenhower administration's reaction to the Soviet Union's successful launch of the space satellite Sputnik 1 in October 1957. But he did warn against putting "fiscal security ahead of national security."

He was very concerned about the Soviet missile capability that was highly likely to be greater than that of America. He called this difference in ballistic missile strength the "missile gap." He believed the Eisenhower administration was weak on defense and the "missile gap" went on to become a major plank of Kennedy's presidential campaign. Eventually, however, it turned out to be purely fictional and based on wrong information.

A NEW BREED OF POLITICIAN

It was highly noticeable that Kennedy had not put his name to a single piece of legislation since he had entered the Senate in 1953. In fact, to his father's great dismay, the only legislation with which he became associated was in the area of labor relations.

In March 1958, he introduced a bill that was designed to limit the use of union funds for improper purposes. It also made independent auditing compulsory. It followed investigations into the Teamster Union leaders Dave Beck (1894 – 1993) and Jimmy Hoffa (1913 – 75) who acted more like gangsters than union men. The bill never made it and anyway, it was seen as a step too far by the

unions while business leaders thought it did not go far enough. Nonetheless, it did no harm to Kennedy's profile with the public.

In the 1958 election to the Senate, Kennedy broke records, winning a massive 73.6 percent of the vote. People may have voted for him in such droves because at the time he seemed to be everywhere, a new breed of politician that graced magazine covers. He and his wife, to whom Kennedy attributed this celebrity, were never out of magazines such as *Life*. Soon there was even more reason for people to be interested in the extraordinary Kennedys. On November 27, 1957, a daughter, Caroline Bouvier Kennedy, was born.

As the crucial presidential election year of 1960 approached, Kennedy was probably more popular outside the Senate and his own party than inside. Many senators disliked him, possibly because they were jealous. He was distrusted by many, including the liberal wing of the Democratic Party and by African Americans. Segregationists, too, were unsure of him. Organized crime bosses and crooked union leaders undoubtedly despised him and his brother, Robert Kennedy.

THE EMBODIMENT OF CHANGE

It was almost inevitable from the start that the 1960 Republican nominee for the presidency was going to be Richard Nixon. The only other contender was moderate New York Governor Nelson Rockefeller (1908 – 79) but when he saw Nixon leave him trailing in the polls, Rockefeller decided against running, and put his efforts into supporting Nixon, trying to insert more moderate policies into the Republican offering.

The Democrats had more choice, maybe because the prospects for a Democratic president looked good. Eisenhower could not run again, but he had been a popular president, and no Republican candidate looked like being able to match him. Moreover, the Democrats had won a majority in Congress four years previously and the mid-term elections had brought them still more gains, giving them an overwhelming majority in the House of 130 and 28 in the Senate.

Things had not been going well for the Eisenhower administration, popular though the man at the top was. The Suez Crisis of 1956 had split the nations signed up to NATO and the Russians had gained ground with Egypt's President Gamal Abdel Nasser (1918 – 70). The United States could only stand and watch as the Soviet Union brutally suppressed the Hungarian Revolution of the same year.

The Russian launch of Sputnik 1, the first artificial Earth satellite, in 1957, was a terrible blow to American technological pride. Then in 1960, as the presidential campaign swung into gear, an American U-2 spy plane was embarrassingly shot down over Russia and its pilot Gary Powers (1929 – 77) was captured and paraded by the Russian authorities before the world's media.

Gloomy economic forecasts added to Republican woes, and the nation needed an injection of energy. John F. Kennedy, the stylish young Democratic senator from Massachusetts, was the embodiment of the change the American people were looking for.

* * * * *

THE 1960 PRIMARIES

Success in the primaries was no guarantee of success in winning the presidential nomination. The convention was where the real decisions were taken. Nonetheless, primary wins for Kennedy could deliver a powerful message to the party bosses that he was the man they should choose.

Behind the scenes, a huge amount of work was instigated. In individual states, Kennedy-people identified the most likely delegates to the convention. Meanwhile, party bosses were sweet-talked in an effort to convince them that Kennedy was the right man to take on Nixon in November.

Hubert Humphrey was extremely unpopular in the South due to his liberal views on civil rights, but hoped African-American votes would make up for the loss of votes there. The unions preferred him to Kennedy and, being from Minnesota, and having consistently supported farm subsidies in his time in the Senate, he had the farm lobby on his side.

However, Minnesota had a mere eleven Electoral College votes. Kennedy's home state, Massachusetts, had sixteen. Furthermore, Humphrey was never a rich man and throughout his political career he struggled to raise funds. The Kennedy pockets were bottomless.

Gary Powers (right) with U-2 designer Kelly Johnson, 1966.

HUBERT HUMPHREY

Hubert Horatio Humphrey Jr. (1911 – 78) was born in Wallace, South Dakota, and attended the University of Minnesota. In 1931, he earned a pharmacist licence and worked in his father's pharmacy until 1937 when he went back to university, graduating with a master's degree from Louisiana State University in 1940. When America entered the war, Humphrey tried to enlist three times but failed due to color blindness. During his political career, he was constantly accused of being a draft dodger.

In 1943 he took the role of assistant director of the War Manpower Commission, and from 1943 to 1944 was a professor of political science at Macalester College in St. Paul, Minnesota.

He unsuccessfully ran for Mayor of Minneapolis in 1943. Around this time, after communists tried to gain control of the Minnesota Democratic-Farmer-Labor Party (DFL), he became a fervent anti-Communist. He again stood for mayor in 1945 and won, remaining in that position until 1948.

At the 1948 Democratic National Convention, Humphrey famously suggested in a pro-civil rights speech that the Democratic Party "walk into the sunshine of human rights." It helped Harry Truman to win the black vote, especially in urban areas and thus secure the presidency for the Democrats.

Humphrey was elected to the Senate for Minnesota in 1948, and was re-elected in 1954 and 1960. He ran unsuccessfully for the Democratic presidential nomination in 1952 and 1960, but became vice president under Lyndon Johnson in 1964. In 1968, following Johnson's announcement that he would not be running, Humphrey announced his candidature and won the nomination. He lost to Richard Nixon in the presidential election. He returned to the Senate and served until his death from cancer in 1978, at the age of 67.

RICHARD NIXON

Richard Milhous Nixon (1913 – 94) was born in Yorba Linda, California, and was brought up a Quaker. His childhood was poor. The family ranch failed in 1922, after which his father opened a grocery store and gas station. After graduating from Whittier College, paid for by a bequest from his maternal grandfather, he studied law at Duke University School of Law, graduating in 1937 and returning to California to practice. During the Second World War, he enlisted in the US Navy, even though as a Quaker he could have claimed exemption from service. He ended the war a lieutenant commander.

Following his naval service, Nixon was elected Republican representative for California's 12th Congressional District. In 1950, he was elected to the Senate for California and gained a reputation as a staunch anti-communist, making him a nationally known political figure.

In 1952, he was on the successful presidential ticket with Dwight D. Eisenhower, serving eight years as vice president. He lost the 1960 presidential election to John F. Kennedy and in 1962 lost to Pat Brown (1905 – 96) to be Governor of California. He finally became US President when he defeated Democrat candidate, Hubert Humphrey in 1968.

Nixon brought America's involvement in Vietnam to an end in 1973. His presidency is also known for his 1972 visit to China and the policy of détente with the Soviet Union. In 1972, he was re-elected in one of the largest election landslides in American history when he defeated Senator George McGovern (1922 – 2012).

His second term as president ended in disgrace and his resignation in the face of impeachment following the Watergate scandal. In retirement, his reputation was somewhat rehabilitated by his writing and by his many trips both at home and abroad. He died at age 81, after suffering a stroke in April 1994.

WINNING WISCONSIN

In April 1960, the Humphrey campaign launched in Wisconsin where he thought he had a good chance. It was a farming state and there was access to television and radio broadcast from Minneapolis-St. Paul. He thought voters would know him from his frequent appearances on Minneapolis media outlets. He hoped also to win the votes of liberal students in Madison and those of the state's industrialized cities.

For Kennedy, on the other hand, Wisconsin provided an opportunity to finish Humphrey's campaign before it had even started. A poor result for the Minnesota senator in a state that bordered his own would suggest that he could hardly expect to perform well nationally.

The Kennedy family turned out in force and could be found everywhere in the state. Humphrey's battle bus was poorly heated and hardly luxurious while the glamorous young Massachusetts senator traveled in a private jet.

Kennedy won 56 percent of the total vote and took six of the ten congressional districts, performing very well in Milwaukee and around Green Bay, suggesting that lots of Roman Catholics switched their votes to his side. The four districts in which he lost were in the west of the state and were predominantly Lutheran. As the media noted, religion played a large part in the voting.

However, they also observed that Kennedy did not do as well as anticipated and that nationally the reliance on the Catholic vote could be a danger to his campaign. It was still widely believed to be impossible for a Roman Catholic to take the White House. The next primary in West Virginia, therefore, took on added importance for Kennedy. He had to prove that he had a broader reach than just to Catholics in order to convince the party bosses to select him.

* * * * * *

MURKY ACCUSATIONS

Humphrey remained in the race with Kennedy supporters claiming that he was there merely to spoil Kennedy's chances. But this was not the case. Humphrey was furious that he had been the victim of some stunts in Wisconsin, such as the distribution of anti-Catholic leaflets in Catholic areas. As it transpired, it was a Kennedy staffer who had posted these, although it was never clear if it was his own initiative or he was acting under orders from above.

West Virginia was going to be a real test for the Kennedy campaign, with only 5 percent of its population being Catholic. Also in Humphrey's favor was the strength in the area of the miners' union. Before the election he declared West Virginia to be "made for my politics and not Jack Kennedy's."

As it happened, religion was not an issue in this primary, especially as 59 percent of West Virginians professed to have no religious feelings whatsoever. West Virginia was a poor state and that meant the candidates had to get out into the communities to press the flesh.

West Virginian politics were notoriously murky and many have since suggested that Joe Kennedy Sr. might have used his money to win the primary for his son. There would be still more accusations, relating to Illinois and Texas, in the general election in November.

* * * * * *

SPENDING SPREE

The contrast in the spending of the candidates was stark. Humphrey had spent around $30,000, of which $2,000 was put into television advertising. Kennedy, on the other hand, had spent more on television—$34,000—than Humphrey had spent on his entire campaign. His total spending in West Virginia was estimated as $200,000.

Humphrey was finding the cash situation intolerable and it was not helped by threats from the Kennedy side to anyone making donations to Humphrey. Unions, too, worked against Humphrey, telling their members, for instance, that if Humphrey won, the vice presidency would be handed to Stuart Symington or Lyndon Johnson, both Southerners and both fervently anti-union.

WINNING WEST VIRGINIA

Kennedy faced the religion issue head-on. "Nobody asked me if I was a Catholic when I joined the United States Navy," he said, playing on his heroic war service. "Nobody asked my brother if he was a Catholic or a Protestant before he climbed into an American bomber to fly his last mission."

West Virginians respected military service and reminding them of the *PT-109* episode was guaranteed to pay dividends in terms of votes. Hinting at Humphrey's lack of military service during the war, Kennedy was often introduced as "the only veteran in the West Virginia primary."

Cleverly, the Kennedy campaign roped in the son of former President Roosevelt to tour the state in support of their man. The people of West Virginia were still grateful to Roosevelt for the help he provided for them in the dark days of the 1930s and welcomed his son with open arms. One journalist reported that it was like "God's son coming down and saying it was alright to vote for a Catholic."

On a rainy election day, Kennedy polled 236,510 votes to Hubert Humphrey's 152,187. The following day Humphrey withdrew from the race for the nomination.

The same day as the West Virginia poll, Nebraska also voted for Kennedy in its primary. Others followed and Kennedy kept on winning. By the time he had recorded victories in all ten of the primary contests he had entered, the Democratic Party chiefs were forced to pay attention.

* * * * * *

STRONG-ARM TACTICS

He still faced opposition from Franklin D. Roosevelt's formidable widow Eleanor Roosevelt, who hated Joe Kennedy Sr. with a passion. After she had claimed in 1959 that Kennedy Senior was spending a fortune to get his son elected president, John Kennedy asked her to prove it. When she was unable to do so, she backed down publicly but she never ceased working to prevent him winning the nomination.

After some strong-arm tactics in negotiations, Ohio Governor Michael DiSalle (1908 – 81) agreed to let Kennedy have the important 64 delegates from his state. Next to pledge their delegates were New York and Michigan. Mayor Richard Daley (1902 – 76) of Chicago also agreed to give Kennedy the Illinois delegation's votes.

Three other Democratic governors refused to commit at this stage—California, Pennsylvania, and New Jersey. Robert Meyner (1908 – 90) of New Jersey would certainly go for Kennedy but it would only be after Meyner's name appeared on the first ballot. Pennsylvania Governor David Lawrence (1889 – 1966) was worried that if he threw his weight behind Kennedy, anti-Catholic sentiment might endanger his own chances of re-election

* * * * * *

CRITICAL BALLOTS

California Governor Pat Brown and Kennedy did not get on, but arrived at a compromise whereby Kennedy promised not to run in the California primary. In return, Brown promised that if Kennedy won the primaries in which he took part, Brown would give him California's delegates at the convention.

This proved difficult in the end as local delegates did not trust Kennedy and wanted to give their votes to Adlai Stevenson. Eleanor Roosevelt was also in the background playing on their mistrust of Kennedy. Eventually Brown said that he would only support Kennedy on the first ballot. That ballot became critically important to the campaign.

Although small in the number of delegates they offered—128—the delegations from North and South Dakota, Nebraska, Kansas, and Oklahoma, as well as the Mountain States that consisted of Utah, Wyoming, Idaho, Montana, Colorado, Arizona, and Nevada, were still very important, especially for Lyndon Johnson.

Johnson should have been able to make these states his own, given that their economies relied on agriculture and oil extraction. But he hesitated about entering the race and when he finally did, he found that Kennedy's people were already in those states, highly organized and effective.

Kennedy's Wordcraft

Kennedy wrote hundreds of speeches, and is remembered as a great communicator who was accomplished in the art of words, but writing did not come naturally to him. He kept a notebook filled with quotations from famous speeches, plays, and works of literature, and borrowed liberally from them. He studied the great presidential speeches of the past, and hired a speech coach to help make his voice deeper and more resounding. He began to speak more slowly and confidently, with an authority that made him appear more "presidential." His speeches were short, never more than 30 minutes long, with simple words and uncomplicated phrases, but they were great pieces of rhetoric that moved audiences, and created a youthful, positive image of America across the globe.

CHAPTER 11

CHASING THE DREAM

✶ ✶ ✶ ✶ ✶ ✶ 🦅 ✶ ✶ ✶ ✶ ✶ ✶

There was always the danger at the Democratic National Convention of 1960 that Adlai Stevenson would be drafted in. Kennedy had already tried to secure Stevenson's endorsement for his bid for the nomination by promising him the role of Secretary of State in a Kennedy administration. Stevenson had turned him down.

Following his victory in the Oregon primary, Kennedy traveled to Illinois to meet Stevenson but he was not prepared to endorse anyone before the convention. He added that neither would he sign up to any movement or effort to stop Kennedy. It looked like he was merely hoping for deadlock and a "Draft Stevenson" moment at the convention or that he could ensure that Lyndon Johnson secured the nomination following a deadlocked convention.

The meeting was fairly acrimonious and Kennedy is reported to have responded to Stevenson's rejection of him with the words, "We are going to have to shit all over you," although some have said that this would have been very uncharacteristic of Kennedy, and sounded more like the reaction of his brother Robert.

✶ ✶ ✶ ✶ ✶ ✶

DAMAGING ACCUSATIONS

With Kennedy so far ahead of every other candidate, the knives were now out for him. Even former President Harry Truman entered the fray. He complained on national television that the convention was being "rigged" so that Kennedy could win.

Truman favored Stuart Symington and brought up all the usual complaints about Kennedy—he was too young, he did not have the necessary experience, his father's money was the only reason he was where he was. Wittily, when Truman was quizzed as

to whether Kennedy's Catholicism was the reason for his antipathy, he replied, "I'm not against the Pope. I'm against the Pop."

Meanwhile, Lyndon Johnson ran newspaper advertisements that highlighted the attitude of Joe Kennedy Sr. toward the Second World War, accusing him of being an appeaser and even a Nazi sympathizer. Critically, however, Johnson's people also brought to the fore the issue of John F. Kennedy's health.

When Democratic politician, India Edwards, told a press conference that Kennedy was suffering from Addison's disease and that but for cortisone he would not be alive, Kennedy furiously denied it. His doctors issued false statements, denying that he suffered from the disease.

ADDISON'S DISEASE

Named after Thomas Addison, the British physician who first described the condition in 1855, Addison's disease is a rare disorder of the adrenal glands which are two small glands that sit on top of the kidneys. They produce two essential hormones: cortisol and aldosterone. In Addison's disease the adrenal glands do not produce enough of these steroid hormones.

Symptoms generally come on slowly and may include abdominal pain, weakness, and weight loss. Over time, these problems may become more severe and sufferers may experience further symptoms, such as dizziness, fainting, cramps, and exhaustion.

1960 DEMOCRATIC NATIONAL CONVENTION

Television coverage was central to the convention. Los Angeles had been chosen as the location for the convention principally so the party could look good in the reflected Hollywood glamor of the city. Events were timed so that the most important moments would play to prime-time TV audiences on the East Coast as well as the West Coast.

There was even a huge television screen behind the podium and tele-prompters were used for the first time. All of this played right into the hands of the media-savvy Kennedy. Young and confident, he looked good on television, especially compared to the crumpled older politicians who were finding it difficult to come to terms with the new medium.

As if it were needed, Kennedy ramped up his media profile during the weekend before the convention, when a number of Kennedy family members were photographed mixing with Hollywood stars. But that weekend signified more than just a photo opportunity. It was the weekend when the larger delegations selected their candidate to take on Richard Nixon.

CHOOSING THE CANDIDATE

Illinois gave Kennedy 59.5 votes with the other candidates in single figures. New York assigned 102 votes to Kennedy and Pennsylvania gave him 64. He needed 761 and looked like he would easily achieve that.

The other task of that weekend was for the Party's platform committee to work out what policies the successful candidate would espouse in his campaign. The chair of the committee was Connecticut Governor Chester Bowles (1901 – 86), a Kennedy supporter and a liberal civil rights proponent. He insisted that the Democratic platform included a demand for federal action to strengthen racial equality in voting, housing, and employment.

They even gave endorsement for the lunch-counter sit-in protests that had broken out across the South earlier that year. The wily Bowles was well aware that Southern delegates would be horrified, but calculated that the move would bring in black votes from the urban North, in key states such as Ohio, Pennsylvania, and Illinois. It was a platform that political rivals of Kennedy, most notably Lyndon Johnson, could publicly support.

John F. Kennedy (left) and Frank Sinatra at the Democratic Committee Dinner, Beverley Hilton Hotel, Los Angeles, California, 1960.

SECURING THE NOMINATION

Johnson was also facing difficulties with organized labor. The American Federation of Labor and Congress of Industrial Organizations (AFL—CIO) instructed members who were delegates not to vote for Lyndon Johnson because of his attitude to unions—"an arch foe of labor" was how they described him.

But Stevenson was still a favorite and there were demonstrations in the convention hall in his favor. During these, he was compelled to take the podium but lost out on a major opportunity by failing to declare that he was a candidate for the nomination. The following day, despite entreaties by Robert Kennedy, Hubert Humphrey the Minnesotan senator, came out in favor of Stevenson.

However, by Wednesday, July 13, Kennedy had the votes required to win on the first ballot. Wyoming gave Kennedy the fifteen votes that took him over the required tally by four votes. In fact, the final number of votes cast for him was 806. In his acceptance speech he laid out his vision:

We stand today on the edge of a New Frontier—the frontier of the 1960s, the frontier of unknown opportunities and perils, the frontier of unfilled hopes and unfilled threats … Beyond that frontier are uncharted areas of science and space, unsolved problems of peace and war, unconquered problems of ignorance and prejudice, unanswered questions of poverty and surplus.

* * * * *

WEIGHING IT ALL UP

With the presidential nomination secured, the Kennedy machine was now faced with securing a vice president. This was a major decision as the vice president would be crucial in bringing on-board with him states where Kennedy struggled.

The strength of the Democratic Party lay in the Southern states and in the industrial cities of the East and Midwest. The multi-ethnic vote was also very important. Formerly made up of Irish and Eastern European voters, it now incorporated African Americans and a growing number of Hispanics.

THE ELECTORAL COLLEGE
➤➤➤➤➤➤➤ ◄◄◄◄◄◄◄

The Electoral College is the method by which the United States elects its president and vice president. When American citizens cast their votes, they are effectively electing representatives called "electors." These are the people whose votes go toward selecting the winning candidate.

Each of the fifty states is given a number of electors in proportion to the number of members of Congress that state has. There are currently 538 electors. This equates to the 435 Representatives and 100 Senators plus three electors that have been given to the District of Columbia (Washington DC).

Apart from Nebraska and Maine, the states give all their votes to the candidate who wins most votes in that state. In Maine and Nebraska, the "congressional district method" is used. One elector within each district is chosen by popular vote while the other two are selected by a vote throughout the entire state. Each elector casts one vote for president and one vote for vice president.

It takes 270 votes to win a majority but if, for some reason, the Electoral College fails to elect a president or vice president, the House of Representatives takes on the task with each state delegation—not each representative—having one vote. The Senate does the same for the vice president. Five times the Electoral College has voted in a president who did not win the popular vote in the country. The most recent was 2016, when Donald Trump defeated Hillary Clinton.

Things looked good in the industrial cities where organized labor would take care of the minority vote. It also looked favorable for Kennedy in the Northeastern and Midwest suburbs where middle-class Catholic voters would almost certainly turn out for him. But where his Catholicism would be beneficial in these areas, it would cause problems with the largely white voters of the South. That was without even considering the strong civil rights platform the Democrats were championing.

Never a supporter of farm subsidies, Kennedy could virtually write off the rural states of the Midwest and Far West. His religion would count against him there, too, as the large number of Protestants among that population were reluctant to see a Catholic in the White House. Put simply, Kennedy absolutely had to win in the largest states because he was unlikely to secure many Electoral College votes from the smaller, rural states.

✶ ✶ ✶ ✶ ✶
MAKE-OR-BREAK IN TEXAS

Texas became a make-or-break state for the Kennedy campaign. It was highly likely that out of the big states, Nixon would take California, Illinois, and Ohio. That would leave Michigan, New York, Pennsylvania, and Texas for Kennedy. If that did indeed happen, Kennedy would be ahead by 121 to Nixon's 97.

However, if Kennedy lost Texas, Nixon would be ahead by 108 to 97 in the bigger states. Given Kennedy's weaknesses elsewhere, that could be a telling advantage for the California senator. Some of the Southern states were hedging their bets. Segregationists were campaigning to elect Electoral College members committed to neither candidate. That way, it would all be up for grabs when the Electoral College assembled in December. They would be in a position to accept the candidate with a viewpoint on civil rights favorable to Southern sensibilities.

✶ ✶ ✶ ✶ ✶ ✶
THE LYNDON JOHNSON PROBLEM

Thus, the choice of running mate was of primary importance to Kennedy. It really had to be Lyndon Johnson who had come second in the nomination stakes with 409 votes, although Stuart Symington would have been Kennedy's preferred choice. Johnson was problematical. He was unpopular with African

John F. Kennedy (left) and Lyndon B. Johnson (center) campaigning in the 1960 presidential election, Wichita Falls, Texas. Senator Ralph Yarborough is on the right.

Americans and organized labor and he would, therefore, be an unpopular choice in the more industrial states.

Of course, there was always the possibility that Johnson would turn Kennedy down. As a hugely powerful senate majority leader, there was every chance that he would see the vice presidency as beneath him. That would be a huge embarrassment to Kennedy and might enable Johnson to make Kennedy look weak.

On the night of July 14, 1960, out of sight of the waiting media, Kennedy sneaked out of his hotel suite and down a set of back stairs to the suite occupied by Johnson and his wife Lady Bird (1912 – 2007).

* * * * * *

CONVINCING JOHNSON

He offered Johnson the position. But the Texan senator told Kennedy he would only take the job if Kennedy convinced Johnson's mentor and House Speaker Sam Rayburn (1882 – 1961) that Johnson should accept it. He also wanted Kennedy to ensure that some notable anti-Johnson union leaders and liberals agreed to have him as vice president.

Robert Kennedy could not stand Lyndon Johnson and was unwilling to see him as his brother's running mate. He insisted that Kennedy merely offer Johnson the job out of politeness and he had fully expected the Texan to say no. He was amazed when Johnson accepted.

But Kennedy's offer to Johnson was more than a mere gesture, and he did talk to Senator Rayburn who was happy with it. Robert Kennedy still worked in the background to stop Johnson being on the ticket, but during the afternoon of July 15, 1960, it was confirmed that Johnson had come on board.

Vintage 1960 Kennedy-Johnson campaign poster.

KEEPING KENNEDY CLOSE

With hindsight, for Johnson it was something of an easy decision, even though he was giving up an extremely powerful position for something with much less influence. A rejection of Kennedy's offer would have left him in the wilderness regarding future presidential ambitions, and Johnson was nothing if not ambitious.

He would still be disliked by labor bosses and African Americans and, after all, Kennedy could be in the White House for the next eight years. If he hitched himself to Kennedy's star, he would at least be close to the presidency and perhaps in a position to launch a bid for the Oval Office when Kennedy stepped down.

There was also the thought that he could make himself a pariah in his party if he were to reject the job and Kennedy lost. Part of the blame for that defeat might be placed at his door, especially by party liberals. Certainly,

Kennedy's health problems must also have occupied Johnson's thinking. Were the young senator to die or become incapacitated in office, the vice president would step into his shoes.

On the evening of Thursday, July 16, 1960, Lyndon Johnson was confirmed by convention chair Florida Governor Leroy Collins (1909 – 91) as the candidate for vice president. The following day the two nominees had a meeting with African American delegates to convince them that they were committed entirely to the civil rights policy that the convention had agreed. Finally, Kennedy gave his acceptance speech in the LA Coliseum football stadium.

* * * * * *

1960 REPUBLICAN NATIONAL CONVENTION

Like the Democrats, the Republicans had major issues in the lead-up to their convention which took place in Chicago. Richard Nixon was faced with a similar task to that of Kennedy, uniting the Goldwater conservatives with the liberals led by Nelson Rockefeller. The tensions lay in what Goldwater and his associates saw as the "creeping socialism" of the two Eisenhower administrations while the liberals favored civil rights reforms and helping the economy through federal spending.

Regarding civil rights, Nixon signed an agreement with Rockefeller that was dubbed "The Treaty of Fifth Avenue," in which he agreed to insert in the platform a civil rights plank such as the Democrats had come up with. The African American vote in the North had become important to both sides in this election. The agreement also incorporated a demand for increased spending on defense. This riled President Eisenhower who for the past two terms as president had been trying to cut defense spending.

* * * * * *

AHEAD IN THE POLLS

Nixon chose Henry Cabot Lodge as his running mate. After losing his Senate seat to Kennedy, Lodge had been appointed

Ambassador to the United Nations, a role that had made him well-known to the American public. The theory was that Lodge would help him to win the votes of Northern liberals and those of minorities, too.

It did not work out well, however, as Lodge was no great campaigner, and appeared arrogant to the voters. In the election, he even failed to deliver his home state, Massachusetts, and in the end did he not even win over the liberals of New York.

Kennedy, in contrast, was able to leave Johnson to campaign in the South which virtually guaranteed Texas. This allowed him to focus his attention on other areas of the country.

Nonetheless, Richard Nixon had a good convention and his acceptance speech was viewed very much as a triumph. Due to his time as vice president, he came across well, as a man experienced in the high office of the presidency. It put him ahead of Kennedy in the polls.

* * * * * *

THE NIXON CAMPAIGN

Unfortunately, Nixon was making fundamental errors in his campaign, such as failing to take care of the journalists who followed him everywhere. Basic formalities such as issuing speech transcripts were ignored, and soon the press and Nixon were at war. Although, in all honesty, Richard Nixon and the press had never seen eye to eye.

Furthermore, the campaign was not helped by an answer Eisenhower gave at a press conference in August. He was asked by journalist, Charles H. Mohr (1929 – 89), for an example of a major idea that Nixon had come up with when he was vice president. Eisenhower replied flippantly "If you give me a week I might think of one."

* * * * * *

THE DAMAGE DONE

Eisenhower later insisted it was a joke, but he had long been unsure about his vice president. Nixon's campaign was seriously damaged by the comment, especially as it went against one of the core strengths of his campaign—that

he had greater experience of decision-making than Kennedy.

Another reason journalists disliked Nixon was that he had promised when he won the nomination, to campaign in each of America's fifty states. It meant very hard work for the press corps following him around. But it all went badly wrong after he banged his knee on a car door in North Carolina. It became infected and Nixon was out of action for two weeks while it healed.

Still he refused to back down on his promise to visit every state and wasted valuable time, therefore, in states that he had no chance of winning or in states with few Electoral College votes up for grabs.

* * * * * *

NOT THE CATHOLIC CANDIDATE

The Kennedy camp received some polling numbers that looked at the issue of his religion. It implied that if someone was not going to vote for Kennedy because of his Catholicism they had already been lost and there was no point trying to win them over.

In fact these poll results told Kennedy that debate about his religion was only going to work to his advantage. They confirmed that Catholics, minorities, and those liberals who were outraged by such prejudice in all likelihood would vote for the Massachusetts senator. Meanwhile, the Nixon campaign exploited Protestant fears but they did it secretly, afraid there would be criticism.

Eventually, it all came out into the open when a committee of Protestant clergy began to clamor for a ban on Catholics standing for the presidency. Kennedy faced it head on and agreed to appear on television talking to the Greater Houston Ministerial Association. He dealt eloquently with a slew of hostile questions and comments and won over even more people to his cause, saying:

> I am not the Catholic candidate for President, I am the Democratic Party's candidate for President who happens to be a Catholic.

CHAPTER 12

THE DAY OF RECKONING

THE TV DEBATES

Having recently endured the "rigged" quiz show scandals of the 1950s, television executives were eager to clean up their image and political debates were just the thing to make them look good. The issue of balance meant that everyone had to be given the same amount of time, and not just the candidates of the two main parties. In a vote, however, in the summer of 1960, Congress decided to suspend the equal time rule and Nixon and Kennedy were offered a primetime slot to have a debate.

Eisenhower advised Nixon to reject the offer. Kennedy was so good on television that it was only likely to be of benefit to him. But the Republicans were reluctant to turn down the chance of free publicity for their candidate. There would also be hostility from the press if Nixon said no. Furthermore, polls had indicated that the American people wanted to see the two candidates stand up against each other. Anyway, Nixon calculated, he was a better debater than Kennedy.

GETTING IT WRONG

It was a complex business and Nixon got it wrong on many levels. He insisted on an empty studio which suited Kennedy more, in the end. The directors showed reaction shots of each candidate to what the other was saying, instead of an audience, and that worked better for Kennedy.

Nixon also agreed to four debates, believing the audience would increase with each week and, therefore, also agreed to having domestic policy as the subject of the first and foreign policy the second. Foreign policy, he believed, was his strongpoint.

The second of the four 1960 presidential TV debates, with Kennedy on the left and Nixon on the right. At the center rear is moderator Frank McGee of NBC.

THE 1950s QUIZ SHOW SCANDAL

In the 1950s, TV viewers went crazy for quiz shows. At the height of their popularity, there were twenty-two different game shows on the air. Viewers discovered their fascination with trivia and the networks discovered rocketing ratings. When contestants became popular, people watched every week to see them win the star prize. In August 1955, almost one-third of the total TV audience tuned in to watch *The $64,000 Question*, which offered the biggest money prizes. The idea that a normal person could win a fortune simply by answering questions was a new one at the time and inspired the nation. Viewing figures soared.

The scandal broke when people found out that many of the shows were fixed. It began to unravel when the new quiz show *Twenty-One* was under pressure due to poor viewing figures. The producers started secretly telling contestants the answers so they could win the show and build up excitement. Returning champion Herb Stempel was coached in what to wear and what to say. The public got behind him and the ratings went up.

Stempel was a perfect champion until the producers decided they wanted someone more photogenic. They introduced Charles Van Doren who was a charismatic college man. Numerous drawn games were set-up between Stempel and Van Doren, and viewing figures went through the roof. Eventually the show scripted Stempel to lose and Van Doren became the new champion.

Stempel was furious and exposed the whole scam of the fake shows. But many thought he was just a sore loser. Eventually a full-scale investigation revealed that *Dotto*, *Twenty-One*, and *The $64,000 Question* were all rigged, with contestants being given the answers so they could win. The networks were forced to cancel all the quiz shows. It was the 1970s before big-money game shows made a comeback to TV.

Jack Barry (center), host of quiz show *Twenty-One*, turns toward Charles Van Doren (right) as fellow contestant Vivienne Nearing looks on.

Nixon also believed that by the second program more people would be watching. He was wrong again. The audience for the first debate was huge as nothing like this had ever been staged before. People switched on out of curiosity.

* * * * *

NEGATIVES FOR NIXON

The first debate took place on September 26, 1960, but Nixon was unwell. Following his knee trouble he had caught a cold and as he walked out to his seat, he had a temperature. He had lost weight and his shirt was ill-fitting around the neck as a result. His eyes looked dark and deep-set and his jowls sagged. In contrast, as a result of a vacation in Florida, Kennedy, or JFK as everyone was calling him, was tanned and healthy-looking. Nixon sweated, his make-up ran and streaked and he was seen several times mopping sweat from his brow and licking it from his top lip.

JFK was cool and relaxed, and taking notes while Nixon looked ill. After the program had ended, the Nixon camp had to rush out a reassuring statement that his health was OK. In fact, despite all the negatives for Nixon, the debates were almost a dead heat, reflecting how close the election was going to be.

* * * * *

KENNEDY FREES KING

Civil rights leader Dr. Martin Luther King Jr. took part in a demonstration in the whites-only snack bar of an Atlanta department store during which he was arrested. Most of the demonstrators were swiftly released from custody, but King was kept in custody, having violated a probation order. Appearing before Judge Oscar Mitchell—an ardent segregationist—King was sentenced to four months' hard labor in the State Prison in Reidsville, Georgia.

King's wife, Coretta (1927 – 2006), who was heavily pregnant at the time, was worried that King would be lynched. She got in touch with John Kennedy's brother-in-law, Sargent Shriver, who asked Kennedy to phone Mrs.

King. On October 27, Robert Kennedy persuaded Judge Mitchell to order the release of the civil rights leader. Martin Luther King Jr. was released on a $2,000 bond.

Tellingly, however, Richard Nixon did nothing during the week King had been incarcerated. African Americans such as the baseball player Jackie Robinson (1919 – 72) pleaded with him to help King but he resolutely refused to comment on the matter.

On the Sunday prior to the presidential election the Kennedy campaign handed out leaflets outside black churches. They were headlined:

"No Comment" Nixon Versus a Candidate with a Heart, Senator Kennedy

Eisenhower blamed Nixon's loss of the election on this incident, saying he had lost it for the want of a couple of phone calls.

* * * * *

ALL THE WAY WITH JFK

Richard Nixon put in a huge effort in the last week of the campaign, spending 25 percent of his television advertising budget. He brought in President Eisenhower who spent an entire day campaigning in the all-important New York with both Nixon and Henry Cabot Lodge. It was a rare event, since Eisenhower's health was really too precarious for vigorous campaigning. It was regrettable for Nixon given Eisenhower's continued popularity. Meanwhile, the Kennedy campaign had finally run out of money

On the evening of Election Day, November 8, 1960, the first result to come in was Connecticut which Kennedy carried by 306,000 votes. By midnight, he was ahead by almost a million votes but that was halved during the next hour as the results of Western states came in. At 3:20 a.m., Nixon almost conceded, but not quite, he told reporters, "If the present trend continues, Senator Kennedy will be the next president." When the nation awoke next morning, Kennedy was indeed the president-elect.

SARGENT SHRIVER

Robert Sargent "Sarge" Shriver Jr. (1915 – 2011) was married to John F. Kennedy's sister, Eunice Mary Kennedy, and was very much a member of the inner circle of the Kennedy family. Born in Westminster, Maryland, he was partly of German ancestry and was descended from David Shriver, a signatory of the Maryland Constitution and Bill of Rights of 1776.

In 1934, Shriver entered Yale University and then went to Yale Law School, gaining a law degree in 1941. Shriver was opposed to America entering the Second World War. Nevertheless, he volunteered for the US Navy before the attack on Pearl Harbor and spent five years on active duty, winning a Purple Heart.

Shriver first became involved with the Kennedys while working as an assistant editor at *Newsweek* magazine. He was later employed by Joe Kennedy Sr. to manage the Merchandise Mart, one of the Kennedy business interests. He practiced law in Washington, Illinois, New York, and at the United States Supreme Court.

Shriver married Eunice Kennedy in 1953 and they had five children. When his brother-in-law ran for the presidency, he worked for the Kennedy campaign in the primaries in West Virginia and Wisconsin.

When Kennedy was president, Shriver founded the Peace Corps. Following Kennedy's assassination he served as Special Assistant to President Johnson. He was the architect of Johnson's "War on Poverty," and from 1968 until 1970 he was US Ambassador to France.

He was vice presidential candidate in the campaign of George McGovern (1922 – 2012) for president in 1972. But they lost to the incumbent Richard Nixon. Shriver was briefly a candidate for the Democratic presidential nomination in 1976.

Sargent Shriver died in 2011, at the age of 95. President Barack Obama said of him in a statement that he was "one of the brightest lights of the greatest generation."

MORE VOTES THAN VOTERS

It had been tantalizingly close. Kennedy had won 49.72 percent of the popular vote and Nixon 49.6 percent. There were questions of foul play and it is on record that in several Texan counties more votes were cast than there were registered voters. There were suspicions, too, about rigged voting in Illinois.

But it was not unusual for Illinois voting to be subject to some irregularities. Stories persisted of the Mafia buying votes on behalf of Joe Kennedy Sr., so the new president would be indebted to them. The Republicans were given an investigation into voting practices but nothing illegal was uncovered and the vote stood.

At midday on November 9, 1960, Richard Nixon conceded the election to John F. Kennedy who became the 35th President of the United States—the youngest-ever elected president, at the age of 43.

OLD AND NEW FACES

As if it was not enough to be president-elect, Kennedy also became a father for the second time on November 25, 1960, when Jacqueline Kennedy gave birth to a son, John Fitzgerald Kennedy Jr. (1960 – 99).

Kennedy now had to form an administration and he enlisted the help of some veterans of the Truman administration—Clark Clifford (1906 – 98), a former legal counsel; Dean Acheson (1893 – 1971), a former Secretary of State; and investment banker Robert Lovett (1895 – 1986) who had worked in the Defense Department. He also pulled in Sargent Shriver, his brother-in-law.

He retained J. Edgar Hoover as Head of the FBI and Allen Dulles at the CIA. In this way, he hoped to pacify those to the right of center. He was also well aware that Hoover had a vast amount of information, gathered through surveillance, that the Kennedy family would rather not be made public.

PLANNING TO KILL THE PRESIDENT-ELECT

Retired postal worker Richard Paul Pavlick (1887 – 1975) was angry because, to his mind at any rate, Kennedy had bought the presidency with his father's money. Pavlick, who had no family, had retired to Belmont, New Hampshire, where he became known for the political anger at public meetings. He took umbrage at the American flag not being flown properly, the government and Roman Catholics. The wealthy Kennedy family ticked a lot of Pavlick's boxes.

Immediately after Kennedy's election victory, Pavlick, now 73, decided he was going to assassinate him. He donated his house to a local youth camp, loaded up his 1950 Buick and drove off. A short while later, postcards from Pavlick began to arrive with Belmont postmaster, Thomas Murphy. In them Pavlick boasted the town would soon hear from him "in a big way." The cards always came from wherever Kennedy was at the time, as Pavlick stalked him. Murphy alerted the police.

Around 10:00 a.m. on December 11, 1960, president-elect Kennedy was preparing to leave for St. Edward church in Palm Beach, Florida. Pavlick waited outside, his car filled with dynamite. His plan was to blow up Kennedy and himself at the same time using the car as a suicide bomb.

When Kennedy emerged, however, he was with his wife Jacqueline Kennedy and their small children. Pavlick could not bear the thought of harming them so he aborted the attempt. He was arrested four days later crossing the Royal Poinciana Bridge leading to Palm Beach, before he could try again.

Pavlick was committed to a mental hospital after a judge ruled that he was unable to distinguish right from wrong. He was eventually released in 1966 and died, at the age of 88, in 1975.

J. EDGAR HOOVER

John Edgar Hoover (1895 – 1972), born in Washington DC, was the first Director of the United States' Federal Bureau of Investigation (FBI), retaining that position from its founding in 1935 until his death in 1972.

He obtained a Master's degree in law from George Washington University Law School, Washington DC, in 1917. He became head of the Alien Enemy Bureau during the First World War and in 1919 took over the Bureau of Investigation's new General Intelligence Division, monitoring radicals and communists.

In 1924, President Calvin Coolidge (1872 – 1933) appointed him Director of the Bureau of Investigation. In 1935, the Federal Bureau of Investigation was founded, assuming responsibility for domestic intelligence. Hoover expanded the FBI's recruitment and established centralized fingerprint and forensic laboratories.

Hoover was particularly concerned about subversion and tens of thousands of suspected radicals were investigated during his time in office. Critics claimed that he often exaggerated the dangers posed by alleged subversives, overstepping the limits of his authority to bring them to justice. He became a controversial figure later in his life as his abuse of power came to light.

It was learned that he collected secret files on political leaders including US presidents, to use as blackmail to ensure he kept his job. President Richard Nixon stated that one of the reasons he did not fire Hoover was to prevent the director from taking reprisals against him. President Harry S. Truman said that Hoover had made the FBI his own secret police force.

Hoover never married and was rumored since the 1940s to be gay, and that his partner was Clyde Tolson (1900 – 75), an associate director of the FBI. J. Edgar Hoover died of a heart attack in 1972.

ALLEN DULLES

Allen Welsh Dulles (1893 – 1969) was the first civilian Director of the Central Intelligence Agency and to this day is its longest-serving head, running it from 1953 until 1961. He was born in 1893 in Watertown, New York, and one of his four siblings, John Foster Dulles (1888 – 1959), went on to be President Dwight D. Eisenhower's Secretary of State throughout Eisenhower's two terms as president.

In 1916, having graduated from Princeton University, Dulles entered the diplomatic service and was initially assigned to Vienna and then moved to Switzerland. He was part of the American delegation to the Paris Peace Conference at the end of the First World War.

In 1926, he left the diplomatic service, took a law degree and began working as an attorney. He worked as director of the Council on Foreign Relations and as legal advisor to the League of Nations, he met Adolf Hitler, Benito Mussolini, and the leaders of the British and French governments.

In 1938 he ran unsuccessfully for the Republican nomination in New York's 16th Congressional district. He was an interventionist and supportive of the strengthening of United States' defenses. He helped numerous German Jews escape from Nazi Germany.

During the Second World War, he worked for the Office of Strategic Services (OSS) in Switzerland. In 1950, he was recruited to work for the CIA, and three years later became Director. As Director of the CIA he oversaw many overseas interventions including the 1954 coup in Guatemala, and the disastrous 1961 Bay of Pigs invasion.

Following the revelation that the CIA played a part in the 1961 Algiers putsch against French President Charles de Gaulle, Dulles was forced to resign. In the aftermath of Kennedy's death, he was a member of the Warren Commission that investigated the assassination. Allen Dulles died in 1969, at the age of 75.

CHAPTER 13

NO LONGER JUST A CANDIDATE

★ ★ ★ ★ ★ ★ ★ 🦅 ★ ★ ★ ★ ★ ★ ★

THE KENNEDY CABINET

John F. Kennedy appointed diplomat and politician C. Douglas Dillon (1909 – 2003)—a Republican—to the Treasury which reassured the financial markets. At the Defense Department, he appointed Robert McNamara (1916 – 2009), one of the so-called "Whiz Kids" who had helped to rebuild the Ford Motor Company after the Second World War.

Kennedy was impressed when his new Defense Secretary insisted on running his own department, hiring and firing his own people. He let the president know he would not be doing much socializing in Washington. These appointments were designed to placate moderate conservatives.

Kennedy was reluctant to offer Adlai Stevenson a role, but realized he had to throw a scrap to the liberals. Therefore, he named Stevenson as ambassador to the United Nations. Chester Bowles was named as under-secretary of state, Arthur Schlesinger Jr. (1917 – 2007) as White House aide and leading economist Walter Heller (1915 – 87) was given the role of Chief of Economic Advisors. The liberal Dean Rusk (1909 – 94), who had worked with Acheson and Lovett in the Truman administration, was made Secretary of State. Kennedy himself would be in charge of foreign policy, however. McGeorge Bundy (1919 – 96) was appointed National Security Advisor.

Swearing-in ceremony of President Kennedy's Cabinet. Chief Justice Earl Warren administers the oath to (left to right) Dean Rusk, Douglas Dillon, Robert McNamara, Robert F. Kennedy, J. Edward Day, Stewart Udall, Jacqueline Kennedy, President Kennedy, Adlai E. Stevenson, Orville Freeman, Arthur Goldberg, and Abraham Ribicoff.

ROBERT F. KENNEDY

Robert Francis "Bobby" Kennedy (1925 – 68) was born in Brookline, Massachusetts, the seventh child of Joe and Rose Kennedy. After serving in the US Naval Reserve from 1944 to 1946 he graduated from Harvard University and the University of Virginia.

He worked for a while as a journalist at the *Boston Post* and as assistant counsel to the Senate committee that was chaired by Kennedy family friend, Joseph McCarthy. But it was as chief counsel of the Senate Labor Rackets Committee from 1957 to 1959 that he first came to national attention when he publicly questioned Jimmy Hoffa, President of the Teamsters Union, over corrupt practices. During this time, he authored the book, *The Enemy Within* that dealt with corruption in organized labor.

Bobby Kennedy managed the successful 1960 presidential campaign for his older brother John F. Kennedy, and was surprisingly appointed Attorney General, working closely with his brother during his 1961 – 63 presidential tenure.

He is remembered for his ardent advocacy of the Civil Rights movement, crusades against the Mafia, and against organized crime. He was also involved in United States foreign policy with regard to Cuba, standing solidly by his brother's side during the difficult days of the Cuban Missile Crisis.

In 1964, he won a seat in the Senate and in 1968 he became a leading contender for the Democratic nomination. However, shortly after midnight on June 5, 1968, having just defeated Senator Eugene McCarthy in the California primary, he was shot by 24-year-old Palestinian, Sirhan Sirhan (born 1944). He died twenty-six hours later.

THE NEW ATTORNEY GENERAL

The position that excited most attention from the media, however, was Kennedy's appointment of his younger brother Robert "Bobby" Kennedy as Attorney General. *The New York Times* and *The New Republic* declared him to be inexperienced and unqualified which was certainly true as he had had no experience in any state or federal court.

Characteristically, Kennedy quipped, "I can't see that it's wrong to give him a little legal experience before he goes out to practice law." But Bobby Kennedy did have considerable experience in fighting organized crime, having established his reputation while engaged as chief counsel to the 1957 – 59 Senate Labor Rackets Committee. As Attorney General, he could continue that work.

Inaugural Address of John F. Kennedy, 35th President of the United States, Washington DC, January 20, 1961.

IRISH MAFIA

In reality, John Kennedy appointed his brother to the Justice Department in order to take charge of his administration's civil rights policy. Civil rights legislation was being held up in Congress by Southerners and it was a continuous cause of embarrassment to the government that legislation could not be progressed beyond committee stages. He was also in charge of the FBI and would be able to keep an eye on J. Edgar Hoover.

He surrounded himself in the White House with people with whom he was familiar, a group that became known as the "Irish Mafia." His appointments secretary was the abrupt Ken O'Donnell (1924 – 77), a close friend of his brother. The devoutly loyal Dave Powers was brought in, more or less to keep Kennedy amused. He was responsible for making sure there was an endless supply of good-looking women surrounding the president.

* * * * *

THE INAUGURAL ADDRESS

The task of writing JFK's inaugural speech fell to Ted Sorensen, a man often referred to as Kennedy's "intellectual blood bank." The brief from Kennedy was for an address that would establish a brand identity for his presidency.

It should identify the president as a member of a new generation and would use the first person pronoun sparingly. The topics would be foreign policy, and civil rights would be mentioned although it was fairly vague in that area, speaking of the new generation's desire to protect human rights both "at home and around the world."

The inauguration took place on January 20, 1961, a cold clear day, the snow of the previous day mercifully staying away. Nonetheless, everyone wore coats and hats to protect against the Washington chill. The top hat was the order of the day, but Kennedy wore his very little on the day and during the ceremony he dispensed with both coat and hat.

* * * * *

THE DEFENSE OF FREEDOM

JFK had worked hard on his speech, taking it everywhere with him, trying to memorize it. He spoke of the defense of freedom:

> *Let every nation know, whether it wishes us well or ill, that we shall pay any price, bear any burden, meet any hardship, support any friend, oppose any foe, to assure the survival and success of liberty.*

HAWKS AND DOVES

He spoke about emergent nations and in 1960 no fewer than seventeen African nations were being granted independence by the colonial powers. In anticipation of these countries becoming a new front line in the Cold War, he promised them American help, America would "help them help themselves," he said.

He reached out to the countries of Central and South America but also warned any power against interfering in the Western Hemisphere—an allusion, no doubt, to Cuba. He threw in enough sabre-rattling to please hawks in his party like Dean Acheson but also placated doves such as Adlai Stevenson and Chester Bowles by saying:

Let us never negotiate out of fear.
But never let us fear to negotiate.

Frequently cited as one of the best speeches in history, it lasted only 13 minutes and 42 seconds. But his most famous phrase rings down through the years:

And so, my fellow Americans, ask not what your country can do for you—ask what you can do for your country.

* * * * * *

RATINGS SOAR

It was a huge success, receiving praise even from Republicans. In fact, Russian Premier, Nikita Khrushchev allowed the entire speech to be printed in the Soviet government organs *Pravda* and *Izvestia*. Kennedy's approval ratings soared.

That night, the new young president partied hard, long after Jackie had gone to bed, but was still at his desk the following morning. The first thing he did was to sign an executive order that provided for an expanded program of food distribution to needy families.

* * * * * *

THE GATHERING STORM

At the time Kennedy took office there were a number of world crises. In Laos in Southeast Asia a civil war was being fought and the communists were starting to make some headway.

The Congo in Central Africa had been given its independence by Belgium in June 1960, but it remained unstable. The Prime Minister whose party had won the newly independent Republic of the Congo's first elections, Patrice Lumumba (1925 – 61), was murdered just a few days before Kennedy's inauguration.

Cuba, led by Fidel Castro and just ninety miles southwest of Florida, was a communist country allied with the Soviet Union. When Kennedy met Eisenhower during the transition of one administration to the other, Eisenhower warned him that he should support the plans of the CIA to eliminate the threat that Cuba posed.

* * * * * *

THE RED SPREAD

In Congress, Kennedy had always been supportive of the nationalist aspirations of nations but Eisenhower believed he needed a dose of reality. Sometimes, he believed, containment was necessary. In his farewell address, Eisenhower warned against what he called the "military-industrial complex"—the informal alliance of a nation's military and the defense industry that supplies it.

Eisenhower was certain that his young successor would be faced with having to use military force to prevent the spread of communism. But he was concerned that unrestricted defense spending could unsettle the economy.

* * * * * *

STATE OF THE UNION

Kennedy revived memories of Abraham Lincoln's Gettysburg Address with his first State of the Union address ten days after his inauguration:

I speak today in an hour of national peril and national opportunity. Before my term has ended, we shall have to test anew whether a nation organized and governed such as ours can endure. The outcome is by no means certain. The answers are by no means clear. All of us together—this Administration, this Congress, this nation—must forge those answers.

THE TIDE MUST TURN

He dealt at length with the economic difficulties America faced but he also touched on the perilous situations in other parts of the world. Khrushchev's Secret Speech, as well as Communist China's ambitions were on his mind.

He announced a reappraisal of the entire defense strategy as well as an expansion of international aid, more rapid deployment of Polaris anti-ballistic missiles and more support for the United Nations in its role in the Congo. He ended with a warning:

Life in 1961 will not be easy. Wishing it, predicting it, even asking for it, will not make it so. There will be further setbacks before the tide is turned. But turn it we must. The hopes of all mankind rest upon us—not simply upon those of us in this chamber, but upon the peasant in Laos, the fisherman in Nigeria, the exile from Cuba, the spirit that moves every man and nation who shares our hopes for freedom and the future. And in the final analysis, they rest most of all upon the pride and perseverance of our fellow citizens of the great Republic.

President John F. Kennedy delivers the State of the Union address. Seated behind him are Vice President Lyndon B. Johnson and Speaker of the House John McCormack.

First official White House photograph of First
Lady Jacqueline Kennedy, 1961.

THE AMERICAN QUEEN

The first thing Jacqueline Kennedy did when she moved into the White House in January 1961, was to announce that the place needed a makeover. Many feared that she would bring her love of French fashion to the old residence, but she opted, instead, for a historic stylish transformation.

She had always championed French couture, but wisely selected a New York designer, Oleg Cassini (1913 – 2006), as her exclusive couturier in 1961. She nicknamed him her "Secretary of Style." His style for her clothes was classic simplicity—clean lines, and beautiful fabrics with pillbox hats and oversize buttons setting off meticulously tailored geometric dresses.

She became closely identified with sophistication and elegance and the "Jackie look" was borrowed by women all over the world. Cassini later wrote that he saw her as an American Queen.

THE NEW GENERATION

Jacqueline's expensive fashion tastes and cultural pursuits were encouraged by the White House press office, but her children and her private life were off limits. She distanced herself from the press and this only made them want more. The images snatched of her on her husband's foreign trips were very much valued.

She was at the forefront of the White House alterations and immediately made plans for each of the seven family rooms. It took her only two weeks to spend the $50,000 refurbishment budget. And that was before she had even started on the State Rooms. She wanted it to be a place of cultural exchange, for the "new generation."

Jacqueline never forgot the value of publicity and her refurbishment was featured in *Life* magazine. At the end of 1961 she took a television audience of sixty million Americans and millions more worldwide on a tour of the White House. It was a huge success and her value to JFK's public image was evident.

Even formal state dinners were different.

Jacqueline hosted a dinner for President Ayub Khan (1907 – 74) of Pakistan, with guests being ferried along the Potomac river and entertained by a Revolutionary War re-enactment before dinner. More music concerts were held at the White House, and there were dinners honoring writers and scholars.

Presidential trips abroad were something of a novelty at the time but the First Lady again proved her worth on these trips, bolstering America's international image as well as that of her husband. In France, she wore Givenchy, a very wise choice. The French press adored her for it. At one point JFK told a press conference that he had been pleased to be "the man who accompanied Jacqueline Kennedy to Paris."

LAVISH LIFESTYLE

Back home, however, there were those who berated her for her overseas trips. Those with more conservative views questioned her time away from her children and many were concerned by their lavish lifestyle.

In 1962 the American press grew more critical of her jet-setting, especially when she spent time in Italy in the company of the heir to the Fiat empire, Gianni Agnelli (1921 – 2003), a notorious playboy. The president is said to have sent her a telegram at this time suggesting that photographs with their daughter Caroline might be slightly more appropriate than photos with Agnelli. "More Caroline, less Agnelli," he wrote.

Following the death of their pre-maturely born son Patrick Bouvier Kennedy in 1963, Jacqueline was excused duties for the remainder of the year. The president allowed her to spend time with her younger sister Caroline Lee Radziwill (née Bouvier, born 1933), on the yacht of Greek shipping magnate, Aristotle Onassis (1906 – 75).

On her return to the White House, she was rejuvenated and eager to help again, which was good news for the president and his prospects for a second term.

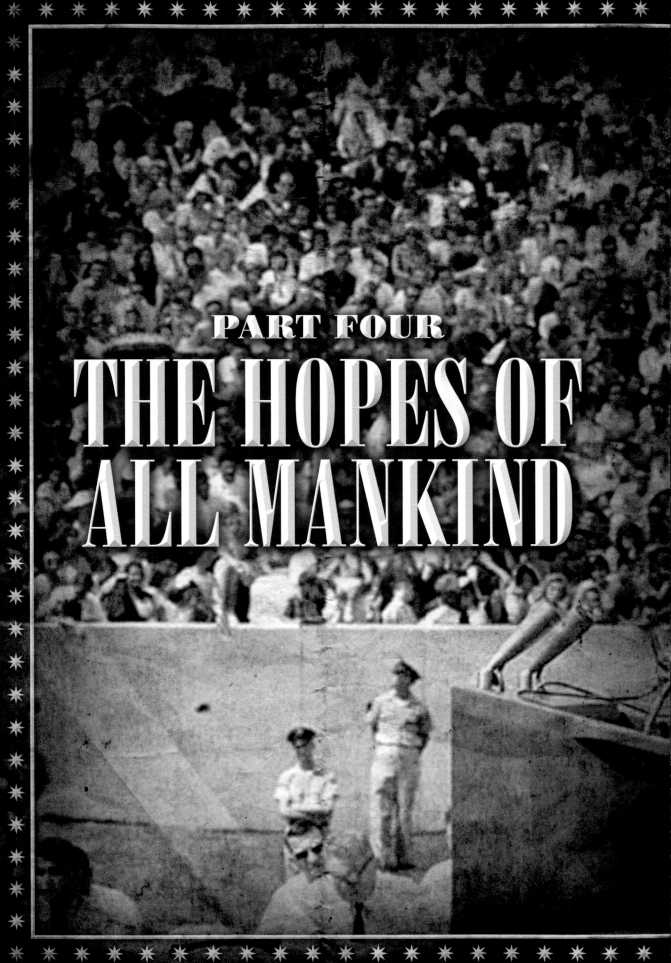

PART FOUR

THE HOPES OF ALL MANKIND

Mankind must put an end to war or war will put an end to mankind.

John F. Kennedy, September 25, 1961
Speech to the United Nations

CHAPTER 14

FIDEL CASTRO AND THE BAY OF PIGS

★ ★ ★ ★ ★ ★ ★ ★ ★ ★ ★ ★

THE BAY OF PIGS

Between April 15 and 20, 1961, a CIA-sponsored paramilitary group—Brigade 2506—led a covert United States military invasion of Cuba to overthrow the communist regime of Fidel Castro. President John F. Kennedy gave the invasion operational approval.

The plan to overthrow Castro was first devised within the CIA in early 1960 under US President Dwight D. Eisenhower. On November 18, 1960, president-elect Kennedy was briefed by Allen Dulles, head of the CIA and his deputy, Richard M. Bissell Jr. (1909 – 94) on an early outline proposal to land anti-Castro, Cuban counter-revolutionaries on Cuban soil and incite an uprising against Castro.

Kennedy had been a long-standing critic of Eisenhower's policy toward Cuba, believing his administration had not done enough to stop Castro. Now that there was a plan of action, he was hardly in a position to refuse.

In all his meetings with the CIA, Kennedy insisted that this would be an operation involving Cuban exiles only. Dulles and Bissell were certain, however, that if the operation looked as if it was not going to succeed, Kennedy would surely intervene with American troops.

Cuban leader Fidel Castro rallies armed revolutionaries, Havana, Cuba, April 16, 1961.

MILITARY-SPEAK MIX-UP

The Joint Chiefs of Staff (JCS) were asked for an evaluation of the operation but they failed to complete the analysis due to missing top-secret information. Their report stated that "the plan has a fair chance of ultimate success," which meant in military-speak that the plan could just as easily fail.

Instead of understanding this as a warning of failure, Kennedy took it as a signal to go ahead with it. What he did not know, however, was that the JCS assessment was based on the original plan that had required both US air and naval support.

The new plan was ill-judged and poorly executed. The CIA had long avoided government supervision and Kennedy's administration was not big on that kind of thing. So, the final plan slipped through without proper analysis and review.

* * * * * *

PRESIDENT UNDER PRESSURE

There is little doubt, too, that Dulles and Bissell overestimated the anticipated response of the anti-Castro fighters. Initially, the plan had the invading force landing at Trinidad in Cuba, a spot that allowed easy access to the mountains. But instead they chose the Bay of Pigs, a couple of hours to the north, a sparsely populated, marshy area that made dispersal of the troops difficult.

Pressure was put on Kennedy. The CIA insisted that the force could only be held together for a short time. If it were dispersed without the invasion taking place the Kennedy administration could suffer considerable criticism. It would appear to the public that his pronouncements on fighting communism were no more than hot air.

Kennedy believed that everyone understood what he wanted. He had unequivocally stated that he wanted it made clear to the Cuban exile invasion force that:

US strike forces would not be allowed to participate in or support the invasion in any way.

SCALING BACK THE BOMBERS

On April 15, 1961, eight B-52 bombers, flown by Cuban pilots who had taken off from Nicaragua, attacked three Cuban airfields but only a few of Cuba's 36 combat planes were destroyed. Kennedy had reduced the number of aircraft involved and fearful of a negative reaction to what would be seen as direct US involvement, also cancelled a dawn air strike on the day of the invasion.

Nonetheless, the B-52s could have come from nowhere but the United States. As soon as Kennedy scaled back the number of bombers, the CIA knew that the entire mission was doomed as the operation only had half the forces it needed.

* * * * * *

INVADING CUBA

On the night of April 16, the main invasion force of Brigade 2506 landed at a beach named Playa Girón in the Bay of Pigs, initially overwhelming local resistance. But Castro threw his revolutionary communist forces against the invasion, taking control of the battle and blocking the invaders. The covert US involvement soon became clear to the world, and to avoid further public embarrassment, Kennedy decided against providing any further military back-up.

By midday on April 18, 1961, the invasion force was in serious trouble, pinned down by Castro's forces. There were repeated demands for Kennedy to deploy US forces, but he refused. On April 20, the Cuban invaders surrendered after only three days of fighting.

* * * * * *

STRONGER THAN EVER

It was a disaster—114 of Brigade 2506 lost their lives and 1,189 were captured with the majority being publicly interrogated and put into Cuban prisons. A report subsequently blamed the CIA for the fiasco:

The Agency became so wrapped up in the military operation that it failed to appraise the chances of success realistically.

Kennedy took the blame, however, stating in a press release that he accepted full responsibility. Although he had little choice in the matter, it was a wise move and it gained him sympathy and support.

At the end of the Bay of Pigs operation, Kennedy's approval rating rocketed to an astonishing 83 percent. However, instead of removing the Cuban leader, the president had managed to make Fidel Castro even stronger than ever.

* * * * * *
DULLES AND BISSELL DEPART

For Dulles and Bissell, it was the end of their CIA careers. Dulles resigned in the autumn of that year after a series of failures and Bissell resigned in February 1962. As Kennedy said to Bissell:

> *In a parliamentary government, I'd have to resign. But in this government I can't, so you and Allen have to go.*

The failure of the operation concerned many who wondered about the new president's competency. But Kennedy learned a lot from the experience, especially with regard to the CIA and the JCS and how much he could trust them. This skepticism would prove beneficial during the Cuban Missile Crisis of 1962. Work to bring down Castro continued, however, with a series of clandestine operations.

* * * * * *
THE CUBAN PROJECT

General Edward Lansdale (1908 – 87) had sought the ambassadorship of Vietnam, but the President did not give it to him. Instead, he placed him in command of the "Cuban Project," part of which was known as Operation Mongoose. It was a covert operation devised by the CIA but controlled, to the dismay of the Joint Chiefs of Staff, by Bobby Kennedy.

Its objective was to incite "a revolt which can take place in Cuba by October 1962." Based in Miami, Lansdale was given a budget of $50 million, 400 CIA personnel and a small navy. Thousands of Cuban exiles were enlisted to be ferried back and forward to the island to commit acts of sabotage, spread propaganda, and gather intelligence.

MRBM FIELD LAUNCH SITE
SAN CRISTOBAL NO 1
14 OCTOBER 1962

ERECTOR/LAUNCHER EQUIPMENT

TENT AREAS

EQUIPMENT

ERECTOR/LAUNCHER EQUIPMENT

8 MISSILE TRAILERS

CONSTRUCTI

One of the first images of missile bases under construction in Cuba, shown to President Kennedy on the morning of October 16, 1962.

Thirty-three plans were assembled that covered a wide range of options to undermine the Cuban government and economy. Some of the plans used US Army Special Forces to mine harbors, and destroy the Cuban sugarcane crop. To help eliminate the Cuban leader, they enlisted the Mafia, whose Cuban casino operations Castro had seized.

* * * * * *

HOW TO KILL CASTRO

During Operation Mongoose, the CIA cooked-up many ideas to assassinate Fidel Castro. One used a ballpoint pen that was rigged up with a hypodermic needle. Others included poisoning his favorite cigars with botulinus toxin, and positioning explosive seashells in his favorite diving spots. There were also plans to contaminate Castro's clothing with thallium salts that would make his beard fall out, thus discrediting him in the eyes of his people.

However, by late August 1962, the Kennedy administration knew of the Soviet military build-up in Cuba. They also feared open Soviet intervention against America in Berlin in retaliation for US actions in Cuba.

By October 1962, the Cuban Missile Crisis was gathering momentum, and President Kennedy demanded the cessation of all CIA agitation.

* * * * * *

THE CUBAN MISSILE CRISIS

The Cuban Missile Crisis was a confrontation between the United States and the Soviet Union that ran from October 16 to October 28, 1962. American Jupiter-2 ballistic missiles had been stationed in both Italy and Turkey within range of the Soviet Union. As a result the Kremlin deployed ballistic missiles in Cuba in retaliation.

The crisis that developed was the most serious of President Kennedy's time in office. In fact, with the future of the world in the balance, it may well have been the most serious crisis faced by any occupant of the Oval Office.

The Soviet Union decided to station nuclear missiles, IL-28 bombers, and around 50,000 troops in Cuba. Russia had a fairly limited first-strike capability and this was Khrushchev's way of leveling the playing field. He planned to put 48 medium-range and 32 intermediate-range missiles in Cuba and bolster those with the bombers which were capable of carrying atomic bombs.

* * * * * *

EYEBALL TO EYEBALL

The Soviets hoped with this move to diminish the chance of an American first strike. They also calculated that it would stop the Americans from launching an invasion of Cuba. They believed that Kennedy would launch an invasion for political expediency around the time of the midterm elections as Kennedy's presidency was unlikely to survive into a second term.

With Kennedy's authorization, the head of Strategic Air Command gave the order to his forces to move to DEFCOM 2, the level just below being at war. The fear was that the Soviets might respond to the blockade with a first strike. But Khrushchev's nerve gave out first. On October 24, six Russian ships that had been bound for Cuba stopped or turned round. Secretary of State Dean Rusk famously said, "We're eyeball to eyeball, and the other fellow just blinked."

On October 26, further aerial surveillance showed that the Russians were working frenetically to complete the installation of the missiles in Cuba. A mobile missile launcher was also spotted. It suddenly seemed possible that there were already tactical nuclear missiles on Cuban soil. This would make an invasion even riskier.

* * * * * *

UNTYING THE KNOT

But while Kennedy was weighing up his options, he received a letter from the Soviet premier. It was long and emotional, drawing on the horrors of the Soviet experience during the Second World War. At one point he said that it was as if the two of them were pulling on a knot that could conceivably become too tight to unfasten:

> ... *let us not only relax the forces pulling on the ends of the knot, let us take measures to untie the knot.*

Khrushchev's letter contained indications that the crisis could be brought to a peaceful conclusion if the United States publicly promised not to invade Cuba in which case the USSR would withdraw its weapons and its ships. The details of the letter were officially confirmed by the head of the KGB—

U-2 DRAGON LADY

The Lockheed U-2, nicknamed "Dragon Lady," is a high-altitude jet aircraft first flown as a spy plane by the CIA, and now operated by the US Air Force (USAF). The U-2 was involved in many Cold War spying missions over the Soviet Union, China, Vietnam, and Cuba, providing high-altitude intelligence, surveillance and reconnaissance (ISR).

In 1960, CIA agent Gary Powers (1929 – 77) was shot down in a U-2C over the Soviet Union, and during the Cuban Missile Crisis, Major Rudolf Anderson (1927 – 62) was shot down over eastern Cuba in a U-2F spy plane.

Anderson was the only American to be killed by enemy fire during that crisis in 1962.

The "Dragon Lady" has served America well during the 50 years its various models have been in service. The current model, the U-2S, had its most recent technical upgrade in 2012. Reaching speeds of more than 475 mph, the U-2 has been used as "eyes in the sky" over Afghanistan and Iraq, and has supported several NATO operations with military intelligence photographed from 70,000 feet (21,336 m), twice the height of commercial airlines.

A U-2 Dragon Lady preparing for take-off on the flight deck of the aircraft carrier USS *America* (CV-66).

the Russians' main security agency—in Washington. Of course, it could have been a trick to buy time for the Soviets to complete the building of the missile bases.

A second letter from Khrushchev arrived. This one demanded the removal of the US missiles from Turkey as well as a commitment to not invading Cuba. It was a smart move as the mutual withdrawal of weapons would appear to the outside world to be a reasonable thing to do. Kennedy worried about Berlin, too. Would the Soviets use an American invasion of Cuba as an excuse to march into Berlin?

* * * * * *

BLACK SATURDAY

October 27, 1962, has become known as "Black Saturday." On that day the Americans and the Russians were on the brink of a nuclear exchange—the closest the world has come to such a catastrophe.

To begin with, a U-2 spy plane was shot down over Cuba and another was tracked by Soviet fighters, having strayed into Soviet air space while engaged in a mission over the Arctic. A letter arrived in Moscow in which Cuban leader, Fidel Castro, pleaded with the Kremlin to launch a pre-emptive nuclear strike before the Americans could begin their invasion of his country.

The shooting down of the U-2 over Cuba infuriated the JCS to such an extent that they demanded that the president order immediate bombing of Cuba the following Monday, with an invasion of the island to be launched within seven days. Meanwhile, the United Kingdom placed its nuclear weapons on a fifteen minute alert.

* * * * * *

PALPABLE RELIEF

Khrushchev wrote a letter to be read on Moscow radio that spoke of the withdrawal of the missiles from Cuba in return for a pledge by the US not to invade. But he also secretly sent a message to Washington promising that he would not make public the removal of American weapons from Turkey. The relief at the White House was palpable when this message was received.

But the JCS was still agitating for military action, considering this move to be just another trick by the Russians. They declared that if there was no evidence by Monday that the missiles were being removed, their plan for air strikes and invasion should proceed.

Horrified by the attitude of the Joint Chiefs, Kennedy instead preferred to wait, retaining the blockade until he was sure that the Russian premier was keeping his promise. It took some time but on November 20, 1962, Kennedy announced that "all known offensive missile sites in Cuba have been dismantled."

The American Jupiter-2 ballistic missiles were quietly removed from Turkey a few months later and were never linked publicly to the Cuban crisis.

But scholars such as Noam Chomsky have commented that "terrorist operations continued through the tensest moments of the missile crisis," remarking that "they were formally canceled on October 30, several days after the Kennedy and Khrushchev agreement, but went on nonetheless." Operation Mongoose formally ceased its activities at the end of 1962.

* * * * * *

A STEEP LEARNING CURVE

Kennedy's handling of the Cuban Missile Crisis is what secured his future reputation. Some presidents have been viewed as great because of their military triumphs or because of their stalwart leadership of America through time of war. John F. Kennedy can be viewed as great because of the restraint he displayed during those difficult few weeks in October 1962.

He refused to be forced into the wrong decision by his hawkish generals and advisors, cannily playing a waiting game and forcing the Soviets to back down. Perhaps he was showing signs of maturing as a statesman. It had certainly been a steep learning curve, but he at last had his first real success as president.

FIDEL CASTRO

Fidel Alejandro Castro Ruz (1926 – 2016) was born into a prosperous sugarcane family in Southeastern Cuba. When he was 19 years old, he attended the School of Law in Havana, but his main interest was politics. In 1947, he was part of a failed attempt to overthrow the president of the Dominican Republic, General Rafael Trujillo (1891 – 1961).

After graduating, Castro practiced law and joined the Cuban People's Party, becoming their candidate for a seat in the Cuban House of Representatives in 1952. Before the election, however, US-backed electoral candidate Fulgencio Batista Zaldívar (1901 – 73) seized power in a military coup and the election was canceled.

Having failed to unseat Batista from power by legal means, Castro assembled a rebel force but was arrested in July 1953 and sentenced to fifteen years imprisonment. A political amnesty released him in 1955.

The rebels formed the 26th of July Movement, waging an urban and rural guerrilla war against Batista's repressive US-funded regime. Eventually, on New Year's Day 1959, 2,000 rebels under the command of Che Guevara defeated Batista's 30,000-strong army at the Battle of Santa Clara. Castro assumed military and political power as Cuba's Prime Minister.

Castro pursued radical policies, nationalizing industry, and seizing agricultural estates and American businesses. America broke diplomatic ties in 1961 and tried to bring down Castro with the catastrophic Bay of Pigs invasion in April 1961. The acquisition of weapons from the Soviet Union brought the world to the brink of nuclear war in 1962 with the Cuban Missile Crisis.

For almost the next five decades, Castro ruled Cuba, ruthlessly suppressing political dissent but expanding the island's educational and health services, and guaranteeing full employment. The economy stalled, however, in the face of sanctions imposed by the United States. Becoming increasingly frail, Castro passed power to his brother Raul in 2006, and died in 2016, at the age of 89.

CHE GUEVARA

Ernesto "Che" Guevara de la Serna (1928-67) was born into a middle-class family in Rosario, Argentina. He studied medicine, but after seeing terrible poverty during a holiday he spent in Latin America, he concluded that the only way to change society was through violent revolution.

He became a Marxist while living in Guatemala in 1953, and began to champion worldwide revolution after the CIA helped to overthrow the progressive Guatemalan government of Jacobo Arbenz.

He first met the Castro brothers—Fidel and Raul—in Mexico and became a member of the 26th of July Movement that they had founded to oust President Batista of Cuba. After the Cuban Revolution had put Castro into power, Guevara took Cuban citizenship and became prominent in the government.

After 1965, however, he disappeared from public life, traveling to the Democratic Republic of the Congo with other freedom fighters in an unsuccessful attempt to help in the civil war being fought there. Around this time, he resigned from the government and renounced his Cuban citizenship.

He next turned up in Bolivia, incognito, where he created and led a guerrilla group in the area of Santa Cruz. Initially successful, soon he and his band were put to flight and in October 1967 they were soundly beaten by the Bolivian army helped by CIA advisors.

Guevara was wounded in the attack and captured. On October 9, 1967, he was executed, his hands were cut off and preserved in formaldehyde so that his fingerprints could be used to confirm his identity. Ironically, after he died, "Che" became an even bigger force for revolution, his iconic image inspiring those on the left for decades to come.

CHAPTER 15

KHRUSHCHEV AND THE BERLIN WALL

On January 6, 1961, Nikita Khrushchev had delivered a speech at a closed meeting at the Kremlin to a gathering of party theoreticians and propagandists. It was an expression of the doctrine of the Communist Party and made it clear that the Soviet Union wanted to spread communism across the world.

He said the acceptance of disarmament and peaceful coexistence was no more than a tactic in the battle to establish world dominance. In the speech he boasted:

> [There is] no force on earth now able to prevent the peoples of more and more countries from advancing to socialism.

Khrushchev assured his audience that the power of the socialist nations would prevent the "imperialists" from starting a world war. But the Soviet Union would wholeheartedly support wars of national liberation. He said that the policy of peaceful coexistence worked to the advantage of the socialists in that it:

> ... promotes the development of the forces of progress, the forces fighting for socialism; and in the capitalist countries it facilitates the work of the Communist parties.

* * * * * *

TIME TO TALK

Kennedy had criticized Eisenhower for not initiating talks with the Soviets, but having just experienced a serious failure of his own with the Bay of Pigs, he was unsure if now was the right time to talk to Khrushchev. A meeting was organized, however, for June 4, 1961 in Vienna. In a congratulatory message after Kennedy won the presidency, Khrushchev had told him that he wished to negotiate on a range of issues:

> disarmament ... a German peace treaty ... and other questions which could bring about an easing and improvement of the entire international situation.

Credibility was at stake for each leader. After the Bay of Pigs, Kennedy needed to reaffirm to the American people his promised tough stance against communism. For Khrushchev it was a matter of dispelling the Chinese belief that his attempts to maintain peaceful coexistence with the West were a betrayal of the principals of the revolution.

Khrushchev also needed to come to some kind of agreement on Berlin, where East German leader Walter Ulbricht had demanded measures to stop his best people fleeing to the West through the city. For Kennedy, however, Berlin was key to the whole of Europe and he did not want in any way to diminish the West's authority in the city.

Khrushchev was determined to solve the Berlin problem within the next six months. He signed a peace treaty with the East German government and the city was sealed off to prevent refugees from escaping to the West. The West, he believed, was as hesitant as Kennedy to initiate a war and they would do nothing, he calculated. German re-unification—an aspiration of the West—would be forever put on hold and NATO would be damaged, the United States' intentions distrusted.

NIKITA KHRUSHCHEV

Nikita Sergeyevich Khrushchev (1894 – 1971) was born into a poor family in the village of Kalinovka, in southwest Russia. When he was 14, he became an apprentice metal-fitter, and later worked in a mine in Rutchenkovo.

In 1917, after the abdication of Tsar Nicholas II, Khrushchev was elected to the Rutchenkovo worker's council, or *soviet*, and soon became chairman. He joined the Bolshevik Party in 1918 and served in the Red Army during the Russian Civil War. In 1921, he was assigned as assistant director for political affairs to the Rutchenkovo mine. In mid-1925 he attended the 14th Congress of the USSR Communist party in Moscow.

He began to rise through the party ranks and became a close associate of Stalin, playing a part in the Great Purge in which millions of Russians were executed or sent to the Gulag labor camps. He returned to the Ukraine in 1937 as head of the Communist Party there, and following his arrival the pace of the purge accelerated.

During the Second World War, Khrushchev served on many fronts, used by Stalin to keep his commanders under tight control. On returning to Ukraine in 1943, he found it devastated by the occupying Germans. He began the work of rebuilding the region. In 1949, he was recalled to Moscow, serving as head of the Moscow Party.

Following Stalin's death in 1953, Khrushchev became leader of the Soviet Union but took several years to consolidate his position. In 1956, at the 20th Party Congress, he delivered the "Secret Speech," revealing Stalin's crimes for the first time, and began a process called "de-Stalinization." He improved living standards, traveled to the West, and invested in the space program, but always kept a tight grip on power in the Kremlin.

But in 1962, facing Kennedy, he backed down over the Cuban Missile Crisis. Party officials were dismayed and, along with some years of poor economic growth and poor relations with China, his enemies had the opportunity to depose him.

Khrushchev served as Soviet Premier until October 14, 1964, but was retired by the party due to his advanced age and poor health. He was given an apartment in Moscow and a villa in the countryside. He died seven years later of heart disease, at the age of 77, on September 11, 1971.

Premier Nikita Khrushchev of the Soviet Union and President John F. Kennedy at the Vienna Summit, June 4, 1961.

THE VIENNA SUMMIT

Kennedy met Khrushchev at the United States ambassador's residence in Vienna and the two leaders spent time together discussing Berlin.

Khrushchev explained the threat that the USSR believed a united Germany would represent. He told Kennedy of the Soviet wish to sign a separate peace treaty with East Germany. If the USA did not support this, the USSR would do it anyway. Kennedy responded that US forces had a right to be there having been on the winning side in the war, saying:

> We are in Berlin not by agreement with the East Germans, but by contractual rights.

President Kennedy told Khrushchev that if he was to remove American troops from Berlin "no one would have any confidence in US commitments and pledges." Kennedy pointed out that signing such a treaty would violate the agreement signed by the four powers at the end of the war.

Khrushchev replied that when the USSR signed the treaty, post-war agreement would be invalidated. He insisted that Berlin should belong to East Germany and, anyway, America would still be occupying West Germany. Kennedy said this was unacceptable but Khrushchev was not backing down from his demand for a treaty.

The only tangible outcome of the Vienna Summit was that Khrushchev finally agreed that a neutral and independent Laos was advantageous to both parties, and the countries agreed a cease-fire.

* * * * * *

THE BERLIN CRISIS

Kennedy became obsessed with the issue of Berlin. He asked ex-Secretary of State Acheson to outline what actions the United States could take. Along with the JCS, he was supportive of a military build-up to emphasize to Moscow how seriously Washington took the situation.

Plans were made to supply Berlin by air as had happened during the Berlin Airlift in 1948 and Kennedy made a televised address to the American people in which he announced

further spending on defense and increased the size of the army to a million men. He said of Berlin:

> Today, the endangered frontier of freedom runs through divided Berlin. We want it to remain a frontier of peace. This is the hope of every citizen of the Atlantic Community; every citizen of Eastern Europe; and, I am confident, every citizen of the Soviet Union. For I cannot believe that the Russian people—who bravely suffered enormous losses in the Second World War—would now wish to see the peace upset once more in Germany. The Soviet government alone can convert Berlin's frontier of peace into a pretext for war.

* * * * * *

BUILDING THE WALL

A couple of weeks later, the East Germans took action. Early on the morning of Sunday, August 13, 1961, barriers were thrown across all the roads between East and West Berlin.

What pleased the Kennedy administration, was it proved that Khrushchev was not planning to seize the whole city, which would undoubtedly have resulted in war. "A wall is a whole lot better than a war," as Kennedy said at the time. Acceptance of the wall was difficult and Kennedy had to reassure the other NATO powers that he was still committed to their security.

Heightening the tension was a Soviet resumption of nuclear arms tests, forcing Kennedy against his will—he had called for a test ban agreement—to resume underground testing. He could not back down again, as he told Adlai Stevenson who hesitated at the renewed nuclear activity. For his part, Khrushchev believed that the only thing Americans responded to was military strength.

* * * * * *

MANKIND MUST END WAR

Many pushed Kennedy to take retaliatory measures but he knew that there was only one outcome in that case—nuclear war. US nuclear capability was superior and Kennedy knew he could lay waste to the Soviet Union, but America would probably have around 15 million fatalities and Western Europe would suffer tens of millions.

Eventually, at a dinner in New York on September 24, 1961, a message from Khrushchev was passed from Soviet delegate Mikhail Kharmalov to Kennedy's press secretary Pierre Salinger (1925 – 2004)—"The storm in Berlin is over." The following day, Kennedy gave a speech to the United Nations in which he said, "mankind must put an end to war or war will put an end to mankind." He challenged the Soviet Union to a peace race rather than an arms race.

But the end of 1961 was a difficult time for the Kennedy family. Now 73, Joe Kennedy Sr. was victim to a massive stroke on December 9. It left him paralyzed down his left side and unable to talk although he remained mentally alert and managed to regain some functions with therapy. However, by this time, there was no one left who thought the old man might still be the power behind the throne.

NUCLEAR TEST BAN

In December 1962, Khrushchev proposed to Kennedy that they could progress nuclear test ban talks by accepting on-site inspections of their respective weapons. But Kennedy was concerned about the Senate's reaction to it and worried that it was unlikely to satisfy the more hawkish among them.

The two countries continued to talk about a test ban into 1963. Kennedy sent the veteran diplomat, Averell Harriman to Moscow as a special envoy, hoping that his presence would smooth the wheels of diplomacy, as he had been US ambassador to the Soviet Union during the Second World War when the two nations had a common purpose. It was also a sign of how eager Kennedy was to make an agreement happen.

The nuclear club was increasing its membership with both China and France about to acquire nuclear capability and Kennedy was keen to sign an agreement before that happened. Meanwhile, Kennedy delivered

POST-WAR BERLIN

By the end of the Second World War, up to a third of Berlin had been destroyed by Allied air raids, Soviet shelling, and fighting on the streets, as the Allies advanced into the city. At midnight on May 8, 1945—"zero hour"—the city was divided into four sections, each controlled by one of the Allied powers.

The Russians had initially occupied all of Berlin and only handed over the various sectors to the other powers in July 1945. In the intervening period, between May and July, they dismantled industry and infrastructure in West Berlin as war reparations from Germany. Even railway tracks were removed. At the time conditions were tough, especially as hundreds of thousands of refugees were flooding into the city from the east. A black market for food and other necessities thrived in the city as people struggled to survive.

The city was governed by the Four Power Allied Control Council, leadership of which rotated among the four Allied powers on a monthly basis. However, as relations between the USSR and the West deteriorated, the Soviets withdrew from this council and governed the eastern zone independently of the others.

When East Germany was formed in October 1949, East Berlin was chosen to be capital of the new state in opposition to the views of Great Britain, France, and the United States. They saw Berlin as an occupied city that was not part of any country. West Germany had been created in May 1949 and its capital located in Bonn.

On June 24, 1948, the Soviet Union blocked access to West Berlin, beginning the Berlin Blockade. A huge logistical effort was put together to supply the city. The Berlin Airlift, as it was called, lasted for a year.

In 1961 the Berlin Wall was built across the city to prevent East Germans from escaping into the West. It remained there until the collapse of East Germany in 1990.

President John F. Kennedy on the steps of Rathaus Schöneberg, Berlin, June 26, 1963.

Ich bin ein Berliner

President John F. Kennedy's "Ich bin ein Berliner" (I am a Berliner) speech is considered among his finest and one of the best in American history. Kennedy used the phrase twice in his speech, together with a phonetically written out note of the German pronunciation—"ish bin ein Bearleener,"—to make sure he got it right.

Two thousand years ago, the proudest boast was "civis romanus sum" [I am a Roman citizen]. Today, in the world of freedom, the proudest boast is "Ich bin ein Berliner!"... All free men, wherever they may live, are citizens of Berlin, and therefore, as a free man, I take pride in the words "Ich bin ein Berliner!"

his famous "Peace Speech" at the American University on June 9, 1963 In it he reiterated that nuclear disarmament was essential to the survival of the planet.

Kennedy's problem was the reaction in Europe to any kind of test ban treaty. France, about to become a nuclear power, would be opposed and Germany was very worried about it. To help, almost two years after the construction of the Berlin Wall, Kennedy went to West Berlin on a visit that would go down in history.

On June 26, 1963, almost half a million Berliners gathered to hear him speak from a platform erected on the steps of Rathaus Schöneberg. He declared "Ich bin ein Berliner," expressing his solidarity with the West German people, who stood right on the front line of the Cold War. A clear statement of intent to the Soviet Union as well as to the rest of the world.

* * * * * *

MAN OF PEACE

It was not likely that a comprehensive test ban treaty would be achieved. A limited treaty was agreed, therefore. Still, conservatives rejected the treaty, seeing it as a sign of weakness and no Republican would agree to attend the signing.

On July 26, 1963, Kennedy addressed the nation, explaining that the treaty, limited though it was, pushed the risk of nuclear conflagration further away. Meanwhile, he told the military top brass that their research facilities were safe and that he viewed the treaty as something to deepen the gulf between the Russians and the Chinese.

The treaty was overwhelmingly ratified by the Senate on September 24, 1963, and to the public it once again appeared that Kennedy had made the Soviets retreat to a position they had not initially wanted. To the American public he was the man who ensured peace for them.

Ultimately, nuclear proliferation continued unabated despite this treaty. Within a few years, India, Israel, and Pakistan had joined the group of powers that had nuclear weapons at their disposal.

PIERRE SALINGER

Pierre Emil George Salinger (1925 – 2004) was born in San Francisco to a mining engineer father and a French-born journalist mother. His maternal grandfather had been a member of the French National Assembly. After attending San Francisco State University, he enlisted in the US Navy in 1943, becoming commanding officer of a submarine chaser in the Pacific.

Completing his studies after the war he worked as a journalist at the *San Francisco Chronicle*. Salinger was an important figure in Kennedy's presidential campaign and when Kennedy became president, he was appointed as his press secretary. Following the assassination, he was retained as President Johnson's press secretary.

At the end of his time in the White House, he ran for the senate in California, defeating California State Controller Alan Cranston (1914 – 2000) in an angry primary. When the incumbent, Clair Engle (1911 – 64), died, Salinger was appointed Senator by the Governor but he was defeated in the election later in 1964 by former Vaudeville song and dance man George Murphy (1902 – 92).

Salinger went on to help manage Robert Kennedy's campaign for the Democratic Party nomination in 1968. He was so devastated by his assassination that he moved to France and resumed his career in journalism as a correspondent for *L'Express*, becoming a popular pundit on French television.

He next worked as a television commentator for ABC Sports and as ABC's Paris Bureau Chief before moving back to Washington to work in public relations. Before the 2000 presidential election he said "If [George] Bush wins, I'm going to leave the country and spend the rest of my life in France." He was as good as his word. Pierre Salinger died in Le Thor in France in 2004, at the age of 79.

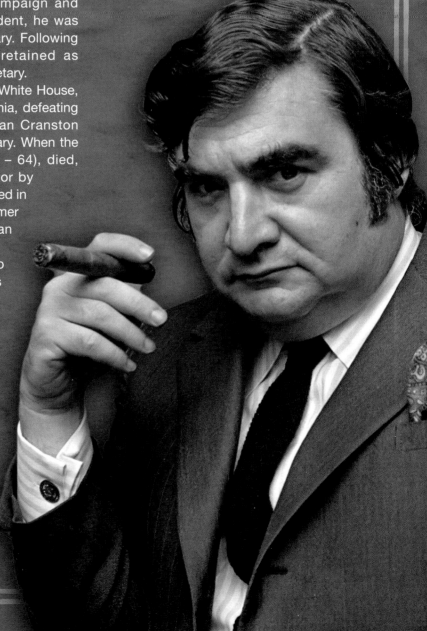

CHAPTER 16

LIGHTING UP THE WORLD

WE CHOOSE TO GO TO THE MOON

Kennedy delivered an unofficial State of the Union address that was full of hope and optimism to a joint session of Congress on May 25, 1961, hoping to restore confidence in his damaged administration after the Bay of Pigs invasion. He emphasized the danger that America faced at that time and said he would be asking for an increase of $700 million in defense expenditure.

He also announced that America should land a man on the moon before the end of the decade. The first US manned space flight had taken place just a few months before, but it was evident that America had fallen behind the Soviet Union in the space race. He famously said:

> *First, I believe that this nation should commit itself to achieving the goal, before this decade is out, of landing a man on the moon and returning him safely to the earth.*

PROBLEMS BEGIN TO GROW

But behind the optimism of the public face, the atmosphere was tense and the president was gloomy as problems mounted up around him. So on May 31, 1961, when he landed at Orly airport outside Paris, on his way to the Vienna Summit, two days after his forty-fourth birthday, Kennedy was not a happy man.

African Americans were being beaten up in city streets as civil rights unrest exploded. The credibility of his presidency had been dented almost before it had started by the poor decision-making of the Bay of Pigs catastrophe. Moreover he was finding it increasingly impossible to control Congress and his domestic plans were getting lost in endless committees. To make matters worse, his back problems had recurred and in private he was again using crutches.

He was taking a wide range of medication, notably procaine for his back and corticosteroids for his Addison's. His sexual exploits aggravated the chance of urinary infections to which he was vulnerable because of the corticosteroids which inhibited his immune system.

TRAVELING WITH DR. FEELGOOD

Ancillary to the President's own medical staff, Dr. Max Jacobson (1900 – 79), a German-born New York physician known as "Miracle Max" or "Dr. Feelgood," traveled with the Presidential entourage to the Vienna Summit in 1961.

Jacobson was a renowned "doctor to the stars," administering amphetamines and other medications to high-profile clients. His "miracle tissue regenerator" shots consisted of amphetamines, animal hormones, bone marrow, enzymes, human placenta, painkillers, steroids, and multivitamins.

But the injections had numerous side-effects including hyperactivity, impaired judgment, nervousness, and wild mood swings. Jacobson gave Kennedy frequent miracle shots to combat his back pain. When questioned about it, the President replied: "I don't care if it's horse piss. It works."

By May 1962, Jacobson had visited Kennedy at the White House thirty-four times. Many suggested that Kennedy's leadership and judgment improved after Jacobson's treatments were blocked by presidential physicians who had realized the inappropriate use of steroids and amphetamines.

* * * * * *

THE DAILY ROUTINE

Kennedy's first year in the White House ended in January 1962. It had been even tougher than he imagined and had taken its toll. Jacqueline Kennedy recalled him crying when the Bay of Pigs operation failed. The only time she had seen him in a worse state was when he had undergone back surgery. His days were full, typically starting with the newspapers early in the morning before a National Security briefing. Then it was the Oval Office for whatever meetings and phone calls had been entered in his diary.

He took a brief respite in the afternoon, often going for a swim in the White House pool with a couple of girls nicknamed Fiddle and Faddle from the White house staff, with each of whom he is said to have had an affair. In the evening, he would spend some time with his children and, if there were no dinners or receptions to attend, he worked on into the night.

* * * * * *

THE ALLIANCE FOR PROGRESS

Kennedy was certain that the USSR was going to target Latin America in its efforts for global domination through communism. In March 1961, he unveiled the Alliance for Progress, an attempt to initiate economic cooperation between the United States and the nations of Latin America. Kennedy said:

… we propose to complete the revolution of the Americas, to build a hemisphere where all men can hope for a suitable standard of living and all can live out their lives in dignity and in freedom … Let us once again awaken our American revolution until it guides the

struggles of people everywhere—not with an imperialism of force or fear but the rule of courage and freedom and hope for the future of man.

The United States provided $20 billion in aid that, it was hoped, would transform the region and bring political and economic reform. This was a huge change from the Eisenhower administration's attitude toward Latin America where some of the most autocratic rulers were applauded. In reality, not much changed regarding the styles of government and many autocratic rulers were accepted and supported by the US government.

Ultimately, the Alliance for Progress failed. There were some gains in education and healthcare provision but even these were no match for the growth in population. The political reform did not last and military juntas were back by the end of the decade. In fact, Kennedy's view became that although a democratic government was desirable, if there had to be a military or autocratic government that kept the communists at bay then that was just as acceptable.

* * * * * *

THE ECONOMY

Kennedy was the first post-war US President to face a decline in American economic power. During his campaign, he had promised economic recovery but there was the danger of the dollar having to be devalued, something he would not countenance. The country had a balance of payments problem that arose out of US commitments around the world, especially in Europe where it had to maintain military bases. Kennedy was forced to ask European allies to share more of the burden of defense. Germany did this by purchasing arms and providing aid to developing countries.

To promote trade, Kennedy asked Congress for permission to negotiate tariff reductions. It was hoped that free trade would help to inspire innovation and thus result in higher productivity but many businesses worried that they would have no protection from cheap foreign imports.

THE PEACE CORPS

The notion of establishing volunteer operations in developing countries was not a new one. While still in the House of Representatives in 1951, John F. Kennedy said, "young college graduates would find a full life in bringing technical advice and assistance to the underprivileged and backward Middle East … In that calling, these men would follow the constructive work done by the religious missionaries in these countries over the past 100 years."

In 1952, Connecticut Senator Brien McMahon (1903 – 52) proposed the creation of an army of young Americans who would act as "missionaries of democracy." In the next decade many young Americans did, indeed, go abroad to provide help, sent by privately funded non-religious organizations.

Kennedy is most often credited with the creation of the Peace Corps during his presidency, but Senator Hubert Humphrey was actually the first to propose its establishment, introducing the first bill on the subject in 1957. Only in 1959, however, did the idea really begin to be taken seriously when a non-governmental study was initiated.

Kennedy talked of what he called the Peace Corps during his 1960 presidential campaign but his opponent Richard Nixon suggested it would become a "cult of escapism" and "a haven for draft dodgers." It was based on Operation Crossroads for Africa, founded by the Reverend James H. Robinson in 1958 to build links between North Africa and the United States.

On March 1, 1961, Kennedy signed Executive Order 10924 establishing the Peace Corps. He put his brother-in-law Sargent Shriver in charge and it began recruiting in July 1962. The Peace Corps now works in 68 countries around the world.

President Kennedy greets Peace Corps volunteers on the White House South Lawn, August 9, 1962.

HOSTILE TO BUSINESS

US producers might be undercut by cheap labor and mass production and this would make the situation with the trade balance even worse. Unfortunately for Kennedy, the benefits from liberalized trade agreements did not accrue. Meanwhile, defense spending was being increased as were deployments of American forces overseas and his problems were only getting worse.

Many began to see Kennedy as hostile to business, a perception that was heightened by his clashes with American steel manufacturers. Kennedy had championed the idea of maintaining a balance between prices and wages in industry.

In keeping with this policy, Secretary of Labor, Arthur Goldberg (1908 – 90) put pressure on the steelworkers' union to accept only a 2.5 percent increase in benefits but US Steel announced a price hike of 3.5 percent, a tactic copied by other steel manufacturers.

* * * * * *

UNLEASHING THE ATTORNEY GENERAL

The president was furious, condemning the price rise as "a wholly unjustifiable and irresponsible defiance of the public interest." He set Bobby Kennedy, the Attorney General, on them, and within days the steel executives' offices were raided by the FBI. It was also made clear that the Inland Revenue would be looking into their personal financial arrangements.

Bobby Kennedy later said: "It was a tough way to operate. But under the circumstances, we couldn't afford to lose." It worked and soon the steel companies were announcing that they would not be increasing their prices to the extent declared previously.

Business leaders were, naturally, horrified, comparing Kennedy to Mussolini. But business confidence was undoubtedly badly damaged and the stock market suffered its worst one-day fall since the Crash of 1929. Kennedy was blamed and the right wing railed at government interference.

THE OTHER SENATOR KENNEDY

The world had been saved from a nuclear conflagration but not a lot really changed, apart from an even more profound distrust of the Russians. President Kennedy was now being pressured to ensure that the terms of the agreement between the United States and the USSR was honored.

The president had been worried about the impact his decisions would have on the midterm elections but the balance of power in Congress changed little. The Republicans gained two seats in the House and the Democrats four in the Senate. The batch of new senators included Kennedy's youngest brother, Edward Moore "Ted" Kennedy.

The president's handling of the crisis had done his party some good, and it also helped his personal standing which went up twelve points to 74 percent. There were some concerns, however, as the president was warned by pollsters. Many Catholics and Jews who had voted for him in 1960 were becoming increasingly Republican the longer they lived in the suburbs. And, like the white Southerners, they were not enamored of civil rights reforms.

On November 20, 1962, integrated federally supported housing had been brought into existence, thus keeping the promise he had made to African Americans while campaigning for the presidency, if a little late. Many white working class people saw advancements such as these coming at a cost to themselves.

* * * * * *

A SECOND TERM?

Who would Kennedy face when he stood for re-election in 1964? Richard Nixon looked an unlikely candidate this time. He had just lost in the election to be governor of California.

Liberal Republican, Nelson Rockefeller, was beginning to look like a good bet. He had just been re-elected governor of New York and had secured a lot of African American votes in doing so.

THE PRESIDENT'S OTHER WOMEN

President John F. Kennedy enjoyed a number of relationships with glamorous and beautiful women before he was married. Among many were the Danish journalist Inga Arvad, German actress and singer "Marlene" Dietrich, and the American actress, Gene Tierney (1920 – 91). Tierney was married to the costume and fashion designer, Oleg Cassini who ended up designing clothes for Jacqueline Kennedy, creating her "Jackie look."

Tierney met Kennedy in 1946 when he visited the set of the film *Dragonwyck* in which she was starring. They dated for a year but broke up after Kennedy informed her he could never marry her because of his political ambitions.

Being married didn't stop Kennedy having relationships with women other than his wife. Among these were Swedish aristocrat Gunilla von Post (1932 – 2011). She met Kennedy on the French Riviera a month before his wedding in 1953.

JUDITH EXNER

Judith Campbell Exner (1934 – 99) claimed in her 1977 memoir *Judith Exner: My Story*, to have been not only the mistress of President Kennedy, but also the mistress of Chicago Mafia bosses Sam Giancana (1908 – 75) and John Roselli (1905 – 76). Singer Frank Sinatra introduced her to Kennedy in Las Vegas during his presidential campaign and she claims to have had a two-year relationship with him.

MARY MEYER

Mary Pinchot Meyer (1920 – 64) was an American painter. After she visited Kennedy at the White House in October 1961, the two began a relationship. A psychologist, writer, and infamous advocate of LSD, she claimed she influenced Kennedy's views on nuclear disarmament and Cuba. A Kennedy aide said, "I think he might have thought more of her than some of the other women and discussed things that were on his mind, not just social gossip."

A close friend of the president described the serious nature of his relationship with Meyer:

> *That was a dangerous relationship. Jack was in love with Mary Meyer. He was certainly smitten with her, he was heavily smitten. He was very frank with me about it.*

The couple apparently met two or three times a week at the White House to which she would be chauffeured and then taken to a bedroom. She is reported to have smoked marijuana in a White House bedroom and is said to have recorded the affair in a diary. The CIA got hold of the diary and burned it after Meyer was murdered in Central Park in 1964. Some have claimed that Kennedy took LSD or Psilocybin with her.

Judith Exner.

MIMI ALFORD

Marion Fay "Mimi" Alford (née Beardsley, born 1943) was a 19-year-old White House intern when she was introduced to Kennedy by Dave Powers who asked her if she'd like to have a swim with the president in the White House swimming pool. Kennedy invited her to a drinks party that evening and while giving her a tour of the residence the two had sex in Jacqueline Kennedy's powder blue bedroom. Their affair lasted eighteen months.

FIDDLE AND FADDLE

Kennedy also had an affair with his wife's press secretary, and another two interns at the White House, Priscilla Ware and Jill Cowen, nicknamed "Fiddle" and "Faddle." His indiscretions created moral issues for the Secret Service agents who were protecting him. As one said:

> You were on the most elite assignment in the Secret Service, and you were there watching an elevator or a door because the president was inside with two hookers … It just didn't compute. Your neighbors and everybody thought you were risking your life, and you were actually out there to see that he's not disturbed while he's having an interlude in the shower with two gals from Twelfth Avenue.

MARILYN MONROE

Of course, his most famous dalliance is the alleged relationship with movie star Marilyn Monroe (1926 – 62). The seriousness of this relationship will never be known, but they are said to have spent a weekend together in March 1962 while Kennedy was staying at Bing Crosby's house in Palm Springs. There were numerous phone calls from her to the White House during 1962. Monroe's masseur, Ralph Roberts told her biographer, Donald Spoto:

Later, once the rumor mill was grinding, Marilyn told me that this night in March was the only time of her "affair" with JFK. Of course she was titillated beyond belief, because for a year he had been trying, through Lawford, to have an evening with her. A great many people thought, after that weekend, that there was more to it. But Marilyn gave me the impression that it was not a major event for either of them: it happened once, that weekend, and that was that.

Marilyn Monroe.

TAX REFORM

Right wing Republican Barry Goldwater would be the choice of the more conservative wing of the party and could be a real threat if white Southerners were upset about Kennedy's support for civil rights. Kennedy had to be careful, therefore, which causes he focused on in the coming months and would have to rein in some of his more liberal leanings.

To help him get re-elected would take a healthy economy and to that end, around the end of 1962, Kennedy was keen to introduce tax reforms that would grow the economy.

Many in both parties, however, would have no truck with tax cuts while there was still a deficit. They insisted on a balanced budget.

Kennedy presented it as being necessary to the security of the United States, taking the terminology of the Cold War into the economy. Prosperity was the only way, he reasoned, for America to be able to fight communism both in a military sense and in providing the world with the perception that the capitalist system was the better of the two. He used the 1963 State of the Union address to make his point but faced a mountain of opposition.

John F. Kennedy, 35th President of the United States in 1961.

CHAPTER 17

THE STRUGGLE FOR CIVIL RIGHTS

FIREBOMBING THE FREEDOM RIDERS

If things had been going badly for the Kennedy administration in foreign policy, it did not look much better on the home front. He had enjoyed success with the Area Redevelopment Act distributing federal aid to ten states that had been experiencing severe poverty.

But other initiatives on college scholarships, federal aid to education, health insurance for the elderly and measures for tax reform were all tied up at the committee stage, held back by the Southern congressmen who overwhelmingly populated these bodies.

Civil rights leaders inevitably criticized what appeared to them to be a lack of action by the new president who had promised so much. One of the main civil rights groups, the Congress of Racial Equality (CORE) initiated Freedom Rides in which Freedom Riders rode interstate buses in the South in mixed racial groups to test whether desegregation of buses and bus terminals—as ordered by the courts—had been complied with.

The organizers had anticipated a violent reaction to their initiative and on May 14, 1961, in Anniston, Alabama, a bus was firebombed by a gang of Ku Klux Klansmen. The riders only just managed to escape with their lives. An hour later, when a second bus arrived in Anniston, eight Klansmen boarded it and assaulted the Freedom Riders.

THE WORLD IS WATCHING

When they arrived in Birmingham they were attacked and beaten by another mob of Klansmen. A further attack took place in Montgomery, Alabama, on a bus carrying Martin Luther King Jr. The world watched on television, further damaging the Kennedy presidency.

Bobby Kennedy intervened in an effort to stop the violence, sending marshals to protect Martin Luther King Jr. in Montgomery and negotiated an armed escort for the Freedom Riders en route to Jackson, Mississippi. However, state administrators only provided this protection for the Freedom Riders on condition that they could put them under arrest when they arrived at their destination.

The Freedom Riders were duly arrested, charged with minor offences and dispatched to a maximum security prison. Kennedy's involvement was a devastating blow to CORE and the Student Nonviolent Coordinating Committee (SNCC) and it launched a climate of distrust of seemingly liberal authorities.

CIVIL RIGHTS REALITY

President Kennedy remained resolutely popular with African Americans. He had made many gestures toward civil rights, such as including African American celebrities on the guest list for White House events. His brother and other members of the Kennedy circle resigned from clubs around Washington if they had a "Whites Only" policy.

But the general public was still not totally supportive of civil rights. A poll in 1961 suggested that two-thirds of Americans disapproved of the activities of the Freedom Riders. Another poll gave the President an 87 percent approval rating among African Americans. The administration tried to focus the civil rights movement away from desegregation activity, such as the Freedom Rides, toward voter registration with the Voter Education Project that was funded by a few liberal philanthropists.

But the reality of civil rights for Kennedy was that it depended on the neutralization of the power of the white South in Congress to make any progress. A civil rights bill would anger Southern congressmen and probably inhibit the other initiatives the president wanted to get through Congress, such as tax and tariff reforms, aid for education, and federally funded health care for the elderly.

* * * * * *

MISSISSIPPI TURMOIL

As it happened, a civil rights *cause célèbre* erupted in Mississippi. James Meredith, a 29-year-old air force veteran, had won a legal battle to be the first African American to attend the University of Mississippi. It was the government's responsibility to ensure that Meredith was admitted. But they were faced with fervent segregationist Mississippi Governor Ross Barnett (1898 – 1987).

A force of US marshals was gathered to ensure that Meredith was peacefully enrolled. Kennedy learned, however, that Barnett had ordered the withdrawal of state troopers. The marshals were on their own against an angry mob. Kennedy addressed the nation on the matter.

But as he spoke things turned very ugly on the university campus. Molotov cocktails and rocks were thrown, and gunshots rang out. The president decided that troops would have to be deployed but it took five hours for them to get there. Only at 5:30 a.m. the following morning was the campus secured. Two people died and many were injured.

Kennedy knew the episode would make life even more difficult with the Dixiecrats—the Southern Democrats—whose campaigns in the fall would be vigorously anti-Kennedy. But his efforts at desegregation helped bring African Americans into the Democratic Party fold and benefited liberal politicians in the North.

Many in the civil rights movement were confused by Kennedy's efforts to placate Southern whites. It created distrust of his motives that prevailed throughout his time in office.

* * * * * *

WALK THE LINE

It was obvious to civil rights activists that the Kennedy administration walked the line between the two sides of the argument. They would act when protests brought out the violent side of Southern segregationists, but at the same time Kennedy always sought to be conciliatory toward the Southerners, afraid to push them too far. Martin Luther King Jr. was particularly vociferous about the administration's lack of action.

James Meredith (center) walking to class at the University of Mississippi, accompanied by US Marshal James McShane (left) and John Doar of the Justice Department, 1961.

King had been trying to get the president to issue a second Emancipation Proclamation that would include desegregation in its terms, but Kennedy rejected the idea. Now King was planning a campaign of mass protest in Birmingham, Alabama, a hotbed of segregation.

Kennedy was against such actions because he feared they would inevitably erupt into violence that would be broadcast to the world on television, undermining the reputation of the United States around the globe. The Communists would exploit it and Southern congressmen would be angered by it and try to block Kennedy's reforms including the tax cut that he saw as absolutely vital.

* * * * * *

BIRMINGHAM, ALABAMA

Nonetheless, King went ahead with his protest, leading marchers in Birmingham, Alabama, on April 12, 1963, Good Friday. He was arrested and everyone waited to see how the president would react, remembering how he got King out of jail in 1960. Kennedy was told, however, that there was no reason that the federal authorities should become involved with the situation.

A few days later, the body of William Moore, a white civil rights protester was found murdered in a town not far from Birmingham. King was released the day the body was found and was concerned that the murder might take the spotlight off his campaign. He was urged by those around him to escalate the protest.

On Thursday, May 2, 1963, he mobilized hundreds of children—some as young as six years old—to march to Kelly Ingram Park in Birmingham where the police waited under the command of the city's Police Commissioner, Eugene "Bull" Connor.

Connor had conspired with the Ku Klux Klan when the Freedom Riders came to Birmingham in May 1961. A symbol of the Segregationist South, Connor was one of the reasons Martin Luther King Jr. chose the city to stage his protest.

* * * * * *

FIGHTING IN THE STREETS

Nearly a thousand people were arrested and the city's jails were full of protesters. As a result, Connor brought in water cannon the following day. Scenes of children being hit by high-powered jets of water filled the pages of the newspapers. A "national disgrace" was the term the *New York Times* used.

Kennedy thought the solution was to bring the opposing parties together and he sent Burke Marshall (1922 – 2003), from the Justice Department, to get the rival sides to come to an agreement. Burke managed to persuade the Senior Citizens Committee to talk, but they would only do so as long as Martin Luther King Jr. was not involved.

Martin Luther King Jr. being arrested by a police officer for leading an anti-segregation march in Birmingham, Alabama, April 12, 1963.

A fragile peace was declared until on May 11, 1963, a bomb exploded outside the house of King's brother and underneath the hotel room at the Gaston Hotel where King had been staying. African Americans took to the streets and went on the rampage.

The White House now feared that this type of violence would spread across the country's inner cities. And, indeed, riots broke out during the next few days in Jackson, Mississippi, Cambridge, Maryland, and Syracuse, New York.

* * * * * *

A DIFFERENT PRESIDENT

Troops were moved close to Birmingham but Kennedy was persuaded that more had to be done. Legislation had to be put forward that dealt with the problems about which African Americans were protesting. The administration had to be seen to be doing something to make things better.

But Kennedy was muddled in his approach to the racial crisis, a different man to the determined, clear-headed president who dealt with the missile crisis. Even Lyndon Johnson realized that a progressive and bold civil rights bill was required. He maintained that it was time for the president to take a moral stand before the nation and force Congress to come to heel.

Johnson told Kennedy that once the bill was proposed he would have to put the full force of his office behind it. This was not what Kennedy wanted to hear. The efforts to get the bill through would last well into the year of the election and his involvement in it would probably not be good for his campaign. Kennedy was more interested in just restoring order than actually addressing the issues.

* * * * * *

STEPS ARE TAKEN

Restoration of law and order began. Jefferson County, Alabama, was targeted for voting rights litigation. Public schools in Prince Edward County, closed since 1959, were ordered to re-open. The Defense Department ordered commanders of bases to tell their men to boycott businesses in areas where segregation and racial discrimination were still customary.

Segregation in reserve military units was banned. This marked the end of the racial discrimination in the military that had been ordered by President Truman in 1948. More African Americans were employed by the federal government.

Kennedy implored business and community and religious leaders to voluntarily make desegregation an important issue, and seek peaceful solutions to the racial tensions. Kennedy expressed his fear:

Our concern is that we do not have a battle in the streets of America in the coming months.

* * * * * *

STANDING IN THE SCHOOLHOUSE DOOR

This quiet quest for peace was in contradiction to the approach of those on both sides of the racial barrier. Staunch segregationists such as George Wallace (1919 – 98) who was Governor of Alabama on three separate occasions, were eager to resist the desegregation orders sent down by the courts and thereby send a message to their supporters. Wallace desperately wanted to preserve segregation saying :

The President [Kennedy] wants us to surrender this state to Martin Luther King and his group of pro-communists who have instituted these demonstrations.

Meanwhile Martin Luther King Jr. and other civil rights leaders believed that it would take incidents such as in Birmingham to grab the nation's attention and drive change. George Wallace was standing firm against a court order saying that he had to allow two African American students to be admitted to the University of Alabama in Tuscaloosa. This became known as the "Stand in the Schoolhouse Door," as Wallace blocked the doorway of the university to prevent the students entering.

The Justice Department tried to mobilize Alabama's most prominent people against

Wallace, emphasizing the need for law and order and the cost of civil unrest to the local economy. It also took out an injunction against Wallace regarding the two students. It worked, and on June 11, 1963, in order to escape a prison sentence, Wallace stepped aside at the door of the university and the students were admitted.

* * * * *

KENNEDY'S CIVIL RIGHTS ADDRESS

Kennedy decided to follow the advice of those around him by delivering a televised address to the nation on the issue of civil rights on the evening of June 11, 1963. He began by explaining what had happened at the University of Alabama that day and then spoke of racial reform, referring to the founding documents of America.

He emphasized the need for the American people to uphold those tenets of equality and freedom, especially because America was being looked to by the rest of the free world for leadership in the Cold War. He went on to say that legislation was needed to diffuse the tensions.

He finished by promising that it was his obligation "to make that revolution, that change, peaceful and constructive for all." It was a speech that elicited praise from civil rights leaders, even Martin Luther King Jr. himself, but the Southern segregationists were distinctly unimpressed.

* * * * *

THE SHOOTING OF MEDGAR EVERS

Tensions on the street exploded just a few hours after the speech. Medgar Evers (1925 – 63), the leader of the National Association for the Advancement of Colored People (NAACP) in Mississippi, was killed by a bullet in the back as he got out of his car at his house. Kennedy was horrified.

To make matters worse that day, a revolt by Southern Democrats had blocked the refunding of the Area Redevelopment Administration. Meanwhile demonstrations by African Americans, some of which developed into riots, were launched in thirty-nine cities across the United States. The televised speech had been good, but not good enough. It was evident that it would take more than that to put things right.

Governor George Wallace stands defiantly blocking the door of the University of Alabama, confronted by Deputy US Attorney General Nicholas Katzenbach.

BULL CONNOR

Theophilus Eugene "Bull" Connor (1897 – 1973), served as Commissioner of Public Safety for the city of Birmingham, Alabama, and was also responsible for the Fire and Police Departments. Connor enforced racial segregation and denied civil rights to black citizens, and became an American symbol of institutional racism.

He directed the use of fire hoses and police attack dogs against children protestors during civil rights rallies. His white supremacy tactics, and support for the Ku Klux Klan, were broadcast nationwide on television, horrifying America, and eventually ushering in major social and legal changes in the South.

GEORGE WALLACE

George Corley Wallace Jr. (1919 – 98) was the 45th Governor of Alabama. The first of four children, he was born in Barbour County, southeastern Alabama.

Wallace is remembered during the Civil Rights struggle in the Southern states, for his declaration that he stood for "segregation now, segregation tomorrow, segregation forever," and for standing in front of the entrance of the University of Alabama in an attempt to stop the enrollment of black students.

He eventually renounced segregationism but remained a social conservative. Historians now tend to view him as a misguided populist politician who used dangerous racist views to attract the votes of the white citizens of Alabama.

In 1972 Arthur Bremer shot George Wallace in an assassination attempt, leaving him paralyzed in a wheelchair for the rest of his life. In the late 1970s, Wallace announced that he was a born-again Christian and apologized to black civil rights leaders for his segregationist past. He spent his final years, trying to explain away his racist attitudes.

Suffering from breathing difficulties as well as complications from his gunshot spinal injury, Wallace died from a bacterial infection in Jackson Hospital, Montgomery, Alabama, on September 13, 1998, at the age of 79.

On June 19, 1963, the day of Medgar Evers' funeral which was attended by 3,000 people, Kennedy sent his civil rights bill to Congress. It was a wide-ranging document that covered voter registration; desegregation of establishments such as hotels, lunch counters, and leisure facilities; stronger litigation powers in cases of desegregation in schools; a new Community Relations Service to deal with disputes of a racial nature; and more powers to force federal contractors and recipients of federal aid to practice non-discrimination.

Southern politicians were inevitably dismayed by the bill, describing it as a "blueprint for the totalitarian state."

* * * * *

THE MARCH ON WASHINGTON

But there was criticism from civil rights leaders, too. They were disappointed by what they saw as the bill's failure to provide measures to ensure federal protection for civil rights activists. Kennedy called a meeting with them at the White House on June 22, 1963.

The president explained that his chances of election had been seriously damaged by the bill, his popularity having plummeted to just 47 percent. But he was still willing to stand up for it and to fight for the votes of the 38 or so moderate senators who could help to defeat the inevitable attempt at filibustering by the Southerners.

Kennedy argued that the passing of the bill meant that the civil rights movement should respond by canceling the March for Jobs and Freedom that was planned for Washington. Moderates, Kennedy warned the leaders, would react badly to what they would view as intimidation and although they might support the bill they would not be forced into seeing it through Congress.

But they rejected his request, telling him that if African Americans were not allowed to express their anger in this way, it might emerge in the form of social unrest and disorder. The march had been due to go to Capitol Hill but as a concession they agreed instead to march to the Lincoln Memorial on August 28, 1963. More than 200,000 Americans were expected for the march, which was destined to become a key moment in the history of the civil rights struggle.

Martin Luther King Jr. at the March on Washington, August 28, 1963.

I HAVE A DREAM

Martin Luther King Jr. originally wrote his speech to echo the biblical tones of Abraham Lincoln, but with the single phrase of "I Have a Dream" he transformed the history of America. It has been judged the finest American speech of the twentieth century in a poll of experts. Toward the end of the speech, urged on by supporters shouting: "Tell them about the dream, Martin!" King abandoned his prepared text and launched into his famous improvisation:

> *And so even though we face the difficulties of today and tomorrow, I still have a dream. It is a dream deeply rooted in the American dream.*
>
> *I have a dream that one day this nation will rise up and live out the true meaning of its creed: "We hold these truths to be self-evident, that all men are created equal."*
>
> *I have a dream that one day on the red hills of Georgia, the sons of former slaves and the sons of former slave owners will be able to sit down together at the table of brotherhood.*
>
> *I have a dream that one day even the state of Mississippi, a state sweltering with the heat of injustice, sweltering with the heat of oppression, will be transformed into an oasis of freedom and justice.*
>
> *I have a dream that my four little children will one day live in a nation where they will not be judged by the color of their skin but by the content of their character.*
>
> *I have a dream today!*
>
> *I have a dream that one day, down in Alabama, with its vicious racists, with its governor having his lips dripping with the words of "interposition" and "nullification"—one day right there in Alabama little black boys and black girls will be able to join hands with little white boys and white girls as sisters and brothers.*
>
> *I have a dream today!*

As King walked off the podium, he handed the original typewritten speech to George Raveling, a college basketball player who was a security guard for the day. Raveling still has the speech, but has no intention of selling, even though he has been offered three million dollars for it.

Martin Luther King Jr. giving his famous "I Have a Dream" speech at the Lincoln Memorial, Washington DC.

I HAVE A DREAM

Kennedy continued to sit on the fence in racial matters, being supportive to the civil rights movement while reassuring Southern whites. For instance, nine black protestors in Albany, Georgia, were prosecuted after picketing a store owned by a white juror in a case in which a racist local police officer had been acquitted.

The accused were linked to the civil rights organization the Student Non-violent Coordinating Committee (SNCC). Its leader John Lewis (born 1940) was scheduled to give a speech during the March on Washington. He planned to articulate the anger African Americans felt at the prosecution of their colleagues while police officers who had been violent toward demonstrators for the last few years had escaped censure.

With such impassioned sentiments surfacing, Kennedy worried that the leaders could keep the event peaceful. In fact, the march was supposed to be all-encompassing, drawing in a wide range of people and interests, both black and white, and Lewis was forced to tone down his speech.

Eventually, the March on Washington was remembered not for John Lewis's angry words, but for Martin Luther King's "I Have a Dream" speech in which he eloquently called for an end to racism in the United States. It became one of the greatest speeches in American history. No wonder that, as he watched King speak on a television at the White House, Kennedy said to those watching with him, "This guy's good."

When the leaders of the march were welcomed at the White House afterward, Kennedy warned them that his bill would only make it through Congress if politicians believed it would stop the shows of violence.

* * * * * *

HORROR IN BIRMINGHAM

On the morning of Sunday, September 15, 1963, a bomb exploded at the northeast door of the Sixteenth Street Baptist Church in Birmingham, killing four young girls—one 11-year-old and three 14-year-olds. Another 12-year-old girl escaped alive but partially blinded, from the debris. Violence erupted almost immediately in an already-tense city. Another two African American teenagers were killed, a 16-year-old was shot by police, and a 13-year-old murdered by a group of white youths.

While this was going on, Kennedy was in Newport, Rhode Island where Jacqueline Kennedy was recovering following the death of their prematurely born baby son, Patrick. He had lived for just thirty-six hours after being born on August 7. Jacqueline had already given birth to a stillborn child in 1956, a daughter whom they named Arabella. Given his present personal situation and the fact that six young lives had been lost so tragically, he reacted very oddly.

* * * * * *

PUTTING THE BLAME ON WALLACE

Returning to the White House, Kennedy issued a statement blaming George Wallace for the current situation, claiming that he was responsible for creating an environment in which the bombers could exist. He announced an FBI investigation but refused to send in federal troops, leaving it to Wallace to take responsibility for clearing up the dangerous situation in Birmingham.

Wallace responded by sending in Colonel Al Lingo (1910 – 69), his Director of the Alabama Department of Public Safety and an ardent segregationist. Kennedy's next broadcast address, a few days after the bombing, made no mention of it or the bereaved families. There was no presidential representation at the funerals of the young people, the White House seemingly indifferent to the tragedy. This apparently uncaring attitude infuriated the civil rights community.

Ever mindful of the election the following year, Kennedy now seemed to focus on placating Southerners and moderates and the steam seemed to have gone out of the civil rights bill. In order to get the bill passed, he had to win round moderate Republicans. And in order to win the election in which he would almost certainly face Barry Goldwater, he had to secure the votes of white Southerners. African American votes seemed assured.

CHAPTER 18

VIETNAM AND SOUTHEAST ASIA

★ ★ ★ ★ ★ ★ 🦅 ★ ★ ★ ★ ★ ★

The problems and hostilities in South Vietnam were escalating. Kennedy had already identified it as "the worst problem we've got" to his advisor, Walt Rostow (1916 – 2003). A report he received early in his presidency warned that the Viet Cong—the Communist-backed National Liberation Front—would bring down the South Vietnamese government of Ngo Dinh Diem (1901 – 63). Diem's administration was plagued by corruption, bribery, and nepotism, but America supported him in an effort to hold back the spread of Communism.

The Vietnamese had defeated the French colonial power in 1954, and North and South Vietnam had been left divided from each other by the Geneva Peace Conference. There were supposed to be elections with the North Vietnamese Communist leader Ho Chi Minh (1890 – 1969) favorite to win, but the United States put its support behind Diem in Saigon. Ho's troops began the armed struggle to topple the Diem government, leaving Vietnam embroiled in the throes of a bloody civil war.

Kennedy publicly denied newspaper comments that America was rapidly slipping deeper into the jungles and paddy fields of Vietnam. But behind closed doors, the administration was well aware of the significance of the escalating hostilities. With

John F. Kennedy in the Oval Office, being briefed on South Vietnam by General Maxwell Taylor, Chairman of the Joint Chiefs of Staff (left), and Robert McNamara, Secretary of Defense (center).

139

support for North Vietnam coming from the Soviet Union, China, and other communist allies, the United States considered Southeast Asia a Cold War-era proxy war.

* * * * * *

THE DOMINO THEORY

Kennedy had in the back of his mind the "domino theory," that President Eisenhower had described during an April 7, 1954, news conference, when referring to communism in Indochina:

> *Finally, you have broader considerations that might follow what you would call the "falling domino" principle. You have a row of dominoes set up, you knock over the first one, and what will happen to the last one is the certainty that it will go over very quickly. So you could have a beginning of a disintegration that would have the most profound influences.*

Kennedy chose to see Vietnam as a military problem instead of an economic or nationalist one and handed responsibility for policy-making to Robert McNamara in the Department of Defense rather than to Dean Rusk in the State Department. Kennedy's method of governing—he had abandoned regular cabinet meetings—meant that decisions were frequently made in isolation and, as a result, policy was often confused.

* * * * * *

TIME TO INTERVENE

Kennedy gave President Diem the funding to recruit another 20,000 local troops and issued orders to increase the number of American "advisors" on the ground in Vietnam training counter-insurgency techniques to the Vietnamese. It made little difference, leading Kennedy to think that Diem had squandered the money. He sent Walt Rostow to Vietnam to investigate where the money had gone and find out what progress the "advisors" were making.

Generally speaking, Kennedy was up against it internationally. The Communists had made headway in both Cuba and Berlin and one more knockdown would have made him look dangerously weak and ineffectual. The task was, therefore, clear to Kennedy, if perhaps not to many around him. He had to prevent the spread of Communism in Southeast Asia without sending in any American forces.

The hawks in the White House who included Walt Rostow and Defense Under Secretary Roswell Gilpatric (1906 – 96) had read reports stating that if the United States was to become militarily involved in Vietnam, the Chinese, and the Soviets would not respond. This left White House aides believing, contrary to Kennedy, that the time for American troops to intervene in Southeast Asia had arrived.

* * * * *

ALL THE PRESIDENT'S MEN

In October 1961, Kennedy sent General Maxwell Taylor (1901 – 87) to Vietnam to assess the situation, making it very clear to him that the independence of South Vietnam "should rest with its people and its government." But despite this, Taylor returned with the suggestion that America should send 8,000 combat troops.

The troops could be sent under the pretense that they were going in to help after serious flooding in the Mekong Delta. The Joint Chiefs and advisors like Rostow and Gilpatric wanted more, however, making plans to send in 200,000 US combat troops and to bomb the North Vietnamese capital, Hanoi.

Kennedy opposed it vehemently, believing it could only lead to even greater escalation. Instead, he again increased the number of military advisors in Vietnam and stepped up the supply of equipment. Disappointed by the caliber of advice he was receiving, he replaced a number of personnel in the State Department and in the CIA.

Veteran diplomat Averell Harriman took over at the Far Eastern desk and Chester Bowles was replaced by George Ball (1909 – 94) as Under Secretary of State. John McCone (1902 – 91) took over from Allen Dulles as head of the CIA.

Ball was about the only person in the State Department who counseled against sending troops to Vietnam. He warned Kennedy:

Within five years, we'll have three hundred thousand men in the paddies and jungles and never find them again.

* * * * * *

FIGHTING FIRE WITH FIRE

In mid-1963, President Kennedy launched a pet project that introduced a new kind of warfare—counter-insurgency. Guerrilla warfare, he believed, would be the strategy of the communists in their battle to dominate the world. He deployed Special Forces commando units from the "Green Berets" to fight fire with fire.

He brought in expertise from around the world to train his troops and used new tactics such as the "strategic hamlets" scheme—the creation of fortified encampments that would keep peasants in the combat zone safe from the incursions of the Viet Cong. But US military funds were still being siphoned off by the South Vietnamese government rather than going to people it was designed to help.

* * * * * *

WINNING MORE SLOWLY

Kennedy tried to dissuade newspaper editors from printing stories that discredited his efforts in Southeast Asia, claiming that they helped the enemy. But it was obvious, however, that the unscrupulous Diem regime was deeply unpopular and out of touch with its people.

Despite the aid given by the United States, the funds had been mishandled and the military effort was a failure.

A situation report by two Kennedy people who had gone to Vietnam on a fact-finding mission, Roger Hilsman (1919 – 2014) and Michael Forrestal (1927 – 89) contained this brief, enigmatic summary:

We are probably winning, but more slowly than we had hoped.

* * * * * *

THE NGO DINH DIEM PROBLEM

Kennedy was caught in yet another dilemma. The Vietnamese military was obviously fairly inadequate, but the US top brass were arguing the case for a greater effort. They claimed that a "surge," an increase in US forces and equipment, would hasten ultimate withdrawal from Vietnam. The problem, however, was President Ngo Dinh Diem.

Diem's brother Ngo Dinh Nhu was a dominating presence in the South Vietnamese government, and it was more often than not that corruption charges fell at his feet. Diem was also faced with claims that he was not interested in democracy and responded with accusations that the United States was breaching Vietnamese sovereignty. Therefore, he said, he would accept no more American military advisors of whom there were now 16,000.

* * * * * *

DIEM AND THE BUDDHISTS

Diem was a Catholic which back in the 1950s had seemed like a boon to the Americans. The Vietnamese, however, were largely Buddhists. Trouble broke out on the day of Buddha's birthday, May 8, 1963 when government troops fired on a crowd that was celebrating the event.

Following this there was a protest march by around 10,000 Buddhists leading Diem to clamp down on the Buddhist leaders, imprisoning them and closing any temples that were perceived to be operating politically.

(Above) A US Army Shawnee helicopter over Vietnam.

At that time, Kennedy was probably too preoccupied with the civil rights problems in the American South to pay much attention to Diem and the Buddhists.

* * * * * *
BUDDHIST INFERNO

But on June 11, 1963, the president's eyes were firmly focussed on Vietnam once more. Elderly Buddhist monk, Thich Quang Duc (1897 – 1963) in protest over the persecution of the Buddhists, sat down at a busy intersection in central Saigon, poured a can of petrol over himself and set himself ablaze.

Diem's brother, Ngo Dinh Nhu, launched nationwide wrecking raids on Buddhist pagodas, seizing Quang Duc's heart, killing monks, and trashing monasteries. Several Buddhist monks followed Quang Duc's example, also immolating themselves.

Photographs of Thich Quang Duc's self-immolation were circulated widely across the world and marked the beginning of the end for the Diem presidency. Referring to one of the photographs of the monk's death, which went on to win a Pulitzer prize for photographer Malcolm Browne, Kennedy said:

No news picture in history has generated so much emotion around the world as that one.

Kennedy had to act fast before irreparable damage was done to his quest for a second term. Diem was warned that if he did not resolve the Buddhist crisis quickly, the United States would withdraw its support from him.

* * * * * *
ULTIMATUM ISSUED

Kennedy reacted to the shocking events in Saigon by appointing Henry Cabot Lodge as ambassador. Meanwhile, he was being told by the military that new initiatives in Vietnam were delivering results, but he was also being informed of the public hatred for Diem, who was seen now as being no more than a US puppet.

Lodge was no fool and quickly concluded that Diem was finished. The corrupt elements of the Diem regime, including Diem's brother, were still in office. Lodge began to show support for a military coup to replace Diem and on August 24, 1963, a telegram arrived from Washington.

Apparently, President Kennedy and most of his top advisors were not in Washington when the telegram was drafted. It basically ordered Lodge to deliver an ultimatum to the South Vietnamese president: if you fail to get rid of your brother and his wife, the United States will no longer support your regime.

* * * * * *
TIME TO BITE THE BULLET

The ownership of this cable is complex. A draft had been prepared and Michael Forrestal had telephoned the president who was in Hyannis Port with his family. Kennedy had also spoken to Under Secretary George Ball about it and was informed that if Secretary of State Dean Rusk and Deputy Defense Secretary Gilpatric were okay with the text, it should be sent.

Rusk assumed that Kennedy had already approved the text and signed off on it. While Gilpatric thought of the telegram as emanating from the State Department and consequently would not stand in its way. CIA head John McCone was not consulted by his deputy director, Richard Helms (1913 – 2002) who said, "It's about time we bit this bullet."

After all this, Kennedy gave the go-ahead for the cable to be sent.

* * * * * *
PRESIDENTIAL SECOND THOUGHTS

Lodge was concerned that the ultimatum he had been asked to deliver would only alert Diem to the fact that there was going to be a coup. He was also certain that Diem would never sack his brother. Therefore, he decided to speak with the Vietnamese generals who were planning the coup.

Before he was able to do this, however, the radio station the Voice of America broadcast a program that cleared the Diem regime of

SELF-IMMOLATION

Self-immolation is an intentional and willing sacrifice of oneself often on behalf of a collective cause. Historically it referred to any suicide method, such as the Japanese ritual act of seppuku or hara-kiri, but nowadays it usually refers to self-death by fire. Often used by the Vietnamese Buddhist monks in the 1960s as a form of radical political martyrdom, it has centuries-old traditions in Southeast Asian cultures.

Thich Quang Duc's self-immolation during the Buddhist crisis in Vietnam. Photographer Malcolm Browne won the 1964 Pulitzer Prize for the picture.

carrying out the raids on Buddhist temples and blaming Ngo Dinh Nhu for the action against Vietnamese Buddhists. This let Diem know what Washington's position was regarding his government.

At this time, there were a number of high officials in Washington who felt they had been cut out of the decision-making process. Robert McNamara, General Maxwell Taylor, and CIA head John McCone were all deeply irritated by the events surrounding the sending of the cable and Kennedy had to pacify them at a particularly stormy White House meeting.

Kennedy hesitated however, worried about the people who were plotting the coup. Ambassador Lodge told him in no uncertain terms that it was the wrong time to be having second thoughts.

* * * * * *

THE DIEM COUP

With a lack of real clarity among his team, Kennedy sent Defense Secretary Robert McNamara and the head of the Joint Chiefs of Staff, General Maxwell Taylor to Vietnam. Their report on returning to Washington, categorically stated that Diem should dissociate himself from his brother Ngo Dinh Nhu and take steps to reform his government. It was thought that cuts in US aid to Vietnam would either bring Diem back into the fold or force a coup.

The report also claimed that there had been progress and plans should go ahead for a reduction of a thousand in the American commitment. Kennedy was delighted with the conclusions.

However, there are two sides to every story, and the personnel on the ground in Saigon believed that the only way forward was to get rid of Diem. While some, such as US General Harkins thought Diem to be the only option available, Ambassador Lodge was making it known that the Americans would not stand in the way of a coup.

Lodge could see first-hand that Diem was not about to make the reforms that the Americans wanted. The possibility of a coup accelerated, amid grave concern in Washington. Finally, on November 1, 1963, Diem was overthrown, and he and his brother were murdered as they tried to escape.

Far from providing stability in Vietnam, the coup merely exacerbated the situation and in 1964 alone there were no fewer than seven different governments. US involvement increased after the coup as the North Vietnamese and the Viet Cong stepped up operations.

* * * * * *

THE HAND OF HISTORY

Part of the Kennedy myth is that he was planning to withdraw from Vietnam. His aide Ken O'Donnell recalls him saying that he had a plan to install a government in Saigon that would request that the Americans withdrew.

The Senate Majority Leader, Mike Mansfield (1903 – 2001) tells how Kennedy assured him that if and when he secured his second term in the White House, he would get America out of Vietnam. In other words, he would never have got America as involved as his successor Lyndon Johnson did.

History tells us, however, that during the summer and fall of 1963, Kennedy had ample opportunity to withdraw. The North Vietnamese had indicated that they might be willing to participate in a coalition of some kind, and Diem had seemed interested.

At that time, the American people were so horrified by Diem's treatment of the Buddhists that they would have been glad to be rid of Vietnam once and for all. But the president dithered, preoccupied with events on the home-front.

Had Kennedy served a second term, he would have been faced with a similar foreign policy catastrophe that he had gone through with the Bay of Pigs. He most certainly did not want to commit combat troops yet he did not want to lose out in another military operation. But would he have been able to withstand the pressure of the US generals? It is a tantalizing question—but the hand of history took an unexpected hold on events, and the answer will never be known.

HENRY CABOT LODGE

Henry Cabot Lodge Jr. (1902 – 85) was born in Nahant, Massachusetts, and came from a long line of senators. In 1924, he graduated from Harvard University and went into the newspaper business. In 1932, he was elected to the Massachusetts House of Representatives. Election to the Senate followed in 1936, where he served until 1944.

During the Second World War, Lodge rose to the rank of lieutenant colonel and he did two tours of duty. When President Roosevelt ordered congressmen to choose between fighting or returning to Washington, Lodge decided to return to the Senate. In 1944 he was back on active duty and single-handedly captured a German patrol of four men. During the war he won the Légion d'Honneur and Croix de Guerre and the Legion of Merit and Bronze Star.

Returning to Massachusetts politics after the war, Lodge was re-elected to the Senate. He was campaign manager for Dwight D. Eisenhower's presidential campaign, but spent so much time with Eisenhower he neglected his own campaign and lost his seat in the Senate.

In 1953, Lodge was appointed United States ambassador to the United Nations, a post he held for seven years. He resigned in order to run for vice president on Richard Nixon's losing ticket against John F. Kennedy.

When Kennedy was elected, he appointed Lodge as ambassador to South Vietnam. Lodge was instrumental in advising Kennedy about events on the ground in Saigon between 1961 and 1963 and continued as ambassador to South Vietnam until 1967 under Lyndon Johnson. More ambassadorial appointments followed in West Germany and the Holy See, until he was appointed head of the American delegation at the Paris negotiations to end the war in Vietnam.

Lodge died in 1985 at the age of 83 after a long illness, and was interred in the Mount Auburn Cemetery in Cambridge, Massachusetts.

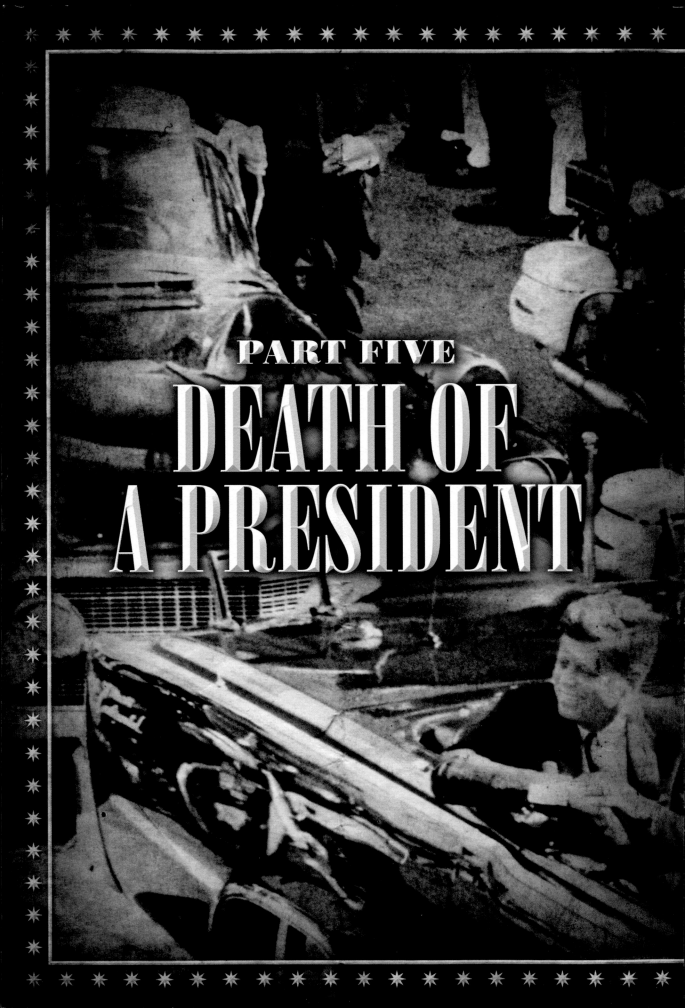

PART FIVE
DEATH OF A PRESIDENT

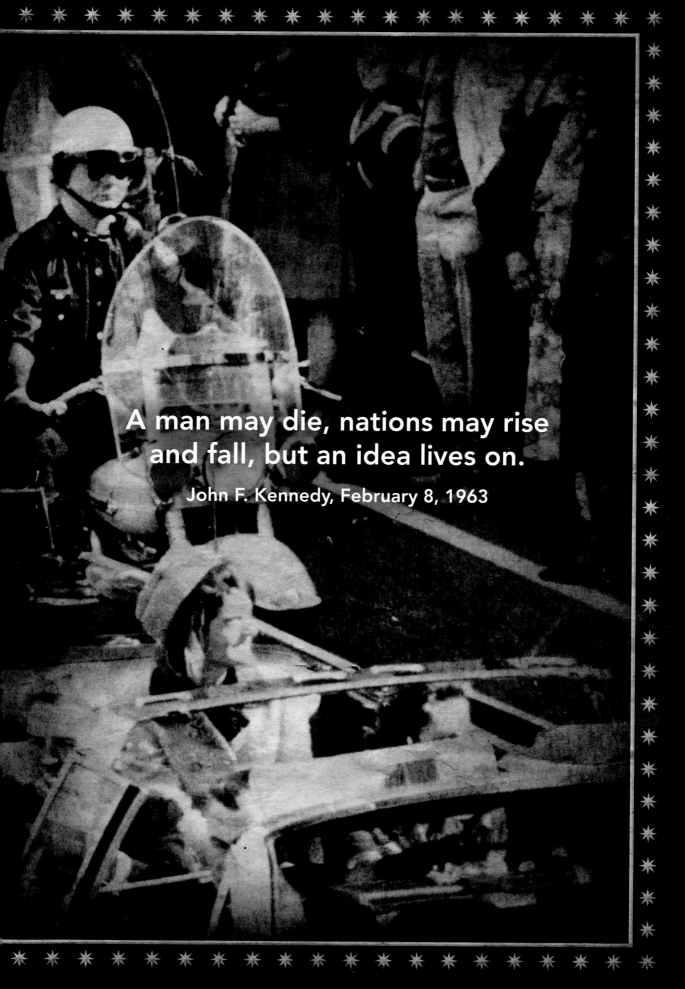

A man may die, nations may rise
and fall, but an idea lives on.

John F. Kennedy, February 8, 1963

CHAPTER 19

WHAT HAPPENED IN DALLAS

✶ ✶ ✶ ✶ ✶ ✶ 🦅 ✶ ✶ ✶ ✶ ✶ ✶

November 22, 1963, Dallas, Texas—the day anyone who was alive at the time remembers as the day the world heard that President John F. Kennedy had been assassinated.

Kennedy was there because Texas had helped him to his narrow victory over Nixon in 1960. Once again it was a key state that the president had to win if he was to obtain a second term in the White House. In the background, the president still faced the never-ending balancing act between civil rights activism and the interests of Southern congressmen which, continued to cause him sleepless nights.

Kennedy was even now holding back from the radical reform of American civil rights. While at the same time he pandered to the wishes of the Southerners whose power in Congress could de-rail anything the president wanted to achieve.

✶ ✶ ✶ ✶ ✶ ✶

GROWING CONSERVATIVE VOTE

Support for Republican Barry Goldwater was so strong before the National Convention that his nomination seemed inevitable. Polls suggested that a race with Kennedy for the White House would be extremely close. Kennedy's situation was summed up by *New York Times* columnist James Reston. Not only did the president face hostility from the South because of civil rights, he faced:

> *an anti-high taxation, anti-integrated housing, anti-job equality movement in the North, even among pro-Democratic labor union members.*

This growing conservative majority would later vote for Richard Nixon, but Goldwater was in at the beginning of this change of attitude and voting habits. He described Kennedy as being a proponent of traditional government interference and espoused a more progressive free market philosophy. The policies of future leaders such as President Ronald Reagan (1911 – 2004) and British Prime Minister Margaret Thatcher (1925 – 2013), would be guided by this philosophy in the 1980s.

✶ ✶ ✶ ✶ ✶ ✶

WHEAT TO RUSSIA

Naturally, the electorate was wary of Goldwater's relentlessly hardline approach to the Soviet Union. Kennedy had shown adroit handling of the Cuban Missile Crisis and had recently negotiated a test ban treaty with the Kremlin, but Republicans still viewed Kennedy as soft on Communism and there were suspicions about him.

Skepticism was exacerbated by the debate surrounding the sale of wheat to the USSR. It would be of great benefit to the American farmers of the Midwest as well as the country's coffers, the administration argued. Kennedy also believed that it would help to build trust between the United States and the Soviet Union.

But anti-communists suggested that the United States would be aiding an immoral regime by helping to alleviate its food crisis. Midwestern farmers might welcome the resultant funds flooding into their bank accounts but it was likely that it would make no difference to their voting. They would still vote Republican.

BARRY GOLDWATER

Barry Morris Goldwater (1909 – 98) was born in Phoenix, Arizona, and was the grandson of Polish immigrants. Goldwater's father owned an up-market department store in Phoenix and on his father's death, he took over the business.

On America's entry into the Second World War, Goldwater was commissioned into the US Air Force, becoming a pilot for the Ferry Command, a unit that delivered supplies to American troops around the world. By the time he retired from the Air Force after the war, Goldwater had reached the rank of major-general.

He entered politics in 1949, being elected to Phoenix City Council, and in 1952 made it to the US Senate. He was a Republican senator in a state that usually voted Democrat. In 1958, he became the first Republican in Arizona history to win a second term.

In 1964, he chose not to run for the Senate so that he could run for his party's presidential nomination. He won a bitterly contested campaign, but his nomination proved unpopular and Goldwater lost to Lyndon B. Johnson by a large margin. He was re-elected to the Senate in 1968 where he remained until his retirement in 1987.

Goldwater was most associated with anti-communism and labor reform, and he opposed the Civil Rights Act of 1964. He was reportedly grief-stricken by the assassination of John F. Kennedy and disliked his successor, Lyndon Johnson. Of Richard Nixon he said he was "the most dishonest individual I have ever met in my life."

Goldwater is credited with the transformation of the Republican Party from an eastern elitist organization, and sowing the seeds for the election of western senator Ronald Reagan as president. He suffered a massive stroke in 1996 and died two years later, at the age of 89.

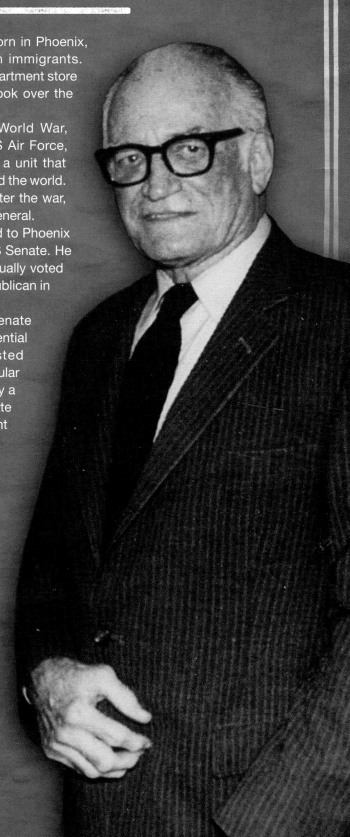

On the other hand, many voters of Eastern European extraction, living in the cities might resent Kennedy's help for the regime that they saw as dominating their ethnic homelands.

* * * * * *

AFRICAN AMERICAN VOTES

Kennedy was desperate to get his tax reform bill through Congress in order to spur economic growth, but his civil rights legislation was more essential to his election campaign. It was becoming increasingly evident that he could not count on the votes of the South, in which case he had to win African American votes in the industrial North.

But, the same old problem persisted. In order to get the tax bill through Congress he needed the support of the Southern congressmen, but they would not reach out and help him while he was adopting a civil rights agenda.

Kennedy was also very aware of the dangers he faced from Goldwater as a candidate, but felt he had the edge on him. He was certain American voters were turned off by Goldwater's radical right opposition to social security and his scary hawkish attitude to foreign policy.

He hoped that economic matters might prove more important in the South than racial issues. He aimed to make the economy an election issue, emphasizing how much better off people were in 1963, than under Eisenhower.

* * * * * *

THE TRIP TO TEXAS

Traveling to Texas in late November had one main purpose—to raise funds for the Democratic Party. The president had earlier sought the help of the Democratic Governor of Texas, John Connally (1917 – 93), to help organize the fund raisers. But the governor was opposed to the civil rights bill and feared any close links to Kennedy would alienate his more conservative supporters. So, instead of hosting a series of fund-raising dinners in August, the governor agreed to stage just one, in November.

Both Governor John Connally and Lyndon Johnson, who was from Texas, had attempted to dissuade Kennedy from spending too much time there. The state was a hotbed of right wing activity and just that summer someone had fired a shotgun into the Democratic Party offices in Dallas.

Civil rights leaders, including Martin Luther King Jr. (fourth from left) and John Lewis (fifth from left, behind) meet with President John F. Kennedy in the White House after the March on Washington.

The city was home to numerous right wing organizations such as the John Birch Society. They supported limited government and opposed wealth redistribution, economic interventionism, collectivism, totalitarianism, communism, and socialism.

United Nations Ambassador Adlai Stevenson faced a hostile crowd when he attended a rally in Dallas celebrating the anniversary of the founding of the UN. He was struck on the head by a placard.

* * * * * *

THE GOLDEN COUPLE ARRIVE

The President and the First Lady were welcomed by enthusiastic, cheering crowds in San Antonio, Houston, and Fort Worth on Thursday, November 21, 1963, the first day of their visit to Texas. Everyone was eager to catch a glimpse of the glamorous Jacqueline Kennedy.

The image of the First Lady was going to be just as important in the 1963 election as it had been in 1960. The president was well aware, and insisted on motorcades in open topped cars in all the cities he and his wife visited—a security nightmare.

On the morning of November 22, 1963, President Kennedy joked with a gathering crowd outside his Fort Worth hotel, telling them that Jacqueline was still getting ready. He said:

It takes her a little longer, but, of course, she looks better than we do when she does it.

Jacqueline Kennedy then appeared in an elegant rose pink Chanel suit with a navy collar, a matching navy blue blouse underneath, and a pink pillbox hat with white gloves. The very personification of early 1960s elegance. The First Lady was given a standing ovation as she entered the ballroom in which 2,000 Southern businessmen and their wives had been patiently waiting for the arrival of the golden couple.

John F. Kennedy and Jacqueline Kennedy arriving at Dallas's Love Field airport, with Lyndon B. Johnson standing behind.

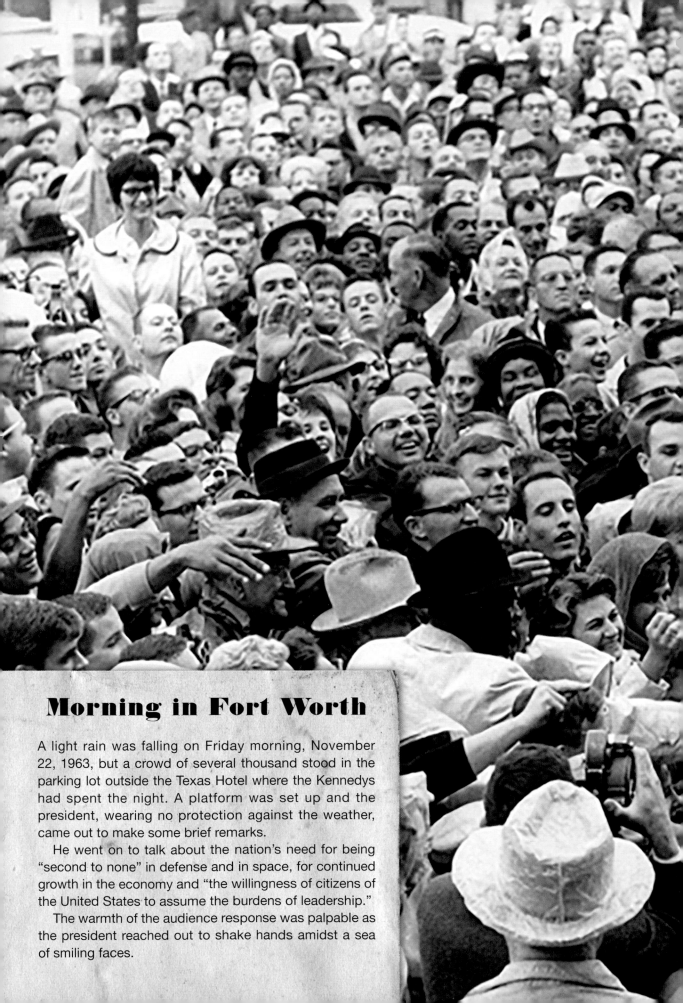

Morning in Fort Worth

A light rain was falling on Friday morning, November 22, 1963, but a crowd of several thousand stood in the parking lot outside the Texas Hotel where the Kennedys had spent the night. A platform was set up and the president, wearing no protection against the weather, came out to make some brief remarks.

He went on to talk about the nation's need for being "second to none" in defense and in space, for continued growth in the economy and "the willingness of citizens of the United States to assume the burdens of leadership."

The warmth of the audience response was palpable as the president reached out to shake hands amidst a sea of smiling faces.

THE OPEN-TOP LINCOLN

Fort Worth's mayor presented the president with a Texan ten-gallon hat, that Kennedy skilfully avoided wearing. In a good mood, the presidential party set off to Carswell Air Force Base for the short hop on Air Force One to Dallas.

Meanwhile in Dallas, Governor John Connally and his liberal rival Senator Ralph Yarborough (1903 – 96) had been at loggerheads for some time. Connally had insisted that Yarborough should play no part whatsoever in the presidential visit.

However, conscious of bad press for party in-fighting, Connally relented, and Yarborough was allowed to ride in the vice president's car.

At Dallas's Love Field airport, the First Lady received a bouquet of red roses. The Kennedys shook hands with the crowds lining the airfield's perimeter fence. Then they took their seats in the back of an open-top Lincoln Continental limousine.

* * * * *

SO PEOPLE CAN SEE

The Lincoln had been custom-built for presidential use and was known to the secret service as X-100. It was unarmored and was to be the third vehicle in the motorcade.

The president sat in the back with the First Lady. In front of Kennedy was Governor Connally. The governor's wife, Nellie Connally (1919 – 2006), sat in front of Jacqueline Kennedy. Secret Service agent Roy Kellerman (1915 – 84) sat next to the presidential driver Bill Greer (1909 – 85).

X-100 was accompanied by four motorcycle outriders and the car behind had a phalanx of secret service agents standing on the running boards. Kennedy had insisted that no agent ride on the running boards or on the rear step of the presidential car, so people could see him and the First Lady more clearly.

* * * * *

SECURITY NIGHTMARE

On the way into Dallas city center, Kennedy spotted some schoolchildren waving to him and his wife. They carried a placard that said:

> **"MR PRESIDENT, PLEASE STOP AND SHAKE OUR HANDS."**

Kennedy ordered the vehicle to stop to the surprise of the delighted children, and the dismay of the security men. He did the same a few blocks later to say hello to some children who were being looked after by a nun.

The crowds grew bigger as they entered the city and the welcoming faces saw a smiling president enjoying himself. Ever mindful of image, he told his wife to remove her sunglasses so the crowd could see her face.

By the time the motorcade entered Dallas's downtown area, the crowds were so thick that the cars could manage a speed of little more than ten miles an hour.

President Kennedy and Mrs. Kennedy with Texas Governor John Connally and his wife in the open-top Lincoln.

DEALEY PLAZA

The clock on top of the Texas School Book Depository building showed 12:30 as the motorcade slowly turned the corner of Main Street onto Houston. The crowds were still yelling and applauding wildly. As they crossed the open space of Dealey Plaza, a breeze began to blow.

The First Lady reached up to safeguard her hat caught in the wind and amid the cheers and clapping, Nellie Connally turned round to reassure the president, saying to Kennedy:

> [There are] some in Dallas who love you and appreciate you.

Police Chief Jesse Curry (1913 – 80) radioed ahead to waiting agents that the motorcade was approaching the Triple Underpass and would arrive in five minutes.

Meanwhile Dallas dressmaker Abraham Zapruder (1905 – 70) switched on his brand new 8-mm movie camera ready to film the approaching motorcade. Behind him stood his receptionist Marilyn Sitzman (1939 – 93) who was holding him steady.

As the vehicles approached from Houston and Elm toward the Triple Underpass, motorcycle patrolman H.B. McClain found the microphone on his bike would not switch off. Both McClain and Zapruder recorded everything that happened next.

* * * * *

THEY'VE KILLED MY HUSBAND

On the film taken by Abraham Zapruder that fateful day, the shooting of President Kennedy and Governor Connally is clearly documented. The two men jerk violently, visibly impacted by the force of the bullets. The president raises his hand to his throat and his wife turns toward him. Six seconds later another gunshot rips into the side of Kennedy's head, making it explode.

Jacqueline Kennedy and a police outrider were splattered with blood and brain matter. The president fell into his wife's lap and Jacqueline Kennedy's words were picked up by H.B. McClain's motorcycle microphone:

> They've killed my husband; I have his brains in my hand!

She repeats it over and over in shock. At one point she crawls onto the back of the car, looking like she is trying to escape. But she was more likely retrieving pieces of her husband's skull.

Still from the Abraham Zapruder home movie showing Mrs. Kennedy crawling onto the back of the car, with FBI agent Clint Hill leaping on board.

AGENTS IN ACTION

Nellie Connally believed her husband was dead, but in reality, the governor had been shot in the chest, wrist, and thigh, and was still conscious. Meanwhile, FBI agent Clint Hill (born 1932) can be seen on the Zapruder film running from the car behind and leaping onto the back of the presidential limousine, to shield Jacqueline Kennedy and the president from further shots.

Hill held onto a small handrail used by agents to steady themselves as they stood on the rear platform. Agents in these rear positions afforded greater protection to passengers. On that day, however, by presidential request, no agents were stationed there. As the *Report of the President's Commission on the Assassination of President Kennedy* said:

> *... the President had frequently stated that he did not want agents to ride on those steps during a motorcade except when necessary. He had repeated this wish only a few days before, during his visit to Tampa, Florida.*

Behind them, in the vice president's vehicle, FBI agent Rufus Youngblood (1924 – 96) had vaulted over the front seat into the back. He pushed Lyndon B. Johnson down onto the floor and shielded him with his body. It was an act later described by Johnson as "as brave an act as I have ever seen."

PARKLAND MEMORIAL HOSPITAL

Nellie Connally recalled that the Secret Service agent yelled for the driver to pull out of the motorcade. On his radiophone he told the motorcyclists to head to the nearest hospital and the cars sped away from Dealey Plaza toward Parkland Memorial Hospital.

Stunned onlookers were pointing at the book depository where they thought the shots had been fired from. Others thought that there had been shots from a fenced off area on top of a grassy knoll above the railway track.

As the vehicles sped toward the hospital, Youngblood was impressed by the vice president's calmness. He told Johnson and his wife that when they reached Parkland Hospital, he would take them immediately to a secure location.

On arrival at the hospital's emergency entrance, no one was waiting for them. But staff and wheeled stretchers were urgently located. As Kennedy was rushed in, Clint Hill quietly covered the president's shattered head with his jacket, hiding it from view.

It was 12:38 p.m.—eight minutes after the shots had rung out in Dealey Plaza.

Agent Clint Hill shielding the occupants of the presidential limousine, moments after the fatal assassination shots.

DEAD ON ARRIVAL

Doctors worked frantically on the president's body for the next 22 minutes, but John F. Kennedy was undoubtedly dead on arrival at Parkland Hospital.

Dr. Marion Thomas Jenkins (1917 – 94), the Texas anesthesiologist who declared the president dead after trying to resuscitate him, observed Jacqueline Kennedy in the emergency room:

I noticed that her hands were cupped in front of her, as if she were cradling something. As she passed by, she nudged me with an elbow and handed me what she had been nursing in her hands—a large chunk of her husband's brain tissues.

* * * * * *

ASSASSINATION!

It fell to the veteran CBS news anchorman Walter Cronkite (1916 – 2009) to announce the assassination of the president to a shocked nation. Cronkite reported the events as they unfolded in a series of newsflashes:

Here is a bulletin from CBS News. In Dallas, Texas, three shots were fired at President Kennedy's motorcade in downtown Dallas. The first reports say that President Kennedy has been seriously wounded by this shooting.

A breaking news bulletin arrived while Cronkite was still reading the first. He read it out with increasing gravitas:

… President Kennedy shot today just as his motorcade left downtown Dallas. Mrs. Kennedy jumped up and grabbed Mr. Kennedy, she called "Oh no!" the motorcade sped on. United Press [International] says that the wounds for President Kennedy perhaps could be fatal. Repeating, a bulletin from CBS News: President Kennedy has been shot by a would-be assassin in Dallas, Texas. Stay tuned to CBS News for further details.

Another more detailed update was read out, and then at 2:38 p.m., Walter Cronkite was handed the bulletin which confirmed the president's death. He looked at it, removed his glasses, and read in his profound tones:

President Kennedy died at 1 p.m. Central Standard Time. 2 o'clock Eastern Standard Time, some 38 minutes ago.

Cronkite paused to gather himself, put his glasses on again, and swallowed deeply to regain some composure. Visibly moved, he read the next part of the bulletin, clearing his throat after the first few words:

Vice President Johnson has left the hospital in Dallas, but we do not know to where he has proceeded; presumably he will be taking the oath of office shortly and become the 36th President of the United States.

Headlines in *The Dallas Morning News*, the day after the assassination.

CHAPTER 20

AFTERMATH

THE SHOOTER

On November 22, 1963, the presidential motorcade passed through Dealey Plaza in downtown Dallas. High above the cheering crowds, a man aimed the telescopic sight of a rifle at the president from a window on the sixth floor of the Texas School Book Depository. At 12:30 p.m., he fired three shots, one of which hit President John F. Kennedy, killing him in front of the onlooking crowds.

The shooter quickly left the scene, hiding his firearm under some boxes, and descended the rear stairwell. Detectives later uncovered the rifle, and found three empty bullet shells, and one intact bullet near the sniper's position, beside the sixth floor window. A ballistics expert subsequently linked the shells to the rifle, and the rifle was plausibly linked to a man called Lee Harvey Oswald.

Oswald had bought a similar 6.5 mm caliber Mannlicher Carcano rifle with a telescopic sight, by mail order in March 1963, along with a .38 Smith & Wesson Model 10 revolver. It is officially accepted that the rifle was the same one that was fired from the Texas School Book Depository to assassinate Kennedy.

Earlier in the day of the assassination, a man resembling Lee Harvey Oswald had been seen on the sixth floor of the Texas School Book Depository by a coworker. He was seen again by his supervisor and a police officer in the second-floor lunchroom, prior to him leaving the building at 12:33 p.m. The supervisor confirmed Oswald was an employee and the police officer let him go. Oswald exited the depository just before it was sealed off by the police.

* * * * * *

KILLING OFFICER TIPPIT

Just after noon on November 22, Officer J.D. Tippit was patrolling his normal beat in south Oak Cliff, a residential district of Dallas. Fifteen minutes after the Kennedy shooting, Tippit was urgently ordered to assist in the search for the suspect.

At 1:15 p.m., Tippit was driving slowly along East 10th Street, when he saw a man fitting the suspect's description and pulled alongside. As he got out of his car, the man suddenly drew a revolver and shot him three times in the chest. He then walked up to the officer as he lay injured on the ground, and fired a bullet into his right temple, killing him.

Witnesses to the shooting later picked out Lee Harvey Oswald in a police lineup as the man they had seen. Others identified Oswald running between the murder scene and the Texas Theater, where he was subsequently found and arrested. Oswald fitted the killer's description.

Four cartridge cases were found at the scene of the murder, and experts testified they had been fired from Oswald's revolver. The gun used in the shooting was a .38 Smith & Wesson Model 10 revolver, the same handgun that Oswald had bought by mail order.

* * * * *

REPEATED DENIALS

When he was arrested, Oswald denied any involvement in Tippit's murder. But based on eyewitness statements, and the gun found in Oswald's possession at the time of his arrest, he was formally charged with the murder of J.D. Tippit at 7:10 p.m. on November 22. During questioning, police began to suspect that Oswald was also involved in the shooting of President Kennedy. At approximately 1:00 a.m. on November 23, Lee Harvey Oswald was also charged with assassinating President John F. Kennedy.

Oswald repeatedly denied any involvement in the two murders during police questioning.

"I didn't shoot anyone," he yelled. He protested his innocence to reporters several times in the corridors of the police station. He would have to be arraigned before a Grand Jury and that meant a transfer from the city to the county jail. There was an anonymous threat to kill him, a call received by the Dallas FBI in the early hours of the morning of November 24, 1963.

* * * * *

RUBY'S REVENGE

Extra security was put in place for the jail transfer as a result. Nonetheless, the media were still permitted to be inside police headquarters. Oswald was escorted to the basement garage purportedly to be put into an armored car that would carry him across town.

As he entered the garage, Oswald was surrounded by seventy police officers as well as photographers and journalists. But they had forgotten to lock the door that led into the basement from Main Street, and nightclub owner Jack Ruby walked in off the street pretending to be a journalist.

The reporters surged forward as the alleged assassin entered, handcuffed to two detectives. Suddenly from Oswald's left a man in a suit and a hat lunged forward. It was Jack Ruby with a gun in his hand. Amid chaotic scenes he shot Oswald in the stomach. It was shown live around the world to a disbelieving television audience.

Lee Harvey Oswald is shot by Jack Ruby, during Oswald's transfer to the Dallas County jail, November 24, 1963.

LEE HARVEY OSWALD

Lee Harvey Oswald (1939 – 63) was born in New Orleans, Louisiana. His father was a First World War veteran who died two months before Oswald's birth. As a child Oswald was withdrawn and temperamental, often truanting from school. A psychiatric assessment suggested that he enjoyed a vivid fantasy life.

Oswald left school early and worked as an office clerk and messenger in New Orleans. He joined the Marines at the age of 17, claimed to be a Marxist and tried to teach himself Russian. In 1959 he had himself discharged and traveled to the Soviet Union and married Marina Prusakova (born 1941).

Back in the United States in 1962, the Oswalds settled in the Dallas/Fort Worth area and began mixing with anti-Communist Russian and Eastern European émigrés. On April 10, 1963, Oswald was strongly suspected of trying to shoot U.S. Major General Edwin Walker.

The couple got out of town and moved to New Orleans on April 24,1963. They joined the Fair Play for Cuba Committee, an organization that supported the Cuban revolution and opposed American attacks on the island's government. In September 1963, Oswald tried to travel to Cuba, seeking an entry visa in Mexico City. Unsuccessful, he returned to Dallas where he took a job at the Texas School Book Depository on October 16, 1963.

On the day of the Kennedy killing, a man resembling Oswald was seen on the sixth floor of the book depository from where the fatal kill shots were fired. Oswald was arrested later the same day and charged with the president's assassination. Two days later, at 11:21 a.m. during a jail transfer, Lee Harvey Oswald was fatally wounded by local nightclub owner Jack Ruby.

JACK RUBY

Jacob Leonard Rubenstein (1911 – 67) was born in Chicago, Illinois, to Orthodox Jewish parents. His childhood was marked by juvenile delinquency and foster homes. He served as an aircraft mechanic during the Second World War, returning to Chicago after his discharge.

In 1947 he moved to Dallas, and shortened his name to Jack Ruby. He managed nightclubs, strip clubs, and dance halls, and befriended many Dallas police officers, supplying them with free drinks and girls. In 1959, he traveled to Cuba to meet a friend of Mafia boss Santo Trafficante Jr., and it is possible that at the same time he met Trafficante himself and set up links with organized crime.

Ruby returned to Dallas and became involved in gambling, narcotics, and prostitution. At the time of the Kennedy assassination, he was working at the Carousel Club in downtown Dallas, and the Vegas Club in the city's Oak Lawn district. After the shooting, he seems to have gone immediately to Parkland Hospital. He was certainly at Dallas Police headquarters several times after Oswald was arrested, pretending to be a journalist on the night of the assassination.

Why did Ruby murder Oswald—was it spontaneous, premeditated, or a contract killing? The report of the House Select Committee on Assassinations was as puzzled as everyone else, and left many questions unanswered:

> … Ruby's shooting of Oswald was not a spontaneous act, in that it involved at least some premeditation. Similarly, the committee believed it was less likely that Ruby entered the police basement without assistance, even though the assistance may have been provided with no knowledge of Ruby's intentions … The committee was troubled by the apparently unlocked doors along the stairway route and the removal of security guards from the area of the garage nearest the stairway shortly before the shooting … There is also evidence that the Dallas Police Department withheld relevant information from the Warren Commission concerning Ruby's entry to the scene of the Oswald transfer.

Jack Ruby was convicted of Oswald's murder and sentenced to death. But his conviction was overturned on appeal. However, while in prison awaiting a re-trial, Ruby became ill in his cell and died of a pulmonary embolism from lung cancer on January 3, 1967.

GUILTY UNTIL PROVEN OTHERWISE

At 3:54 p.m. on the day of the Kennedy shooting, NBC newsman Bill Ryan had announced on national television that "Lee Oswald seems to be the prime suspect in the assassination of John F. Kennedy." The day after Ruby shot Oswald, the *New York Times* headlined its front page, "President's Assassin Shot to Death."

A fever akin to mass hysteria gripped America after Kennedy's killing. The nation's press, television, and radio, acted as prosecutor, judge, and jury, presenting the evidence and persuading the world that Lee Harvey Oswald was without doubt the man who shot Kennedy.

* * * * * *

SOME CELEBRATE THE DAY

Of course, not everyone was sad to see the end of the Kennedy presidency. It is reported that in one part of Texas, where he was deeply unpopular, a class of fourth grade schoolchildren shockingly burst into spontaneous applause when the president's death was announced.

Jimmy Hoffa, the leader of the Teamsters Union, to whom Robert Kennedy had given such a hard time, could barely conceal his delight, describing the president to a lawyer over the phone as "a son of a bitch." His joy was laced with relief, as he also imagined that Robert Kennedy's tenure as Attorney General would now end.

The same lawyer that Hoffa spoke to, recalled a celebration party being thrown on the day of the assassination by the Mafia boss, Santo Trafficante Jr. (1914 – 87) at which toasts to Kennedy's death were drunk.

* * * * * *

JOHNSON TAKES THE OATH

The local medical examiner was legally bound to carry out a post-mortem on a victim of a violent or suspicious death, but Kennedy's people wanted to take their dead leader back to the White House immediately. The dispute over the body's release delayed its delivery to the airport until 2:14 p.m.

Everyone was surprised to find Lyndon Johnson on Air Force One, having presumed he would have been immediately whisked back to Washington. Johnson had wanted to return to the White House with the body and Kennedy's entourage, after he had been sworn in as president.

The makeshift ceremony was carried out by an old friend of the new president, federal district judge Sarah Hughes. Surrounded by members of the press, Johnson gave his oath of allegiance in the cabin of Air Force One, with a dazed Jacqueline Kennedy standing beside him, still wearing her bloodstained pink suit.

A Bible could not be found and a Roman Catholic missal from the desk of President Kennedy was used for the swearing of the oath. John F. Kennedy had been dead for two hours and eight minutes.

* * * * * *

A NEW PRESIDENCY BEGINS

The immediate task for Johnson was to create the perception that the United States government was continuing and was in control. Thus, a rapid transition of power was needed. The photographed swearing-in was an effort to reassure shocked and grieving Americans.

There was also the fear, shared by the FBI, that a conspiracy was afoot and Johnson could well be a target of that. Therefore, they did their utmost to get him back to Washington. This was seen by some, however, as the new president showing indecent haste to get his hands on the reins of power.

He had also telephoned Robert Kennedy to obtain the precise wording of the oath, which some saw as very insensitive. Even the inclusion of the former First Lady in the swearing-in was seen as indelicate. He needed, however, to return things to normal as soon as possible, to put a lid on any speculation of a Communist plot or a conspiracy from elsewhere.

THE STATE FUNERAL

President Kennedy's body was brought back to Washington from Dallas and taken straight to Bethesda Naval Hospital for a post-mortem to be carried out. He was then taken to the White House at around 4:30 a.m. the following morning, November 23, 1963. The coffin was placed in the East Room where it remained for twenty-four hours surrounded by a guard of honor. Jacqueline Kennedy asked that two Catholic priests remain with the body.

Jacqueline Kennedy had insisted the casket remain closed, probably because of the gaping wound to the president's head. She still wore the bloodstained suit she wore in Dallas. She had not left her husband's side since his death. But once the casket had been placed in the East Room, she retired to her private quarters.

A Mass was said at 10:30 on Saturday morning and there followed a series of visits by family, friends, and government officials. Presidents Truman and Eisenhower both paid their respects. The other living president, Herbert Hoover, was too ill to be there. Meanwhile, crowds had gathered in pouring rain outside the White House.

* * * * * *

THE FALLEN LEADER

On Sunday, November 24, 1963, the flag-draped casket was taken on a horse-drawn two-wheeled military carriage to the Capitol to lie in state in the rotunda. It was followed by the traditional riderless horse, an animal named Black Jack, with a pair of boots reversed in the stirrups—the symbol of a fallen leader.

Around 300,000 people lined the streets silently watching it pass. Hundreds of thousands of people waited day and night in freezing temperatures to pay their respects. At times the line stretched for about ten miles.

* * * * * *

DAY OF MOURNING

The day of the state funeral was declared a national day of mourning by President Johnson. It took place on Monday, November 25, 1963, with representatives from more than ninety countries present.

Around a million people lined the route of the procession while many millions more watched on television around the world. Led on foot by Robert, Edward, and Jacqueline Kennedy, the cortege went from the Capitol, back to the White House, and then on to a Requiem Mass at St. Matthew's Cathedral.

Lyndon B. Johnson taking the presidential oath of office aboard Air Force One, witnessed by Jacqueline Kennedy (right).

Behind them in a limousine came the children, Caroline and John F. Kennedy Jr.

The remainder of the Kennedy family waited at the cathedral, apart from Joe Kennedy Sr. who was ill. Controversially, the new president also walked in the procession. He had been advised against it by the secret service, fearful of another assassination. Jacqueline Kennedy thanked him in a letter for his courage. Johnson said later:

Walking in the procession was one of the most difficult decisions I ever had to make … [but it was something I] could do, should do, would do, and did so.

THE FINAL FAREWELL

After leaving the cathedral, Jacqueline Kennedy whispered to her son John F. Kennedy Jr., and the three-year-old famously stepped forward and saluted his father's coffin as it passed. The resulting photograph became an icon of the 1960s.

The motorcade made its way to Arlington National Cemetery and John Fitzgerald Kennedy was laid to rest at 3:34 p.m. on November 25, 1963. He was 46 years old. At the end of the proceedings, Jacqueline Kennedy lit an eternal flame that burns at the graveside to this day.

Three-year-old John F. Kennedy Jr. saluting his father's coffin, alongside his sister Caroline, with his mother Jacqueline in a black veil, flanked by Edward (left) and Robert Kennedy.

CHAPTER 21

COVER-UPS AND CONSPIRACIES

THE WARREN COMMISSION

The President's Commission on the Assassination of President Kennedy is popularly known as the Warren Commission. Its name derived from its chairperson, Chief Justice Earl Warren (1891 – 1974). Set up by Kennedy's successor, President Lyndon Johnson, just a week after Kennedy's death, its brief was to listen to the testimony of witnesses to the incident and examine evidence.

As well as Warren, it was made up of Senator Richard Russell Jr. (1897 – 1971), Senator John Sherman Cooper (1901 – 91), Representative Hale Boggs (1914 – 72), Representative and later 38th president of the United States, Gerald Ford (1913 – 2006), Allen Dulles, former Director of the CIA and John J. McCloy (1895 – 1989), former President of the World Bank.

★ ★ ★ ★ ★

OSWALD ACTED ALONE

It began meeting on December 5, 1963, and published its 889-page report on September 24, 1964. The committee had taken testimony from 552 witnesses and had examined more than 3,100 exhibits. It concluded that the president had been killed by Lee Harvey Oswald and that he had acted alone. It further concluded that Jack Ruby, Oswald's killer had also been acting alone.

Members of the Warren Commission present their report to President Lyndon B. Johnson. (Left to right) John McCloy, J. Lee Rankin, Richard Russell, Gerald Ford, Earl Warren, President Lyndon B. Johnson, Allen Dulles, John Sherman Cooper, and Hale Boggs.

In the years since the commission published its report, it has been the subject of severe criticism for the way it conducted some of its business and for important omissions. Its conclusions have been discredited over time. As the 1992 Assassination Records Review Board said:

> *Doubts about the Warren Commission's findings were not restricted to ordinary Americans. Well before 1978, President Johnson, Robert Kennedy, and four of the seven members of the Warren Commission all articulated, if sometimes off the record, some level of skepticism about the Commission's basic findings.*

* * * * * *

CONSPIRACY THEORIES

The multitude of conspiracy and cover-up theories are part of the enduring legacy of the Kennedy years. It has been estimated that more than a thousand books have been written about Kennedy's assassination and most of those espouse conspiracy theories. A majority of Americans believe that there was a conspiracy to kill him and only around 20 to 30 percent believe Oswald acted alone.

The theories are many and varied, involving many people and numerous organizations. The CIA, President Lyndon Johnson, Cuban President Fidel Castro, and the KGB, are just some of the entities and individuals that people have suggested had something to do with the president's death. In fact, around 42 groups, 82 assassins and 214 individuals have been named by the conspiracy theorists over the years.

The Warren Commission concluded in 1964 that Lee Harvey Oswald was solely responsible for Kennedy's death but in 1979, the House Select Committee on Assassinations (HSCA) concluded that a second gunman had probably also fired at the president in his motorcade that day.

LOCATION OF EYEWITNESSES TO THE MOVEMENTS OF LEE HARVEY OSWALD IN THE VICINITY OF THE TIPPIT KILLING

Warren Commission exhibit showing the movements of Lee Harvey Oswald around the time of J.D. Tippit's killing.

That person and any organization to which he might have belonged remained unidentified by the HSCA. However, the acoustic evidence on which their conclusion was based has since been discredited. Nevertheless, it has not stopped people believing it.

* * * * * *

FAILINGS AND OVERSIGHTS

The Dallas Police made numerous mistakes, or, as conspiracy theorists would say, deliberately failed to carry out investigations that might have provided a different version of the assassination. For instance, reports of the shots from the grassy knoll were never taken seriously by the Dallas PD and were not investigated by them.

Then, the post-mortem failed to follow the direction of the bullets through the president, establishing points of entry and possibly enabling them to work out from which direction they came. But this may have happened because of the rush. The post-mortem at Bethesda Naval Hospital was carried out as quickly as possible to allow the First Lady and the nation to get on with grieving for the president.

Shots from the grassy knoll would indicate that Oswald had not been the only shooter. The lack of investigation into these areas has fueled the conspiracy claims. They probably discredited the grassy knoll because they quickly discovered the sniper's nest in the Book Depository, complete with three shell casings. Many witnesses pointed to the Book Depository as the source of the shots that killed Kennedy. Conspiracy theorists say that it was all too convenient and was designed to lead everyone away from investigation of the grassy knoll.

Oswald's death, too, can be seen in two ways. Were the police just trying to allow the press access to what were obviously historical events? Or was it part of a plot to frame Oswald so that a much bigger conspiracy would not be uncovered?

MURDER BY LEFT OR RIGHT?

Some immediately blamed the Russians and the Cubans. Oswald's connection with communism and Cuba fed this suspicion. But the Russians themselves suggested it was a right-wing plot. After all, the test ban treaty had not been welcomed by those of the right and Dallas was known to be a hotbed of right-wing activity and attitudes. Kennedy's civil rights legislation was opposed by the segregationists of the South, and elsewhere. Liberals immediately raised the possibility that an attempted coup had come from these forces. The variations on these themes are limitless.

* * * * *

THE GRASSY KNOLL SHOOTER

This is the main piece of evidence used by conspiracy theorists to prove that Lee Harvey Oswald was not acting alone. The grassy knoll was on the north side of Elm Street. Witnesses report seeing a flash of light and a character known as "Badgeman" has been isolated by examination of film from the day. He is said to be wearing a badge and holding a rifle, but the footage has never been completely proven to show that image.

Shortly after the assassination, three vagrants were found in a train carriage behind the knoll. However, they were clean-shaven and far too well dressed. It has been suggested that these men, never charged by the police, were actually CIA agents and not hobos.

A large number of staff at Parkland Hospital reported that a large piece of the back of the president's skull had been blown out. This suggests strongly that the bullet that did this was fired from in front of him.

* * * * *

THE NEW ORLEANS CONSPIRACY

Three days after the president's death, New Orleans lawyer Dean Andrews told the FBI about a telephone call. On the day of the

SINGLE-BULLET THEORY

How did Oswald do so much damage with just three bullets? The Warren Commission's theory, credited to assistant counsel Arlen Specter, suggested that both Kennedy and Governor Connally were wounded by a single bullet. It entered Kennedy's upper back, exited his throat, and then struck Connally, breaking a rib and shattering his wrist, and finally coming to rest in his thigh.

Doubters responded that it would be impossible for a bullet to take such a trajectory and re-named the Warren Commission's hypothesis the "magic bullet theory." But over the years, various re-enactments, computer analyses, and in-depth research, including frame by frame scrutiny of Abraham Zapruder's film, have given increasing credibility to the single-bullet theory.

After 10 years of research, Dale Myers produced a 3D computer-generated re-enactment of the assassination, released in 2003. With Governor Connally sitting in a middle-row jump seat, as much as 6 inches to the left and 4 inches lower than Kennedy, the animation allowed the assassination sequence to be viewed from any point of view with absolute geometric accuracy.

Myers calculated that the position of the two men at the time of the shooting, meant a single bullet could indeed have inflicted the wounds on Kennedy and Connally. By following the bullet's straight line trajectory backwards, it could, in addition, be seen to have been fired from the sixth floor of the Texas School Book Depository. Myers used a close-up examination of the Zapruder film as the basis for his animation.

Zapruder's 26 seconds of footage has become one of the most watched and controversial films of all time. The single shot, and the responses of Kennedy and Connally to the bullet, were captured on frames 210 through 225. But frame 313 records an even more shocking event, when a second shot hits Kennedy's head, and his skull explodes. Due to its horrific content, frame 313 was not seen by the general public until 1975. The single-bullet theory does not exclude any other shots, or additional bullets hitting the president. Most witnesses and analysts believe that a total of three shots were fired.

Whether Oswald was a lone gunman, or was set up to take the blame, may never be known, nonetheless, theories surrounding the assassination show no sign of subsiding. A recent poll found that 61 percent of Americans think there was a conspiracy to kill the president.

Arlen Specter of the Warren Commission reproducing the assumed alignment of the single-bullet theory in 1964.

assassination a man calling himself Clay Bertrand phoned to ask him to defend Lee Harvey Oswald.

Meanwhile, Jack Martin who worked for New Orleans private detective Guy Banister claimed that another of Banister's employees, David Ferrie (1918 – 67), had been involved in the assassination. Ferrie had made plans to kill Kennedy and may even have given Oswald training in the use of a rifle with a telescopic sight.

Ferrie knew Oswald from the time that Oswald lived and worked in New Orleans. They had been in the Civil Air Patrol together in the 1950s. When questioned, Ferrie denied that he had ever made Oswald's acquaintance.

Oswald distributed leaflets on behalf of the Fair Play for Cuba Committee in New Orleans in spring 1963. Stamped on them was an address that was located in the same building as Guy Banister Associates. Some have said that Oswald knew Banister and was often to be seen in his office but this has never been authenticated.

* * * * * *

OSWALD WAS A PAWN

In 1966, New Orleans DA, Jim Garrison, began an investigation into the involvement of certain prominent New Orleans citizens in Kennedy's assassination. He came to the conclusion that a bunch of right-wing extremists that included Guy Banister and David Ferrie had put together a plot to kill Kennedy, in concert with elements of the CIA.

The reason, Garrison claimed, was that they did not like Kennedy trying to establish peace in both Cuba and Vietnam. Garrison also believed New Orleans businessman Clay Shaw to be part of the plot and that he had been the "Clay Bertrand" that had telephoned Andrews. It was Garrison's contention that Oswald was merely a pawn, and had been set up.

Garrison went so far as to have Clay Shaw arrested in March 1967. Shaw has the distinction of being the only person to be tried for Kennedy's murder. He was acquitted by the jury after only one hour's deliberation.

THE CIA

Kennedy had said that he wanted to "splinter the CIA into a thousand pieces and scatter it to the winds." Conspiracy theorists suggest those words made him an instant target for the CIA. It is often said that one of the three vagrants was E. Howard Hunt (1918 – 2007), a former CIA agent who had connections to the Bay of Pigs operation. After his death in 2007, Hunt's sons released a deathbed confession by him that he had knowledge of a conspiracy to kill the president.

The CIA was also particularly angered by Kennedy's actions regarding the Bay of Pigs fiasco. He had refused to follow advice to provide air support or to launch a full-scale invasion and elements were deeply irritated by this.

The Warren Commission found no evidence that Oswald was ever employed or had any connection with the agency. But one investigator for the HSCA claimed that there was pressure not to investigate this angle. He named a CIA agent that he believed had connections with Oswald before the assassination.

Former US Army Intelligence officer, John M. Newman believed that only the CIA's Chief of Counter-intelligence, James Angleton, "had the access, the authority, and the diabolically ingenious mind to manage this sophisticated plot." But he also named CIA chief Allen Dulles as being responsible. Dulles had been dismissed by Kennedy over the Bay of Pigs but sat as a member of the Warren Commission.

* * * * * *

THE SECRET SERVICE

There is little doubt that the Secret Service did a bad job in Dallas. The protection they gave the president was inadequate, and it had not prepared properly for the visit, failing to analyze information that it had. Furthermore, Agent Roy Kellerman did not give Kennedy the full body protection that was the norm, failing to cover the president's body with his own when the shooting started.

CARLOS MARCELLO

Carlos Marcello (1910 – 93) was born Calogero Minacori (or Minacore) to Sicilian parents in Tunis, North Africa. His family emigrated to America in 1911 and settled in New Orleans. He got involved in petty crime, and became leader of a gang of teenage armed robbers. In 1929, he was arrested for assault and served five years. After marrying the sister of New Orleans Mafia underboss Frank Todaro, Marcello kept moving up within the ranks of the crime syndicate. By 1947, he was the undisputed leader, and became "The Godfather" in New Orleans for the next 30 years.

Hounded by Robert Kennedy and the senate committee investigating the Mafia, Marcello was deported to Guatemala in 1961, but he didn't take long to get back to New Orleans. His grudge against the Kennedys was well known. Strangely enough, after the president's assassination, the FBI found no evidence that he was any more than "a tomato salesman and real estate investor," with no links to the killing.

Attorney Frank Ragano claimed in his book *Mob Lawyer*, that in July 1963, on behalf of union leader Jimmy Hoffa, he asked Marcello and Santo Trafficante to hire an assassin to kill the president. After Kennedy was shot, Marcello apparently told Ragano: "When you see Jimmy (Hoffa), you tell him he owes me and he owes me big." Subsequently Hoffa vanished in 1975, and his body was never found.

In 1981, Marcello was convicted and sent to prison for bribery and racketeering. While in prison he had suffered several strokes. In July 1989, he was released when his sentence was overturned. Marcello went home to his mansion in New Orleans, into the care of his family and a team of nurses. He died in 1993, at the age of 83.

SANTO TRAFFICANTE JR.

Santo Trafficante Jr. (1914 – 87) was the powerful Florida-based mobster who was extensively involved in the Mafia's lucrative gambling operations in pre-revolution Cuba.

Every night in Havana, Trafficante paid Cuban dictator Fulgencio Batista ten percent of the profits from his syndicate's casinos. Legend has it that Batista took as much as thirty percent from other casinos. Over the years millions of Mafia dollars were deposited in Batista's Swiss Bank accounts.

When Fidel Castro seized power, he impounded all the Mafia's Cuban business assets and expelled Trafficante. Thereafter, approached by US agents looking for an anti-Castro partner, Trafficante worked with the CIA between 1960 and 1961 on plans to assassinate the Cuban Communist leader.

In a 1963 meeting with Jose Aleman, an undercover FBI informant and Cuban exile, Trafficante allegedly predicted that President Kennedy would be killed before serving a second term. In 1978, Aleman told the House Select Committee on Assassinations (HCSA) investigating links between Lee Harvey Oswald and anti-Castro Cubans that Trafficante had told him:

> "You see this man, he is not going to be re-elected, there is no doubt about it … he is not going to be re-elected … he is going to be hit."

Testifying before the same investigating committee, Trafficante denied he had ever said it. He refuted any connection with the Kennedy killing, and claimed that he had never met Jack Ruby or Lee Harvey Oswald. He did, however, admit his anti-Castro activities.

On the other hand in 1975, after Sam Giancana, the Chicago Outfit boss was found shot dead, Trafficante and New Orleans Mafia boss, Carlos Marcello, were recorded in conversation by an undercover FBI bugging operation. Trafficante is on tape saying to Marcello, "Now only two people are alive, who know who killed Kennedy."

But the hidden meaning behind the cryptic comment was to remain a secret that both men took to their grave. At the age of 72 years old, and in poor health, Trafficante died on March 17, 1987, and after a series of strokes, Carlos Marcello died in 1993.

Some point out that Kennedy had asked for discretion from the Secret Service. However, another source has reported that it was not Kennedy who had asked for the roof bubble to be removed from the Lincoln. Neither did he request the reduced number of motorcycle outriders or the lack of agents on the rear bumper step. One agent, Abraham Bolden, who was the first African American on the White House Secret Service detail, claimed that he had heard other Secret Service agents say that they would not go out of their way to protect Kennedy from a would-be assassin.

* * * * * *

THE MAFIA

The HSCA summed up its views regarding the involvement of organized crime in the assassination:

> *The committee believes, on the basis of the evidence available to it, that the national syndicate of organized crime, as a group, was not involved in the assassination of President Kennedy, but that the available evidence does not preclude the possibility that individual members may have been involved.*

One such individual, it is suggested, was New Orleans Mafia boss, Carlos Marcello (1910 – 93). The Mafia, with its pre-Castro interests in casinos on the island, had almost as big an interest in bringing down the Castro government as the CIA, and several Mafiosi became involved in plots to eliminate Fidel Castro. Carlos Marcello, Sam Giancana, and Santo Trafficante Jr. all had long ties with Cuban exiles.

* * * * * *

A BLOOD FEUD OF HATRED

The Mafia hated the Attorney General Robert Kennedy, because of his pursuit of organized crime and corruption in labor unions. In particular Jimmy Hoffa, president of the Teamsters Union, described his relationship with Kennedy as a "blood feud of hatred." Prosecutions of senior Mafia figures had increased since Robert Kennedy had been appointed Attorney General giving them ample reason to want revenge against his family.

The Mafia who thought they had a deal with Joe Kennedy Sr. to help his son get elected as president, felt double-crossed. The FBI released information in 2006 that led people to believe that Marcello had confessed to his cellmate in a Texas prison, that he had organized the assassination.

A further "proof" of organized crime involvement was that Oswald's killer, Jack Ruby made a number of calls to associates of leading organized crime figures in the months prior to Dallas.

* * * * * *

CUBAN EXILES

It would seem obvious that this group would be considered as potential killers of a president who had prevented them from achieving their dream of re-capturing Cuba. They blamed the president for the failure of the Bay of Pigs invasion.

* * * * * *

THE CUBAN GOVERNMENT

The Warren Commission investigated many allegations that Oswald was involved with agents of the Cuban government but claimed that the allegations were all unfounded.

The main reason for the assassination, supporters of this theory believe, was revenge by Fidel Castro for the attempts on his life by agents of the US Government. One source intimated around the time of the assassination that there was "a Cuban Communist assassination team at large and Oswald was their hired gun."

Again this allegation was unproven but Lyndon Johnson was of the opinion that Castro was responsible, telling one broadcaster that "Kennedy was trying to get to Castro, but Castro got to him first." In 1977, Castro denied any involvement:

It would have been absolute insanity by Cuba … It would have been a provocation. Needless to say, it would have been to run the risk that our country would have been destroyed by the United States. Nobody who's not insane could have thought about [killing Kennedy in retaliation].

* * * * *

THE USSR

The Soviets had been humiliated by their climb-down during the Cuban Missile Crisis. One theory had it that Oswald had been recruited by the KGB. He had, of course, spent time in the Soviet Union and spoke Russian. The Russians would have had plenty of opportunities to plan an assassination with him.

* * * * *

LYNDON B. JOHNSON

Incredibly, a poll by Gallup in 2003 showed some 20 percent of Americans believed that President Johnson had some sort of involvement in a conspiracy to murder Kennedy.

The reasons, it is suggested, were that he was ruthlessly ambitious and wanted nothing more than to be president. It is also believed that Kennedy was about to drop Johnson from his ticket for the 1964 election.

It is claimed that even Jacqueline Kennedy believed Johnson was working in concert with a group of Texan millionaires to kill the president so that he could take his place. These views are said to have been recorded by Jacqueline Kennedy a short time after her husband's death and locked in a vault not to be released until fifty years after her death.

* * * * *

FRIENDLY FIRE

According to this theory, one of the president's own bodyguards accidentally fired the fatal bullet that killed the president. Secret Service agent, George Hickey, is said to have raised his automatic rifle to return fire after the shooting started, but the vehicle in which he was traveling stopped suddenly and he pulled the trigger by mistake.

* * * * *

SURGICAL ALTERATIONS

One theory has it that on Air Force One, Kennedy's body was clandestinely removed from its bronze casket while flying from Dallas to Washington. It was then taken to a place where it could be surgically altered to make it appear that the president was only shot from the rear. A lab technician observed that the president's brain was missing when it arrived at Bethesda and there were only small pieces of brain matter in the skull.

* * * * *

KENNEDY ASSASSINATION RECORDS REVIEW BOARD

In 1993 President Bill Clinton appointed a Kennedy Assassination Records Review Board, whose job was to assess whether the Warren Commission report was complete. They spent four years chasing Kennedy documents all over the world, even acquiring some from the Soviet Union and from Cuba. Professor Henry Graff of Columbia University who was a member of the Review Board concluded:

Almost all assassinations of leaders raise questions, and there's always the thought that there can't be a simple explanation. People wondered if the men who shot Garfield and McKinley acted alone. As for Oswald, the question was how could this know-nothing, incompetent little man kill the president of the United States? Ultimately we picked up four million documents that are housed in the National Archives now, and there was no evidence that anybody other than Oswald was involved in that assassination.

CHAPTER 22

THE KENNEDY LEGACY

★ ★ ★ ★ ★ ★ ★ ★ ★ ★ ★ ★

Americans, when asked, consistently give John Fitzgerald Kennedy the highest approval rating of any president of the United States since Franklin D. Roosevelt. It shows the interest that his name still evokes. Every year there are 350,000 visitors to the Texas Book Depository building from which Lee Harvey Oswald is said to have shot him on November 22, 1963. The depository is now a museum.

It is strange because he occupied the Oval Office for a mere three years, the first of which include the disastrous Bay of Pigs invasion and a poor summit in Vienna when Nikita Khrushchev humiliated him. Meanwhile at home, he was unable to get his legislation through Congress. Things improved with the Cuban Missile Crisis when Kennedy registered a stunning achievement that changed international relations in the world.

★ ★ ★ ★ ★

STRATEGY OF PEACE

His 1963 "Strategy of Peace" speech at the American University was delivered at the height of his rhetorical powers with his speechwriter, Ted Sorensen, at the top of his game. He outlined a plan to restrict nuclear weapons as well as a route to world peace just as the USA and USSR were engaged in a potentially catastrophic arms race. He said that he wanted:

… to discuss a topic on which too often ignorance abounds and the truth is too rarely perceived—yet it is the most important topic on earth: world peace … I speak of peace because of the new face of war … in an age when a singular nuclear weapon contains ten times the explosive force delivered by all the allied forces in the Second World War … an age when the deadly poisons produced by a nuclear exchange would be carried by wind and air

and soil and seed to the far corners of the globe and to generations yet unborn … I speak of peace, therefore, as the necessary rational end of rational men … world peace, like community peace, does not require that each man love his neighbor—it requires only that they live together in mutual tolerance … our problems are man-made—therefore they can be solved by man. And man can be as big as he wants.

Kennedy was able to add that the Russians had expressed a desire to negotiate a nuclear test ban treaty and that the United States had postponed planned atmospheric nuclear tests. As well as easing people's worries, this speech took a large step toward easing some of the tensions of the Cold War.

★ ★ ★ ★ ★

CIVIL RIGHTS LEGISLATION

Kennedy was caught between a rock and a hard place regarding civil rights. Push too hard and he would antagonize the Southern congressmen who had a stranglehold on Congress committees with the power to block any legislation the president wanted to pass through.

Racial tensions had blighted America for decades and had now begun to explode in violent confrontations on the streets of the nation's cities. The day after his American University speech, Kennedy launched a push for a civil rights bill.

★ ★ ★ ★ ★

MONUMENT TO THE FALLEN

Kennedy also put forward a voting-rights bill and federal programs that would provide health care for the elderly and the poor. It was a huge disappointment that none of these bills made it through Congress and into law during his lifetime. However, most of what he proposed became law after his assassination and was seen as a monument to the fallen leader.

★ ★ ★ ★ ★ ★
THE NEW FRONTIER

Kennedy was the prototype of the modern leader—witty, charming, good-looking, and made for the television age. He and his wife presented to the world a new White House as well as a new type of presidency.

They welcomed artists and performers to glittering events. White House invitations were extended to people such as Pablo Casals, the poet Robert Frost, and the French intellectual André Malraux.

The Second World War was beginning to recede into the past as the 1960s dawned. Much of America was eager to believe that this dynamic young figure was the man to "get the country moving again."

He berated the previous administration, presided over by the oldest man elected president since 1856, for eight years of stagnation:

> *I have premised my campaign for the presidency, that the American people are uneasy at the present drift in our national course … and that they have the will and the strength to start the United States moving again.*

It was the "New Frontier" that he had described in his acceptance speech at the Democratic National Convention in 1960.

★ ★ ★ ★ ★ ★
VITAL REFORMS

Despite his problems with Congress, during his presidency, more new legislation was passed into law than at any other time since President Roosevelt's first term in the 1930s.

The New Frontier did, indeed, deliver the passage of a wide variety of vital social and economic reforms. Unemployment benefits were expanded. Federal aid helped improve housing and transport in American cities. Money was provided to continue the construction of the national highway system begun under the previous administration. A water pollution act was passed. An agricultural act raised farmers' income. Anti-poverty legislation was passed.

★ ★ ★ ★ ★ ★
THE SKEPTICS

Henry Graff, Professor Emeritus of History, taught one of the first courses on the American Presidency at Columbia University. In 2013 he was skeptical about Kennedy's legacy:

> *Kennedy was, of course, a myth created in large measure by his father. I must add that JFK was a faker in many ways. The Pulitzer Prize he won [in 1957 for Profiles in Courage] was probably not deserved; many people helped him write it. Nobody knew then how ill Kennedy was all his life. Nobody knew the extent to which he was not an ideal husband. We did not know that the missile crisis ended in part because we made a deal with Khrushchev to give up our missiles in Turkey in exchange for removing theirs from Cuba. The public didn't know any of this. They saw only this young man who was standing up to the Soviet Union and presumably was not going to go on with that fight in Vietnam. That's all pure conjecture.*

Anti-Soviet demonstration in front of the Soviet embassy, New York, 1960.

In 1993, Noam Chomsky, Institute Professor Emeritus at the Massachusetts Institute of Technology, and well–known critic of the US government's policies, had his own philosophical theory. He suggested commentators erroneously pinpoint the Kennedy assassination as a significant factor in causing contemporary world problems:

> … A lot of things have gone wrong in the last thirty years, for all sorts of independent reasons. I mean, the Civil Rights Movement made great achievements, but it never lived up to the hopes that many people invested in it … Real wages have been declining for twenty years. People are working harder, they have to work longer hours, they have less security — things are just looking bad for a lot of people, especially young people. … And in this kind of situation, it's very easy to fall into the belief that we had a hero, and we had a wonderful country, and we had this guy who was going to lead us, we had the messiah — then they shot him down and ever since then everything's been illegitimate. So really there have to be serious efforts to get past this, I think.

* * * * * *

ONE OF THE GREATEST

So Kennedy's legacy according to Professor Graff, even his political career, was bought and paid for by his father, who brought powerful people to his son's side. Professor Chomsky is unconcerned about the assassination, seeing no long-term significance in the event. But, many saw Kennedy's legacy differently.

Over the years, Kennedy's private life and his many sexual conquests both before and after becoming president, have become public knowledge, but still his reputation remains intact and, despite his moral failings, the American people still consider him one of their greatest leaders.

* * * * * *

WHAT UNITES US

He also seemed to have given Americans a future mission, the idea of pursuing a national purpose. A Defense Department policy document of the time captured this notion:

> The United States needs a Grand Objective … We behave as if our real objective is to sit by our pools contemplating the spare tires around our middles … The key consideration is not that the Grand Objective be exactly right, it is that we have one and that we start moving toward it.

Jeff Sachs in his book *To Move the World: JFK's Quest for Peace* characterized Kennedy as a visionary for us all:

> John F. Kennedy represents for us the hopes and potential of our own lives, and of an America that we believe, as JFK famously said, can truly light the world. Listening to JFK's speeches one feels powerfully that he is speaking directly to us as peers—fellow warriors in valiant causes. Most fundamentally, JFK told us about our common purpose as human beings, always emphasizing that what unites us is vastly deeper than what divides us.

* * * * * *

LOST MOMENT IN TIME

Most scholars concur that Kennedy was a good president but not a great one. A poll of historians in 1982 ranked him 13th out of the 36 presidents included in the survey. Thirteen such polls from 1982 to 2011 put him, on average, 12th.

Richard Neustadt, the prominent presidential scholar, revered Kennedy during his lifetime but in the 1970s, even he described the president as "… a flicker, forever clouded by the record of his successors."

But to the American people he is altogether more than that. More than fifty years after his death in Dallas, one hundred years after his birth, John F. Kennedy is still a symbol of hope and idealism, of youth and dynamism, of energy and grace. A lost moment in time, that subsequent generations are forever trying to recapture.

President John F. Kennedy speaks at the American University commencement in Washington DC on June 10, 1963.

THE CAMELOT MYTH

The term "Camelot" came to be used to describe the Kennedy administration and to represent the hope and idealism of his presidency. It described him, his family and the insiders that he worked with. It was first publicly used by the First Lady during an interview, after her husband's assassination, with Theodore H. White (1915 – 86), a Kennedy biographer for *Life* magazine. White might have thought he had got her at her most vulnerable, but Jacqueline Kennedy had an unspoken agenda.

She wanted to preserve her husband's legacy by enshrining his short presidency as the mythical Camelot. She explained that she and her late husband enjoyed the Broadway musical *Camelot*, which was popular at the time. Written by Alan Jay Lerner (1918 – 86) and Frederick Lowe (1901 – 88) it told the story of King Arthur's mythical court and castle.

Theodore H. White later claimed that he had unwittingly become "her instrument in labelling the myth." She picked out the closing lines of the title song and they resonated in people's minds with the Kennedy administration. The media latched on to the name and the legend was born.

Don't let it be forgot, that once there was a spot, for one brief, shining moment that was known as Camelot.

[Just in case White didn't get her meaning, she spelled it out, saying:]

There'll be great presidents again … but there will never be another Camelot.

Jacqueline Kennedy watches the new President addressing the meeting after the presidential election results, November 1960.

CAROLINE KENNEDY

Born in New York City, Caroline Bouvier Kennedy was three years old when her father became President of the United States in 1961. Two weeks after her father's assassination in 1963, her mother Jacqueline Kennedy moved Caroline and her brother John Jr. (1960 – 99) out of the White House and into a home in Georgetown, Washington DC. By the summer of 1964, the family had moved to New York City to escape the press, and in September 1964, Caroline was enrolled at the Sacred Heart School in Manhattan.

In 1968, the Kennedy family's lives were in turmoil again when Caroline's uncle, US Senator Robert F. "Bobby" Kennedy, was assassinated. Jacqueline became frightened for the safety of her family and four months after Bobby's death, she married Greek shipping magnate, Aristotle Onassis. But he was never accepted as a father figure by the children, and Caroline often turned to her other uncle, US Senator Edward "Ted" Kennedy.

In 1969, Caroline enrolled at The Brearley School, an exclusive all-girls school in Manhattan. She next attended Concord Academy in Massachusetts. Then in 1975, Aristotle Onassis died, and Jacqueline moved back to New York City. In 1980, Caroline received a Bachelor of Arts from Radcliffe College at Harvard University and began work at the Metropolitan Museum of Art where she met Edwin Schlossberg, whom she married in 1986. She went on to study at Columbia Law School and gained a Juris Doctor degree in law.

In 1994, after battling with lymphatic cancer, Jacqueline Kennedy passed away. Caroline took up her mother's role as the guardian of the Kennedy name and spent several months trying to settle her mother's $200 million estate.

Caroline and her brother John Jr. were very close, especially following their mother's death. After John Jr. died in a plane crash in 1999, Caroline became the sole survivor of the former President's immediate family.

She spoke at the 2000 Democratic National Convention and campaigned for Barack Obama when he ran for president in 2008. President Barack Obama named her US ambassador to Japan in July 2013, a position in which she served until January 2017.

In 2007, singer Neil Diamond (born 1941) revealed that the inspiration for his 1969 pop hit *Sweet Caroline* was Caroline Kennedy. He performed the song for Kennedy via satellite at her 50th birthday celebration.

CHAPTER 23

KENNEDY IN POPULAR CULTURE

KENNEDY ON FILM

There are possibly more films about John F. Kennedy than any other president. They explore his life, his presidency and, of course, the mystery of his death. The most famous film about John F. Kennedy is the 26-second film shot by Dallas businessman Abraham Zapruder. It became a vital piece of evidence in the Warren Commission's investigation of the assassination and has been analyzed endlessly by conspiracy theorists in the decades since Kennedy's death.

PT-109 (1963)

This film tells the story of the torpedo boat Kennedy commanded during World War Two and the heroism shown by him and members of his crew. Starring Cliff Robertson as Kennedy, it was released just five months before his assassination. Joseph Kennedy Sr. had used his influence in Hollywood to negotiate the film rights to the book *PT109: John F. Kennedy in World War II*, by Robert J. Donovan. The White House had full approval for casting and many other aspects of the film. It received a lukewarm reception on release.

RUSH TO JUDGMENT (1967)

Based on a book of the same name by Mark Lane, *Rush to Judgment* was one of the first films to question the findings of the Warren Commission. A documentary, it features interviews with witnesses, including Abraham Zapruder who captured the shooting on film. It may be responsible for launching the discussion of conspiracy theories around the assassination.

EXECUTIVE ACTION (1973)

Like Oliver Stone's *JFK* of 1991, this film investigates what factions and individuals could have conspired to kill the president. Written by acclaimed screenwriter Dalton Trumbo and starring Burt Lancaster and Robert Ryan, it was extremely controversial as it was released just ten years after Dallas. Like *JFK*, it implies that Oswald was no more than a pawn of the real conspirators.

JFK (1991)

Oliver Stone's gripping film *JFK* tells the true story of New Orleans District Attorney Jim Garrison who tries to discover the truth about Kennedy's death. The film's premise that Lyndon Johnson was part of a *coup d'état* to unseat Kennedy proved controversial. Kevin Costner plays Garrison and Gary Oldman is Lee Harvey Oswald.

THIRTEEN DAYS (2000)

The thriller *Thirteen Days* stars Kevin Costner as Kennedy's aide Kenneth P. O'Donnell. The film tells the story of the Cuban Missile Crisis seen from the point of view of the US administration. It was the second film made about the crisis, the first being *The Missiles of October* that was made in 1974 and was based on a book by Robert F. Kennedy.

PARKLAND (2013)

This film looks at the assassination from the point of view of ordinary people who were present in Dallas on the fateful day, including the staff of Parkland Hospital to which Kennedy was rushed immediately after the shooting. It features the stories of Oswald's brother, the FBI agents who were visited by

Oswald prior to the assassination and Dallas's chief of the Secret Service, among others.

KENNEDY ON THE SMALL SCREEN

JACKIE (2016)

Jackie is a bio-drama seen through the eyes of Jacqueline Kennedy. The film covers the immediate chaotic days following John F. Kennedy's assassination. Jacqueline Kennedy, played by Natalie Portman, is interviewed by Theodore H. White for *Life* magazine, and consciously starts to sow the seeds in the minds of the media of her husband's image and the legacy of the "Camelot" presidency.

KENNEDY (1983)

This five-hour film followed Kennedy's life from childhood through his career in Congress right up until just before his assassination. Martin Sheen (born 1940) who went on to portray President Josiah Bartlet in *The West Wing*, was widely praised for his portrayal of JFK.

Natalie Portman stars as Jacqueline Kennedy in *Jackie* (2016).

THE KENNEDYS (2011)

This Canadian miniseries courted controversy with its portrayal of JFK and its historical accuracy. It chronicles the lives of the Kennedy family through its important triumphs and tragedies. Kennedy speechwriter Ted Sorensen described it as "character assassination."

* * * * * *

KENNEDY ON THE PAGE

Strangely enough, for a man who produced so much primary source material and several of his own works, there is no single "official" story. Most presidents have an "endorsed" biographical account, but Kennedy does not.

His closest advisors have their version of the story. Jacqueline Kennedy's friends have their version. The Kennedy family has another version. Perhaps Kennedy himself would have told his own story. But he did not have time.

Kennedy's premature death meant everyone was left wondering what might have been—what would he have done if he had lived? Unsurprisingly therefore, there are around 40,000 books about President John F. Kennedy. The following are just a small selection.

BIOGRAPHIES

ONE THOUSAND DAYS

The nation was still mourning the loss of its leader two years after the assassination, when this book was published in 1965. Written by loyal White House insider, Arthur J. Schlesinger, this book reminds us of the hope and optimism of Kennedy's brief presidency, but is not remotely critical.

THE DEATH OF A PRESIDENT

Jacqueline Kennedy initially offered author William Manchester her support but withdrew it on reading the final draft, angered by his treatment of LBJ. Published in 1967, the book provides a highly detailed account of Kennedy's death and the events leading up to his funeral. It makes clear the antipathy many Texans felt toward Kennedy and how a number of his staff advised against the trip to Texas. Manchester had access to many of the key people in the Kennedy administration.

Katie Holmes and Greg Kinnear star as Jackie and Jack in *The Kennedys* (TV Mini-Series 2011).

KENNEDY: THE CLASSIC BIOGRAPHY

Written in 1970 by Kennedy confidante, advisor and speechwriter, Ted Sorensen, this book deals with the failures as well as the successes of the Kennedy presidency.

THE DARK SIDE OF CAMELOT

In a meticulously documented and researched biography, Seymour Hersh in 1997 told the controversial behind-the-scenes story of the Kennedy White House as it had never been seen before—the prostitutes, the affairs, the attempts to assassinate Fidel Castro, and the associations with organized crime, among much else.

JOHN F. KENNEDY: AN UNFINISHED LIFE

A frank examination of JFK's life and presidency, not shying away from the issues of his sexual appetite and his health problems. Robert Dallek's 2003 biography also assesses the political achievements and the legacy of John F. Kennedy.

JFK'S LAST 100 DAYS

A 2013 examination by Thurston Clarke of the last months of Kennedy's life that offers hints as to the sort of leader he was becoming. The dramatic period begins with the death of the Kennedys' son, Patrick, shortly after birth. The book follows Kennedy's efforts afterward to be a better husband and father, and the political struggles that preoccupied him before his untimely death.

* * * * * *

FICTION

THE PARALLAX VIEW

Later adapted as an excellent film by Alan J. Pakula, Loren Singer's book was among the earliest to claim that the Warren Commission's report was not the real story of the assassination. In this 1970 novel, a journalist investigating the murder of a politician becomes embroiled in a vast corporate conspiracy.

LIBRA

Don DeLillo insisted that he was not trying to find answers to the questions surrounding Kennedy's assassination. In this 1988 work, he re-imagines the events and the personalities surrounding the incident, focusing on Oswald, some former government agents who are unhappy with Kennedy's presidency and Nicholas Branch, a CIA archivist trying to analyze the information after the president's murder.

NO SAFE PLACE

Richard North Patterson, a friend of Edward Kennedy, wrote a series of novels about a politician whose brother was killed while campaigning. In this 1991 story, the protagonist, Kerry Kilcannon, is himself campaigning for the presidency, but knows he may be a target.

A SEASON IN PURGATORY

Thirty years after the assassination, the glow around the fallen president is fading as revelations about his sex life become public. In this 1993 book, Dominick Dunne narrates the story of the Bradleys, a fictional Irish-American political dynasty, incorporating the facts and the rumors about the real-life Kennedys.

OSWALD'S TALE: AN AMERICAN MYSTERY

In one of the best of his later works written in 1995, Norman Mailer investigates the character and the life of Lee Harvey Oswald. He uses KGB papers released after the end of the Soviet Union and arrives at a striking conclusion as to whether Oswald acted alone.

AMERICAN TABLOID

In James Ellroy's 1995 blend of fiction and history, the author tells the story of the political and legal corruption in America between the years 1958 and 1963. The book unravels the interconnecting associations between the FBI, CIA, and the Mafia, eventually leading to Dallas and the Kennedy assassination. It is the first novel of the Underworld USA Trilogy, followed by *The Cold Six Thousand* (2001) and *Blood's a Rover (2009),* that go on to trace what happened after Dallas.

For time and the world do not stand still. Change is the law of life. And those who look only to the past, or the present, are certain to miss the future.

John F. Kennedy, June 25, 1963

FURTHER READING

This biography of President John F. Kennedy is designed to be an informative and entertaining introductory text. There are many more academic publications available should the reader wish to delve more deeply. Publications that were especially useful during the preparation of this book are listed below, and contemporary newspaper and magazine articles are cited at the point where they appear within the text.

Bedell Smith, Sally, *Grace and Power: The Private World of the Kennedy White House*. London, Aurum Press, 2011

Blair, Joan and Clay Jr., *The Search for JFK*. New York, Putnam, 1974

Bryant, Nick, *The Bystander: John F. Kennedy and the Struggle for Black Equality*. New York, Basic Books, 2006

Bugliosi, Vincent, *Reclaiming History: The Assassination of President John F. Kennedy*. New York, Norton, 2007

Burleigh, Nina, *A Very Private Woman: The Life and Unsolved Murder of Presidential Mistress Mary Meyer*. Bantam, New York, 1999

Collier, Peter, and Horowitz, David, *The Kennedys; An American Drama*. New York, Summit Books, 1984

Dallek, Robert, *John F. Kennedy: An Unfinished Life 1917-1963*. London, Allen Lane, 2003.

Damore, Leo, *The Cape Cod Years of John Fitzgerald Kennedy*. Englewood Cliffs, New Jersey, Prentice Hall, 1967

Davis, John H., *The Kennedys: Dynasty and Disaster, 1848-1983*. New York, McGraw-Hill, 1984

Dobbs, Michael, *One Minute to Midnight. Kennedy, Khrushchev and Castro on the Brink of Nuclear War*. London, Arrow, 2009

Donaldson, Gary, *The First Modern Campaign: Kennedy, Nixon, and the Election of 1960*. New York, Rowman & Littlefield, 2007

Farris, Scott, *Inga: Kennedy's Great Love, Hitler's Perfect Beauty and J. Edgar Hoover's Prime Suspect*. New York, Lyons Press, 2016

Freedman, Lawrence, *Kennedy's Wars: Berlin, Cuba, Laos, and Vietnam*. New York, Oxford University Press, 2000

Goodwin, Doris Kearns, *The Fitzgeralds and the Kennedys*. New York, Simon & Schuster, 1987

Hamilton, Nigel, *JFK: Reckless Youth*. New York, Random House, 1992

Hersh, Seymour, *The Dark Side of Camelot*. Boston, Little Brown, 1997

Kennedy, John F., *Profiles in Courage*. New York, Harper & Brothers, 1957

Kennedy, Rose Fitzgerald, *Times to Remember*. New York, Doubleday, 1974

Leamer, Laurence, *The Kennedy Men: 1901–1963*. New York, William Morrow, 2002

Leaming, Barbara, *Jacqueline Bouvier Kennedy Onassis: The Untold Story*. New York, Thomas Dunne Books, 2014

Leaming, Barbara, *Mrs. Kennedy: The Missing History of the Kennedy Years*. New York, Free Press, 2001

Ling, Peter, *John F. Kennedy*. London, Routledge, 2013

Maier, Thomas, *The Kennedys: America's Emerald Kings*. New York, Basic Books, 2003

Manchester, William, *The Death of a President*. New York, Harper & Row, 1967

Marrs, Jim, *Crossfire: The Plot That Killed Kennedy*. New York, Carroll & Graf, 1989

Matthews, Chris, *Jack Kennedy: Elusive Hero*. New York, Simon & Schuster, 2011

Oliver, Willard; Marion, Nancy E., *Killing the President: Assassinations, Attempts, and Rumored Attempts on U.S. Commanders-in-Chief*. Santa Barbara, Praeger, 2010

Reeves, Richard, *President Kennedy: Profile of Power*. New York, Simon & Schuster, 1994

Rust, William J., *Kennedy in Vietnam*. De Capo, New York, 1985

Sabato, Larry J., *The Kennedy Half-Century: The Presidency, Assassination, and Lasting Legacy of John F. Kennedy*. New York, Bloomsbury USA, 2013

Salinger, Pierre, *With Kennedy*. New York, Doubleday, 1966

Schlesinger, Arthur, Jr., *A Thousand Days*. Boston, Houghton Mifflin, 1978

Spoto, Donald, *Marilyn Monroe: The Biography*. Arrow, London, 1994

Thomas, Evan, *Robert Kennedy: His Life*. New York, Simon & Schuster, 2000

Watts, Steven, *JFK and the Masculine Mystique: Sex and Power on the New Frontier*. New York, Thomas Dunne Books, 2016

White, Theodore H., *The Making of the President, 1960*. New York, Atheneum, 1961

President John F. Kennedy and
First Lady Jacqueline Kennedy,
New York, October 12, 1961.

INDEX

Page numbers in italic denote an illustration

Inspiring | Educating | Creating | Entertaining

© 2017 Oxford Publishing Ventures Ltd.

This edition published in 2017 by Chartwell Books, an imprint of The Quarto Group, 142 West 36th Street, 4th Floor, New York, NY 10018, USA
T (212) 779-4972 F (212) 779-6058 www.QuartoKnows.com

Chartwell Books titles are also available at discount for retail, wholesale, promotional, and bulk purchase. For details, contact the Special Sales Manager by email at specialsales@quarto.com or by mail at The Quarto Group, Attn: Special Sales Manager, 401 Second Avenue North, Suite 310, Minneapolis, MN 55401, USA.

10 9 8 7 6 5 4 3 2 1

ISBN: 978-0-7858-3508-0

Printed in China

PICTURE CREDITS

Many of the images in this book are released via the White House Photographic Collection (WHPC) and, as works of the US federal government, the images are in the public domain. Others are from the public archives of the Library of Congress (loc.gov). The publishers are also grateful to the John F. Kennedy Presidential Library and Museum (jfklibrary.org). The images listed below are all in the public domain unless otherwise stated.

Cover images: Granger Historical Picture Archive / Alamy / Victor Hugo King / WHPC / Walt Cisco / dpa picture alliance / Alamy.

Internal images: 1 RedDaxLuma / Alamy / 2 WHPC 1961 / 4 Granger Historical Picture Archive / Alamy/ 6 Cecil W. Stoughton WHPC 1962 / 7 NASA US-gov 1961 / 8 Pictorial Press Ltd / Alamy/ 11 Old Paper Studios / Alamy / 12 jfklibrary.org 1900 /13 Bain News Service 1906 / loc.gov / 14 Wide World Photos 1938 / 15 Ridpath's History of the World 1907 / Internet Archive Book Images / 16 Old Paper Studios / Alamy / 18 Richard Sears 1931 / jfklibrary.org / 21 jfklibrary.org 1934 / 23 Pictorial Press Ltd / Alamy / 24 princeton-archives 1935 / 26 Everett Collection Historical / Alamy / 27 jfklibrary.org 1962 / 29 World History Archive / Alamy / 31 Publisher Wilfred Funk first edition 1940 / 33 Keystone Pictures USA / Alamy / 34 alchetron.com / 36 US Naval Historical Center 1943 / 40 RBM Vintage Images / Alamy / 42 jfklibrary.org 1939 / 43 nypost.com 1943 / 42 jfklibrary.org 1942 / 48 Yale Joel 1946 / 52 jfklibrary.org 1946 / 53 Associated Press 1948 / 55 Keystone Pictures USA / Alamy / 57 Roger Higgins 1951 / loc.gov / 60&61 Abbie Rowe WHPC 1961 / 62 Hy Peskin Life Magazine 1953 / 66 Harper & Brothers New York first edition 1956 / 67 WHPC 1964 / 68 oldpoliticals.com / 69 eleanor-roosevelt 1934 / loc.gov / 70 ABC Television 1959 / 71 US Army 1957 / army.mil / 72 Dick DeMarsico 1964 / loc.gov 1964 / 73 Associated Press 1960 / loc.gov / 74 US Information Agency 1960 / 77 US Air Force 1966 / nationalmuseum.af.mil / 78 hubert-humphrey 1966 / loc.gov / 79 Oliver F. Atkins WHPC 1971 / 82 Everett Collection Historical / Alamy / 85 MediaPunch Inc / Alamy / 87 White House Photo / Alamy / 88 Shawshots / Alamy / 91 United Press International 1960 / 92 Orlando Fernandez 1957 / loc.gov/ 94 Rowland Scherman Peace Corps 1961 / jfklibrary.org / 96 Marion S. Trikosko 1961 / loc.gov / 97 RBM Vintage Images / Alamy Stock Photo / 98 Abbie Rowe WHPC 1961 / 99 Keystone Pictures USA / Alamy Stock Photo /100 Donald Mingfield US Army Signal Corps 1961 / jfklibrary.org / 103 Cecil W. Stoughton 1963 / jfklibrary.org / 104 Ian Dagnall Computing / Alamy / 106 jfklibrary.org 1962 / 108 Alpha Historica / Alamy / 110 national-archives.gov 1962 / jfklibrary.org / 112 US Navy 1984 / 114 Zuma Press, Inc. / Alamy / 115 Alberto Korda 1960 Museo Che Guevara / 117 World History Archive / Alamy / 120 Keystone Pictures USA / Alamy / 121 Bert Verhoeff / Anefo 1970 / Nationaal Archief / 124 Stocktrek Images Inc. / Alamy / 126 alchetron.com / 127 Milton H. Greene 1957 / 128 Pictorial Press Ltd / Alamy / 130 Marion S. Trikosko 1962 / loc.gov / 131 Granger Historical Picture Archive / Alamy / 133 Warren K. Leffler 1963 / loc.gov / 134 City of Birmingham Alabama 1960 / 134 George C Wallace / loc.gov / 135&136 national-archives.gov 1963 / 139 Granger Historical Picture Archive / Alamy / 141 US Army 1963 / 143 Malcolm Browne Associated Press 1963 /145 John T. Bledsoe 1959 / loc.gov / 146 Walt Cisco Dallas Morning News 1963 / 149 barry-goldwater 1986 /150 Warren K. Leffler 1963 / loc.gov /151 jfkassassinationgallery.com / 152 Cecil W. Stoughton WHPC 1963 / 154 Victor Hugo King 1963 /155 Abraham Zapruder 1963 / 156 Justin Newman 1963 / 157 Richard Levine / Alamy/ 159 Zuma Press Inc. / Alamy Stock / 160 Marina Oswald 1963 / 161 Everett Collection Historical / Alamy/ 163 Cecil W. Stoughton WHPC 1963 / 164 nydailynews.com / 165 Cecil W. Stoughton WHPC 1964 / 166 Everett Collection Historical / Alamy / 168 Warren Commission exhibit 903 / 170 Bettmann / Getty / 171 tribune.com / 175 Interfoto / Alamy / 177 dpa picture alliance / Alamy / 178 Photo 12 / Alamy/ 179 William Ng US Department of State 2013 / 181 Moviestore collection Ltd / Alamy / 182 Photo 12 / Alamy / 184 Granger Historical Picture Archive / Alamy / 186 Keystone Pictures USA / Alamy